ABSOLUTE BEGINNER'S GUIDE

Minecraft® Mods Programming

No experience necessary!

Second Edition

Rogers Cadenhead

800 East 96th Street,
Indianapolis, Indiana 46240

Absolute Beginner's Guide to Minecraft® Mods Programming

Copyright © 2016 by Pearson Education, Inc.

ISBN-13: 978-0-7897-5574-2
ISBN-10: 0-7897-5574-2

Library of Congress Control Number: 2015948680

Printed in the United States of America

First Printing: October 2015

Trademarks

Minecraft is a trademark of Mojang Synergies / Notch Development AB. This book is not affiliated with or sponsored by Mojang Synergies / Notch Development AB.

All terms mentioned in this book that are known to be trademarks or service marks have been appropriately capitalized. Que Publishing cannot attest to the accuracy of this information. Use of a term in this book should not be regarded as affecting the validity of any trademark or service mark.

Warning and Disclaimer

Every effort has been made to make this book as complete and as accurate as possible, but no warranty or fitness is implied. The information provided is on an "as is" basis. The author and the publisher shall have neither liability nor responsibility to any person or entity with respect to any loss or damages arising from the information contained in this book.

Special Sales

For information about buying this title in bulk quantities, or for special sales opportunities (which may include electronic versions; custom cover designs; and content particular to your business, training goals, marketing focus, or branding interests), please contact our corporate sales department at corpsales@pearsoned.com or (800) 382-3419.

For government sales inquiries, please contact governmentsales@pearsoned.com.

For questions about sales outside the U.S., please contact international@pearsoned.com.

Acquisitions Editor
Mark Taber

Managing Editor
Kristy Hart

Project Editor
Andy Beaster

Copy Editor
Apostrophe Editing Services

Indexer
Lisa Stumpf

Proofreader
Sarah Kearns

Technical Editor
Boris Minkin

Publishing Coordinator
Vanessa Evans

Cover Designer
Matt Coleman

Compositor
Nonie Ratcliff

Contents at a Glance

Table of Contents

About the Author

Rogers Cadenhead is a writer, computer programmer, and web developer who has written more than 20 books on Internet-related topics, including *Sams Teach Yourself Java in 24 Hours.* He maintains the Drudge Retort and other websites that receive more than 20 million visits a year. This book's official website is at www.javaminecraft.com.

Dedication

This book is dedicated to the kids out there who have been inspired by Minecraft to learn computer programming, whether they're 10, 20, or 50. There's a lot of great experiences ahead of you, not only in writing mods for a video game but in what you do with your skills beyond the game world.

Acknowledgments

To the folks at Pearson, especially Mark Taber, Andy Beaster, Lori Lyons, Boris Minkin, and San Dee Phillips. No author can produce a book like this on his own. Their excellent work will give me plenty to take credit for later.

To my wife, Mary, and my sons, Max, Eli, and Sam.

We Want to Hear from You!

As the reader of this book, *you* are our most important critic and commentator. We value your opinion and want to know what we're doing right, what we could do better, what areas you'd like to see us publish in, and any other words of wisdom you're willing to pass our way.

We welcome your comments. You can email or write to let us know what you did or didn't like about this book—as well as what we can do to make our books better.

Please note that we cannot help you with technical problems related to the topic of this book.

When you write, please be sure to include this book's title and author as well as your name and email address. We will carefully review your comments and share them with the author and editors who worked on the book.

Email: feedback@quepublishing.com

Mail: Que Publishing
ATTN: Reader Feedback
800 East 96th Street
Indianapolis, IN 46240 USA

Reader Services

Visit our website and register this book at quepublishing.com/register for convenient access to any updates, downloads, or errata that might be available for this book.

IN THIS CHAPTER

- Explore how Minecraft programs are created
- Download a Minecraft server to run mods
- Set up a command to start the server
- Run the server and fix any problems that arise
- Start a Minecraft client to connect to the server
- Fix connection problems between the client and the server
- Try out a brand-new Minecraft world

DIG INTO MINECRAFT PROGRAMMING WITH JAVA

As a Java programmer and father in a house full of teen-aged sons who are avid gamers, I was pleasantly surprised when they began asking me questions about Java.

They wanted to know how hard the language is to learn, what kind of software is required to develop programs, and whether that software is free.

The interest of my sons in my favorite programming language had come from an unusual place: a game world of infinite dimensions where players build cool structures, dig mines, hunt for food, and watch out for creatures who want to kill them and blow up their stuff.

Minecraft, an indie game from Sweden that has become a massive cult phenomenon in recent years, is transforming my sons and many other young players into aspiring Java programmers.

If I meet anyone under the age of 20 who learns that I write books about Java, I always get the same question: Will your book show me how to create Minecraft mods?

This book answers that question with an emphatic "Yes!"

Minecraft mods, extensions to the game designed and shared by players, are created using Java, the same language in which the programmer Markus "Notch" Persson originally wrote the game.

This book enables you to learn the Java language and put that knowledge to use creating mods that do entertaining, useful, and bizarre things in Minecraft.

To get started, this chapter covers how to download, install, and run your own Minecraft server on your computer. You need one to have a place where you can run mods. After that server is running, the next chapter will walk through the process of creating, deploying, and testing a Minecraft mod.

Some of this might sound difficult, but as I told my sons, the Java language is not hard to learn. Software like NetBeans streamlines the task of writing programs and everything—Java, NetBeans, and the Minecraft server—is free!

It all begins with a Minecraft server and a brand-new world.

Setting Up a Minecraft Server

Developing mods requires access to a Minecraft server. The best way to do this when you're starting out as a mod programmer is to install and run a server on your own computer. Because there's not yet a standard way to add mods to the game, different servers have different ways to make this possible.

The easiest to use when creating mods is a server from the Spigot Project designed specifically for this purpose.

Using Spigot requires two things: The server and the Spigot API, a set of Java classes that enables you to write mods. Both are free to download and use. This book uses Spigot version 1.8.7, the most current as it went to press.

Spigot's Minecraft server and the Spigot API are packaged together as a single JAR file. (A JAR is a Java archive file, which stores files together in a manner similar to ZIP files.)

The Spigot API is a collection of more than 700 Java classes that will be used when creating mods.

The Spigot API and server can be downloaded from this book's website at www.javaminecraft.com/spigot.

The server and API JAR file are named `spigotserver.jar` and will be approximately 20MB in size.

Use the link to download the JAR file.

When you have downloaded the file, create a new folder on your computer and store the file in it. On my Windows PC, I created `c:\minecraft\server` and copied the JAR file into it.

The file `spigotserver.jar` is the one you run to launch the Minecraft server.

CAUTION If you visit the Spigot Project's official website at www.spigotmc.org, you may find versions of Spigot higher than 1.8.7. Though it is likely all of this book's mods will work with later versions, it would be best to use 1.8.7 while you are starting out and creating the programs in these pages.

After you've completed the book, it will be easier to understand the installation and use of new versions of the Spigot API and server.

The following command starts the server:

```
java -Xms1024M -Xmx1024M -jar spigotserver.jar
```

This command tells the Java Virtual Machine to run the application packaged as the JAR file `spigotserver.jar`, allocating 1024MB of memory to the program.

To avoid typing this command every time you run the server, you can create a batch or shell file that contains it, and then run that file instead.

On Windows, open a text editor such as Notepad and enter the text of Listing 1.1 into the file, saving it as `start-server.bat` in the same folder where you put `spigotserver.jar`.

When typing in the listing, don't enter the `1:` and `2:` in the file because these are line numbers used in this book to refer to specific lines as concepts are explained.

LISTING 1.1 The Full Text of `start-server.bat`

```
1: java -Xms1024M -Xmx1024M -jar spigotserver.jar
2: pause
```

Save the file and double-click its name or icon to run the server.

The first time you run it, you will see an error message, "Failed to load eula.txt," as shown in Figure 1.1. Don't freak out—this is supposed to happen.

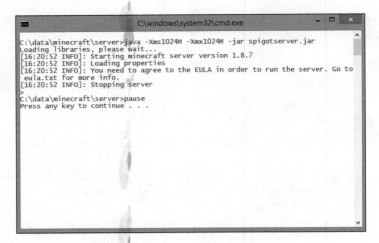

FIGURE 1.1

The server fails (on purpose) because of the EULA check.

Minecraft has an end-user license agreement (EULA) that you must read and agree to before you can run the server. Visit the following web page to review this agreement: http://account.mojang.com/documents/minecraft_eula.

There's now a file called eula.txt in the same folder as the server. This file has a line that contains the following text:

```
eula=false
```

If you agree to the EULA, change this line to `eula=true`, save the file, and run the server again.

If it runs successfully, a window opens that displays what the server is doing as it starts. The first time the server runs, it creates more than a dozen files and subfolders and builds the Minecraft world map. If it is successful, you see a final message that begins with the text " `[Info] Done`." The next line is a blinking cursor next to a `>` prompt. Commands can be typed on this line.

The `help` command lists commands you can use that control the server and the game world. The `stop` command shuts down the server (don't do this yet!).

Figure 1.2 shows a running Spigot server.

This window must be kept open while the server is running.

If your server window looks like this, you can skip the next section and proceed in this chapter to "Connecting to the Server."

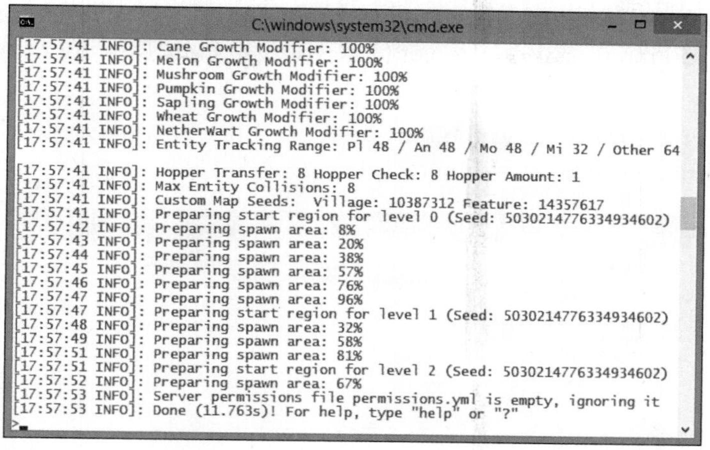

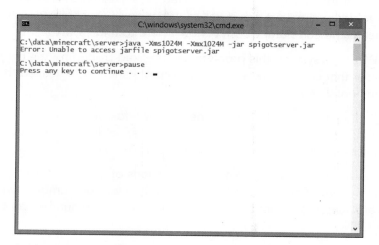

FIGURE 1.2

Running a Minecraft server for the first time.

Fixing Problems Running the Server

Two common errors prevent a server from running successfully after you download and install it.

The first error displays the message `Unable to access jar file spigotserver.jar`, as shown in Figure 1.3.

FIGURE 1.3

The Spigot server's JAR file can't be found.

To fix this problem, make sure the file `spigotserver.jar` is in the same folder as the file you ran to start the server (`start-server.bat`). Then try to start the server again.

The second error displays the message `'java' is not recognized as an internal or external command` as in Figure 1.4.

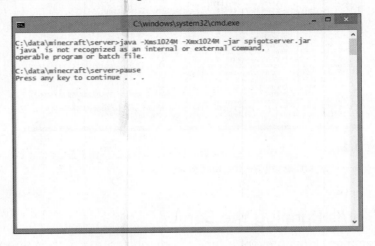

FIGURE 1.4

The Java Virtual Machine can't be found.

The Java Virtual Machine is in a file called `java.exe`, which is in the `bin` subfolder of the folder where Java was installed. When the `java` command is not recognized, this means the computer doesn't know where to find `java.exe`.

On a Windows system, this problem can be fixed by adding the name of the folder that contains `java.exe` to a Control Panel setting called the Path environmental variable.

First, find your Java folder. Go to the top-level folder of your main hard drive; then open the `Program Files` or `Program Files (x86)` folder to see whether either one contains a `Java` subfolder. If you find it, open that folder.

The `Java` subfolder can contain several versions of the Java Development Kit (JDK) or Java Runtime Environment (JRE), each with a version number. On my computer, there are `jdk1.7.0_21` and `jdk1.8.0` folders. The higher number contains the most current JDK.

NOTE Java programs can be run on your computer by the JRE and JDK. You might be wondering why there are two programs filling this purpose and how they differ from each other.

The JRE is a Java Virtual Machine for anyone who wants to run Java programs on a computer or other device. You can make sure your computer has one, and update the one you have, by visiting the website www.java.com. If you have been playing Minecraft on your computer, it has a version of the JRE.

The JDK is a set of programs for developing Java programs. You might have one on your computer, but it's less likely than having the JRE. When you begin writing Java programs in the next chapter, you will be installing NetBeans, which is software that uses the JDK behind the scenes.

Open that folder, and then open its `bin` subfolder. There should be a couple dozen applications, including one called `java`.

Your computer's Path variable needs to be updated to include the full name of this folder, which is something like `C:\Program Files\jdk1.8.0\bin` (with your own JDK version number).

To add the Java Virtual Machine to the Path, perform these steps:

1. Open the Control Panel.

2. Look for a View By drop-down. If it is set to Category, look for the System and Security heading on the panel and select it.

3. Select the System item, then select Advanced System Settings. The Advanced dialog opens.

4. Click Environment Variables. A dialog opens that lists a group of user variables and a group of system variables.

5. In the System Variables panel, scroll down until you find Path, click it, and then click the Edit button below the panel. The Edit System Variable dialog opens (see Figure 1.5).

6. In the Variable Value field, carefully place your cursor at the end of the text in this field.

7. Add a semicolon character (;) followed by the folder where you found the `java` program. This already has been done in Figure 1.5, where the text `;C:\Program Files\jdk1.8.0\bin` was added. (Don't forget that semicolon!)

8. Click OK to close each of the three dialogs; then close the Control Panel.

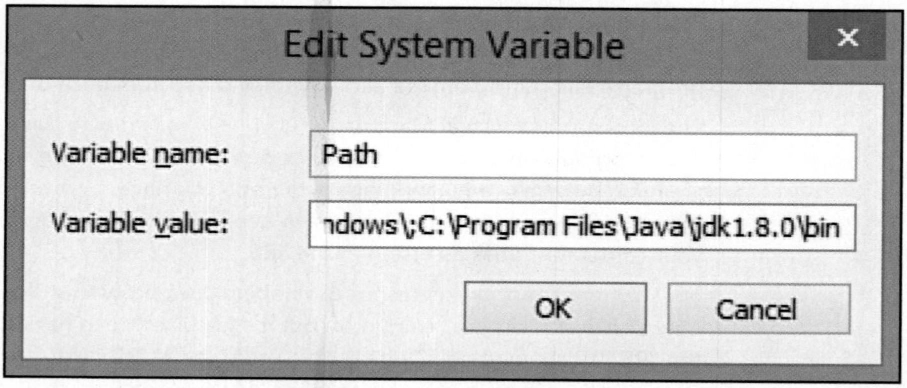

FIGURE 1.5

Editing the Path environmental variable on Windows.

Try running the server again. If it still isn't working, you might be able to fix the problem by installing the JDK. Visit Oracle's website at www.oracle.com/technetwork/java/javase/downloads and click the JDK Download button. A page opens with links to get the JDK for several operating systems.

In the JDK section that matches your operating system, click one of the links for the 32- or 64-bit version of the JDK. (For Minecraft, the 64-bit version is better, but your computer and operating system must support it.)

After installing the JDK, reboot your computer and try to run the Minecraft server again.

If all else fails, visit www.javaminecraft.com and look for the link to the help forum, a message board I've set up where there are sections devoted to helping readers who have trouble getting the server to run.

Connecting to the Server

After you have successfully started a Minecraft server and you can see from its window that it is running, you must connect to it with a Minecraft client.

Because you want to make Minecraft mods, you presumably already have a Minecraft client on your computer. If you didn't, you couldn't be playing the game.

If you don't have the game, you can buy and download it from the website www.minecraft.net. The current price is $26.95. The game is available for

Windows, Mac OS, videogame consoles, and mobile devices, but mod programming requires the Windows or Mac OS versions.

Start Minecraft and select Multiplayer. You should see your new server as one of the options (see Figure 1.6).

FIGURE 1.6

Your new Minecraft server is ready for connections.

The server is called "Minecraft Server" (you can change this to something cooler later). The client will send a ping message to the server and report back the speed, which is displayed as a set of green connection bars. This is identified in Figure 1.6.

These green bars mean you are ready to connect. If you see them, select the server (by clicking it) and click the Join Server button. You now have a new Minecraft world running on your own server.

When the client can't connect to the server, a red X is displayed instead of green connection bars. The next section describes how to troubleshoot this issue.

Fixing a Server Connection Problem

Sometimes a Minecraft client has a problem sending a ping to the server and getting a response back. This is indicated by the red X shown in Figure 1.7.

Connection Error

FIGURE 1.7

Your new Minecraft server has a connection problem.

The most common cause of this problem is that the server is running a different version of Minecraft than the client. In the server window, the first message indicates the version the server is running. You can return to the server window and use the scrollbar to see the first messages that display as the server starts. One of them indicates the Minecraft version in use on the server. If you used the version downloaded from the book's website, one line near the top of the server window reads `Starting Minecraft version 1.8.7`.

The Minecraft client normally runs the most up-to-date version of the game. You can edit your profile to use an older version instead. Exit the Minecraft client completely. You need to reload it to change this.

Follow these steps to choose a different version in your profile:

1. Run the Minecraft client.

2. In the Minecraft Launcher window, click the Edit Profile button, which is in the lower-left corner. The Profile Editor dialog opens (see Figure 1.8).

3. Look for the Use Version field, which probably has Use Latest Version as its value.

4. Change this to match the server's version number. Because you are running version 1.8.7 of the Spigot server, the same version of the Minecraft client should be chosen. In Figure 1.8, Release 1.8.7 is selected.

Profile Editor		
Profile Info		
Profile Name:	rcaden	
☐ Game Directory:	C:\Users\caden_000\AppData\Roaming\.minecraft	
☐ Resolution:	854	x 480
☑ Automatically ask Mojang for assistance with fixing crashes		
☐ Launcher Visibility:	Close launcher when game starts	
Version Selection		
☐ Enable experimental development versions ("snapshots")		
☐ Allow use of old "Beta" Minecraft versions (From 2010-2011)		
☐ Allow use of old "Alpha" Minecraft versions (From 2010)		
Use version: release 1.8.7		
Java Settings (Advanced)		
☐ Executable:	C:\Program Files\Java\jre1.8.0_45\bin\javaw.exe	
☐ JVM Arguments:	-Xmx1G -XX:+UseConcMarkSweepGC -XX:+CMSIncrementalMode -XX:-UseAdaptiveSizePolicy -Xmn128M	
Cancel	Open Game Dir	Save Profile

FIGURE 1.8

Editing your Minecraft player profile.

5. Click Save Profile.

A welcome message in the lower right will indicate which version your profile is set up to play.

Click Play, and then select Multiplayer. You should see your server with green connection bars.

 CAUTION   Changing your player profile affects all Minecraft servers you use, including the ones you play when you're not creating and testing mods. Be sure to change the profile back to Use Latest Version when you aren't connecting to your own server (or create a second player profile so one is for mod work and one is for playing).

THE ABSOLUTE MINIMUM

If everything went well, you now have a Minecraft server running on your computer. You can use this server to play the game.

If you've never had your own server before, you might be tempted to set this book down for a while and explore a completely unspoiled Minecraft world never before seen by another player.

Give in to that temptation.

Cut down a tree and make some tools. Build a shelter before nightfall. Make a crafting table and furnace. Kill some zombies. Dig for iron ore.

Just don't get carried away and find yourself three years later putting the final touches on a complete re-creation of the city of King's Landing from *Game of Thrones*. You are here to write mods.

When you're done exploring a new world for a while, you are ready to install a programming environment where you will develop your first mod.

2

USE NETBEANS FOR MINECRAFT PROGRAMMING

Although it's possible to create Minecraft mods and other Java programs with nothing more than the Java Development Kit and a text editor, the experience is considerably more pleasant when you use an integrated development environment (IDE).

This book employs NetBeans, a free IDE offered by Oracle for Java programmers. NetBeans is a program that makes it easier to organize, write, compile, and test Java software. It includes a project and file manager, graphical user interface designer, and many other tools. One killer feature is a code editor that automatically detects Java syntax errors as you type.

Now in version 8.0.2, NetBeans has become a favorite of professional Java developers. It's also one of the easiest IDEs for Java novices to use.

There are specific requirements for how to organize the source code of a Minecraft mod when you deploy it on a Minecraft server. NetBeans makes this as simple as possible.

In this chapter, you learn enough about NetBeans to install the software and put it to use throughout this book.

Installing NetBeans

From inauspicious beginnings, the NetBeans IDE has grown to become one of the leading programming tools for Java developers. James Gosling, the creator of the Java language, gave it the ultimate vote of confidence in his foreword to the book *NetBeans Field Guide*: "I use NetBeans for all my Java development." I've become a convert as well.

NetBeans supports all facets of Java programming for the three editions of the language—Java Standard Edition (JSE), Java Enterprise Edition (JEE), and Java Micro Edition (JME). It also supports web application development, web services, and JavaBeans.

You can download the software, available for Windows, MacOS, and Linux, from http://netbeans.org. Look for the Download button. The version to choose for this book is the JSE. NetBeans is available for download bundled with the Java Development Kit (JDK) and can be downloaded separately. You must have NetBeans and the JDK installed on your computer.

If you'd like to ensure that you're downloading the same versions of NetBeans and the JDK used in the preparation of this book, visit the book's website at www.javaminecraft.com. Click the cover of this book to open the site for this edition, and then look for the Download JDK and Download NetBeans 8.0.2 links. You'll be steered to the proper sites.

Creating a New Project

The JDK and NetBeans are downloaded as installation wizards that set up the software on your system. You can install the software in any folder and menu group you like, but it's best to stick with the default setup options unless you have a good reason to do otherwise.

When you run NetBeans for the first time after installation, you see a start page that displays links to news and programming tutorials (see Figure 2.1). You can read these within the IDE using NetBeans' built-in web browser.

New Project

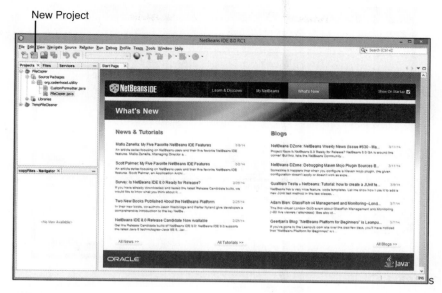

FIGURE 2.1

The NetBeans user interface.

A Java program also is called a class. A NetBeans project consists of a set of related Java classes, files used by those classes, and Java class libraries. Each project has its own folder, which you can explore and modify outside of NetBeans using text editors and other programming tools.

To begin a new project, click the New Project button shown in Figure 2.1 or select the File, New Project menu command. The New Project Wizard opens, as shown in Figure 2.2.

NetBeans can create several types of Java projects, but during this book and in your Minecraft programming, you can focus on one type: Java Application.

For your first project (and all the projects in this book), select the project type Java Application and click Next. The wizard asks you to select a name and location for the project.

The Project Location text field identifies the root folder of the programming projects you create with NetBeans. Click the Browse button next to Project Location. A file dialog opens. Use it to find and select the folder where you installed the Spigot server; then click Open. All projects you create are stored inside this folder, each in its own subfolder.

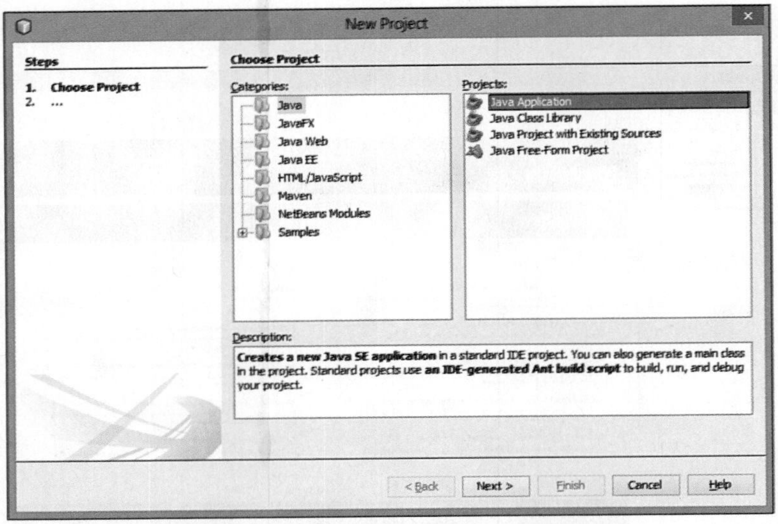

FIGURE 2.2

The New Project Wizard.

In the Project Name text field, enter **Minecraft**. The Create Main Class text box changes in response to the input, recommending `minecraft.Minecraft` as the name of the main Java class in the project. Change this to **Spartacus** and click Finish, accepting all other defaults. NetBeans creates the project and its first class.

Creating a New Java Class

When NetBeans creates a new project, it sets up all the necessary files and folders and creates the main class. Figure 2.3 shows the first class in your project, `Spartacus.java`, open in the source editor.

`Spartacus.java` is a bare-bones Java program that consists only of a `main()` method. All the light gray lines in the class are comments that explain the purpose and function of the program. Comments are ignored when the class is run.

To make the new class do something, add the following line of code on a new line right below the comment `// TODO code application logic here`:

```
System.out.println("I am Spartacus!");
```

The method `System.out.println()` displays a string of text, in this case the sentence "I am Spartacus!"

Projects Pane

Save All Files

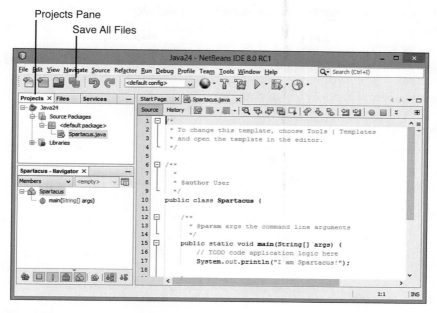

FIGURE 2.3

The NetBeans source editor.

Be sure to enter this exactly as it appears. After you make sure you've typed the line correctly and ended it with a semicolon, click the Save All Files toolbar button to save the class. (Or choose the menu command File, Save All.)

 NOTE As you type, the source editor figures out what you're doing and pops up helpful information related to the System class, the out instance variable, and the println() method. You'll love this helpfulness later, but for now try your best to ignore it.

Java programs must be compiled into executable bytecode before you can run them. NetBeans tries to compile classes automatically. You also can manually compile this class in two ways:

- Select the menu command Run, Compile File.

- Right-click Spartacus.java in the Projects pane to open a pop-up menu, and select Compile File.

If NetBeans doesn't allow you to choose either of these options, it already has compiled the class automatically.

If the class does not compile successfully, a red alert icon appears next to the filename `Spartacus.java` in the Projects pane. To fix the error, compare what you've typed in the text editor to the full source code of `Spartacus.java` in Listing 2.1 and save the file again. The line numbers in Listing 2.1 should not appear in your program—they're used in this book when describing how the code works. (Also, Line 8 will have your own username in place of the word "User.")

LISTING 2.1   The Full Text of `Spartacus.java`

```
 1: /*
 2:  * To change this template, choose Tools | Templates
 3:  * and open the template in the editor.
 4:  */
 5:
 6: /**
 7:  *
 8:  * @author User
 9:  */
10: public class Spartacus {
11:
12:     /**
13:      * @param args the command line arguments
14:      */
15:     public static void main(String[] args) {
16:         // TODO code application logic here
17:         System.out.println("I am Spartacus!");
18:
19:     }
20:
21: }
```

The class is defined in Lines 10–21. Everything above Line 10 is a comment included by NetBeans in every new class when you choose Java Application as the project type. These comments help explain things about the program to humans reading the source code. The compiler ignores them.

Running the Application

After you've created the Java class `Spartacus.java` and compiled it successfully, you can run it within NetBeans in two ways:

- Select Run, Run File from the menu.

- Right-click `Spartacus.java` in the Projects pane, and select Run File.

When you run a Java program, its `main()` method is called by the Java Virtual Machine. The string "I am Spartacus!" appears in the Output pane, as shown in Figure 2.4.

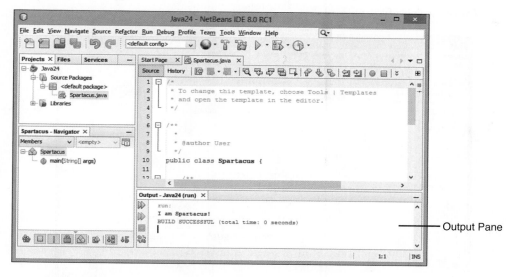

FIGURE 2.4

Output of the Spartacus application.

A Java program must have a `main()` method to be run. If you attempt to run a program that lacks one, NetBeans responds with an error.

After you're done reviewing the program's output, close the Output pane by clicking the X on the pane's tab. This makes the source editor larger, which comes in handy when you are creating a program.

Fixing Errors

Now that the Spartacus application has been written, compiled, and run, it's time to break something to get some experience with how NetBeans responds when things go terribly wrong.

Like any programmer, you'll have plenty of practice screwing things up on your own, but pay attention here anyway.

Return to `Spartacus.java` in the source editor and take the semicolon off the end of the line that calls `System.out.println()` (Line 17 in Listing 2.1). Even before you save the file, NetBeans spots the error and displays a red alert icon to the left of the line (see Figure 2.5).

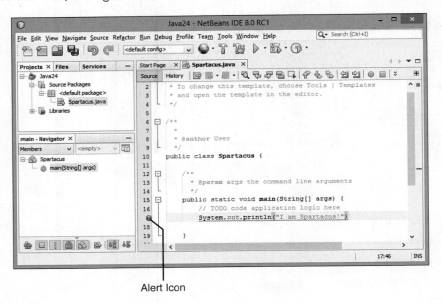

Alert Icon

FIGURE 2.5

Flagging errors in the source editor.

Hover over the alert icon to see a dialog appear that describes the error NetBeans thinks it has spotted.

The NetBeans source editor can identify most of the common programming errors and typos that it encounters as you write a Java program. The detection of an error stops the file from being compiled until the error has been fixed.

Put the semicolon back at the end of the line. The alert icon disappears, and you can save and run the class again.

THE ABSOLUTE MINIMUM

These basic features are all you need to create and compile the Java programs in this book.

NetBeans is capable of a lot more than the basic features described here, but you should focus on learning Java before diving too deeply into the IDE. Use NetBeans as if it was just a simple programming project manager and text editor. Write classes, flag errors, and make sure you can compile and run each project successfully.

When you're ready to learn more about NetBeans, the Start page offers resources to learn how to use it. Oracle also offers training and documentation resources at http://netbeans.org/kb.

In the next chapter, you use NetBeans to develop a Minecraft mod and run it on your new Spigot server. Each mod is its own project in NetBeans. The IDE makes it easier to develop mods because of how it organizes project files and folders and packages everything into a JAR file that can be loaded by the Minecraft server.

3

CREATE A MINECRAFT MOD

Now that you have a Spigot server for Minecraft set up and running and have installed the NetBeans integrated development environment (IDE), you're ready to create and deploy a mod.

Mods are special Java programs that run on a Minecraft server. They can't be run anywhere else.

Writing a mod requires the use of the Spigot API, a set of Java programs that do all of the background work necessary for the program to function inside a Minecraft game. A Java program also is called a *class*, so the Spigot API is called a *class library*.

The Spigot class library handles things like determining the (x,y,z) location of any object in the game, including a player. Everything you interact with in the game is represented in Spigot.

Before this book takes a full trip through Java, from the basics of the language into advanced features, this chapter demonstrates how a mod is created. This will give you a chance to see where all this material is headed. Many programming concepts will be unfamiliar to you, but all will be fully explained in subsequent chapters.

Creating Your First Mod

Mods are packaged as Java archive files, also called JAR files. NetBeans, the free integrated development environment from Oracle used throughout this book, automatically creates JAR files every time you build a project.

When you have finished writing a mod, you will be storing it under the server's folder in a subfolder named `plugins`.

The mod you are creating is a simple one that demonstrates the framework you'll use in every mod you create for Spigot. The mod adds a `/petwolf` command to the game that creates a wolf mob, adds it to the world, and makes you (the player) its owner.

 CAUTION There are two very similar terms you encounter a lot when doing Minecraft programming: *mod* and *mob*. A *mod* is a Java program that runs on a server to add something cool to the game. A *mob* is any living creature in the game, such as a creeper, chicken, cow, cave spider, or catoblepas.

Actually, there are no catoblepases in Minecraft. I was just making sure you were paying attention.

Each mod will be its own project in NetBeans. To begin this project, follow these steps:

1. In NetBeans, select the menu command File, New Project. The New Project Wizard opens.

2. In the Categories pane, select Java, and in the Projects pane, select Java Application. Then click Next.

3. In the Project Name field, enter `PetWolf` (with no spaces and capitalized as shown).

4. Click the Browse button next to the Project Location field. The Select Project Location dialog appears.

5. Find the folder where you installed the Minecraft server. Select it and click Open. The folder appears in the Project Location field.

6. Deselect the Create Main Class check box.

7. Click Finish.

The PetWolf project is created, and two folders appear in the Projects pane, `Source Packages` and `Libraries`, as shown in Figure 3.1.

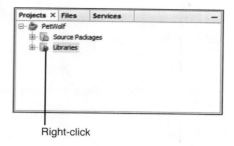

Right-click

FIGURE 3.1

Viewing a project in the Projects pane.

On each mod project, you must add a Java class library before you begin writing Java code: the Spigot server's JAR file, which includes the Spigot API. Here's how to do this:

1. In the Projects pane, right-click the Libraries folder and select the menu command Add Library. The Add Library dialog opens.

2. Click the Create button. The Create New Library dialog appears.

3. In the Library Name field, enter `spigot` and click OK. The Customize Library dialog opens.

4. Click the Add JAR/Folder button. The Browse JAR/Folder dialog opens.

5. Use the dialog to find and open the folder where you installed the server. You see a file in that folder named `spigotserver`.

6. Click that file.

7. Click Add JAR/Folder.

8. Click OK.

9. In the Add Library dialog, the Available Libraries pane now has a Spigot item. Select it and click Add Library.

The Projects pane now contains the JAR file for the Spigot API in the Libraries folder, so you're ready to begin writing the mod program.

Follow these steps to create the program:

1. Click File, New File. The New File wizard appears.

2. In the Categories pane, select Java.

3. In the File Types pane, select Empty Java File; then click Next.

4. In the Class Name field, enter `PetWolf`.

5. In the Package field, enter `com.javaminecraft`.

6. Click Finish.

The file `PetWolf.java` opens in the NetBeans source code editor.

Before you begin entering any code, this section explains the basics of how a mod is structured. Don't type in anything yet.

Every mod you create for Spigot begins with a framework of standard Java code. Here's the main part of that code, customized in a few places for this project:

```java
public class PetWolf extends JavaPlugin {
    public static final Logger LOG = Logger.getLogger(
        "Minecraft");


    public boolean onCommand(CommandSender sender,
        Command command, String label, String[] arguments) {


        if (label.equalsIgnoreCase("petwolf")) {
            if (sender instanceof Player) {
                // do something cool here
                LOG.info("[PetWolf] Howl!");
                return true;
            }
        }
        return false;
    }
}
```

Looking at this framework, the only things that will change when you use it for a different mod are the three things that refer to PetWolf because those are specific to this project:

- The name of the program is `PetWolf`.

- The argument inside `label.equalsIgnoreCase("petwolf")` is the command the user will type in the game to run the mod. This program implements the command `/petwolf` (commands in a mod are preceded by a slash (/) character). The `label` object, which is sent as an argument to `onCommand()`, is a string that holds the text of a command entered by the user.

- The statement that calls `log.info("[PetWolf] Howl!")` sends a log message that is displayed in the Minecraft server window.

Everything a mod does when its command is entered goes at the spot marked by the comment `// do something cool here`. *Comments* are messages in a program that explain what it does to humans reading the code. They're ignored by the computer when the program runs.

The first thing the PetWolf mod needs to do is learn more about the game world, using these three statements:

```
Player me = (Player) sender;
Location spot = me.getLocation();
World world = me.getWorld();
```

A `Player` object called `me` is the character controlled by the person playing the game.

With this `Player` object, you can call its `getLocation()` method to learn the exact spot where the player is standing. A *method* is a section of a Java program that performs a task. Here, the method retrieves the player's current location as a `Location` object. Three things you can learn about a location are its (x,y,z) coordinates on the three-dimensional game map.

The `Player` object has a `getWorld()` method that responds with the `World` object that represents the entire game world.

Most of the mods you create need these three `Player`, `Location`, and `World` objects.

This mod creates a new mob that's a wolf, using the `spawn()` method of the `World` object:

```
Wolf wolfie = world.spawn(spot, Wolf.class);
```

There's a class for every type of mob in the game. The two arguments to the `spawn()` method are the location where the wolf should be placed and the class of the mob to create.

This statement creates a `Wolf` object named `wolfie` at the same spot as the player.

The color of the wolf's collar is set in this statement:

```
cat.setCollarColor(DyeColor.PINK);
```

After the wolf has been created, the player becomes its owner by calling the wolf's `setOwner()` method with the `Player` object `me` as the only argument:

```
wolf.setOwner(me);
```

Now you can begin typing. Put all this together by entering Listing 3.1 into the source code editor and clicking the Save All button in the NetBeans toolbar (or select File, Save).

LISTING 3.1   The Full Text of `PetWolf.java`

```
 1: package com.javaminecraft;
 2:
 3: import java.util.logging.*;
 4: import org.bukkit.*;
 5: import org.bukkit.command.*;
 6: import org.bukkit.entity.*;
 7: import org.bukkit.plugin.java.*;
 8:
 9: public class PetWolf extends JavaPlugin {
10:     public static final Logger LOG = Logger.getLogger(
11:         "Minecraft");
12:
13:     public boolean onCommand(CommandSender sender,
14:         Command command, String label, String[] arguments) {
15:
16:         if (label.equalsIgnoreCase("petwolf")) {
17:             if (sender instanceof Player) {
18:                 // get the player
19:                 Player me = (Player) sender;
20:                 // get the player's current location
21:                 Location spot = me.getLocation();
22:                 // get the game world
23:                 World world = me.getWorld();
```

```
24:
25:                    // spawn one wolf
26:                    Wolf wolf = world.spawn(spot, Wolf.class);
27:                    // set the color of its collar
28:                    wolf.setCollarColor(DyeColor.PINK);
29:                    // make the player its owner
30:                    wolf.setOwner(me);
31:                    LOG.info("[PetWolf] Howl!");
32:                    return true;
33:                }
34:            }
35:            return false;
36:        }
37: }
```

The import statements in Lines 3–7 of Listing 3.1 make five packages available in the program: one from the Java Class Library and four from Spigot. *Packages* are groups of Java classes that serve a related purpose. For instance, the org.bukkit.entity package referenced in Line 6 is a group of classes for the mobs in the game (which in Spigot are called *entities*).

NOTE These classes are used in the PetWolf program: Logger from java.util.logging.Logger, Location and World from org.bukkit, Command from org.bukkit.command, Wolf and Player from org.bukkit.entity, and JavaPlugin from org.bukkit.plugin.java.

You learn more about these packages as you use them to create more mods beginning in Chapter 18, "Spawn a Mob."

The return statements in Lines 32 and 35 are part of the standard mod framework. A method in Java can return a value when its task is completed. Your mods should return the value true inside the onCommand() method when the mod handles a user command and false when it doesn't.

You have created your first mod, but it can't be run yet by the Spigot server. It needs a file called plugin.yml that tells the server about the mod.

This file is a YAML file, which you also can create with NetBeans using these steps:

1. Select File, New File. The New File dialog opens.

2. In the Categories pane, scroll down and select Other.

3. In the File Types pane, select YAML File and click Next.

4. In the File Name field, enter **plugin**. (Don't put .yml on the end; this is done for you by NetBeans.)

5. In the Folder field, enter **src**.

6. Click Finish.

A file named plugin.yml opens in the source code editor with two lines in it:

```
## YAML Template.

---
```

Delete these lines. They aren't needed in this file. Enter the text of Listing 3.2 into the file, and be sure to use the same number of spaces in each line. Don't use tab characters instead of spaces.

LISTING 3.2   The Full Text of This Project's plugin.yml

```
 1: name: PetWolf
 2:
 3: author: Your Name Here
 4:
 5: main: com.javaminecraft.PetWolf
 6:
 7: commands:
 8:     petwolf:
 9:         description: Spawn a wolf as the player's pet.
10:
11: version: 1.0
```

Replace Your Name Here with your own name. Telling people you wrote a mod is the first step toward becoming a legendary Minecraft coder.

To double-check that you have entered the spaces correctly, there are four spaces in Line 8 before the text petwolf and eight spaces in Line 9 before description.

The plugin.yml file describes the mod's name, author, Java class file, version, command, and a short description of what the command does.

This file must be in the right place in the project. Look in the Projects pane, where it should be inside the Source Packages folder under a subheading called <default package>. This is shown in Figure 3.2.

FIGURE 3.2

Checking the location of plugin.yml.

If the plugin.yml file is in the wrong place, such as under the com.javaminecraft heading, you can use drag and drop to move it to the proper location. Click and hold the file, drag it to the Source Packages folder icon, and drop it there.

You're now ready to build your mod. Select the menu command Run, Clean and Build Project. If this is successful, the message Finished Building PetWolf (clean, jar) will appear in the lower-left corner of the NetBeans user interface, way down at the bottom edge.

The mod is packaged as a file called PetWolf.jar in a subfolder of the project. To find it, click the Files tab in the Projects pane, expand the PetWolf folder (if necessary), and then expand the dist subfolder. The Files tab lists all the files that make up the project, as shown in Figure 3.3.

FIGURE 3.3

Finding the PetWolf mod's JAR file.

This PetWolf.jar file needs to be copied from the project folder to the Minecraft server. Follow these steps:

1. If the Minecraft server is running, stop it by going to the server window and typing the command **stop**; then press the spacebar or any other key to close that window.

2. Outside of NetBeans, open the folder where you installed the Minecraft server.

3. Open the `PetWolf` subfolder.

4. Open the `dist` subfolder.

5. Select the `PetWolf` file (a JAR file), and press Ctrl+C to copy it.

6. Go back to the Minecraft server folder.

7. Open the `plugins` subfolder.

8. Press Ctrl+V to copy `PetWolf` into it.

You have deployed your new mod on the Minecraft server. Start the server the same way you did before—by clicking the `start-server.bat` file you created. If you look carefully at the messages that display in the server window as the server loads, you see two new messages in the log file that display as it runs:

```
[PetWolf] Loading PetWolf v1.0

[PetWolf] Enabling PetWolf v1.0
```

These messages do not appear together. One appears close to the top and another close to the bottom.

If you don't see these messages, but instead see some long, complicated error messages, double-check everything in `PetWolf.java` against Listing 3.1 and `plugin.yml` against Listing 3.2 to ensure they were entered correctly; then rebuild and redeploy the mod.

 TIP   Still having problems making the PetWolf mod work? The source code, `plugin.yml` configuration file, and all other files for each book project can be found on www.javaminecraft.com. Visit the website to see files that were compiled successfully and run on a server.

After you run the Minecraft client and connect to your server, enter the command `/petwolf`. You now have a new wolf who will follow you around. Enter the command as many times as you like to keep adding wolves.

Figure 3.4 shows me and 20 wolves. Hostile mobs don't last long against us. We will rule this world. Hoooooooooooooooooooowl!

FIGURE 3.4

Your own wolf pack, courtesy of your own mod.

THE ABSOLUTE MINIMUM

This chapter was a sprint through the subject of how to write a Minecraft mod. The rest of the book will be at a much gentler pace that explains all the concepts in Java programming and the Spigot API that are necessary to create sophisticated mods.

There are a lot of different ways to learn Java. Doing it inside Minecraft is one of the most entertaining. You will put your programming abilities to use in a three-dimensional world where you fight monsters, dig tunnels, build houses, and dodge the legions of the living dead—including some who ride chickens.

Minecraft is an excellent way to learn about object-oriented programming, one of the toughest aspects of the Java language to master. Everything you do in Java is accomplished with objects. You create them in constructors, give them knowledge in variables, and tell them to do things by calling methods. Objects indicate the tasks they can perform by implementing interfaces.

All these concepts are new to you now, but as you learn them in the next 14 chapters, you will find they directly relate to mod programming. Need a zombie? Create a `Zombie` object. Want the player to move to a new spot? Call his `teleport()` method. Did you lose your horse? Call its `getLocation()` method.

So dig as deep into Minecraft mod programming as you like. You're going to use these skills far beyond the mines.

IN THIS CHAPTER

- Type a Java program in a source code editor
- Organize a program with bracket marks
- Store information in a variable
- Display the information stored in a variable
- Save, compile, and run a program

4

START WRITING JAVA PROGRAMS

A computer program is a set of instructions that tells a computer what to do. These instructions are given to a computer using a programming language.

During this chapter, you create a simple program with the Java language by entering it into a text editor. When that's done, you save the program, compile it, and test it. Then you break it on purpose and fix it again, just to show off.

What You Need to Write Programs

To create Minecraft mods or any other Java programs, you must have a programming tool that supports the Java Development Kit (JDK) such as the NetBeans integrated development environment (IDE). You need a tool that can compile and run Java programs and a text editor to write those programs.

With most programming languages, computer programs are written by entering text into a text editor (also called a *source code editor).* Some programming languages come with their own editor. NetBeans includes its own editor for writing Java programs.

Java programs are simple text files without any special formatting, such as centered text or boldface text. The NetBeans source code editor functions like a simple text editor with some extremely useful enhancements for programmers. Text turns different colors as you type to identify different elements of the language. NetBeans also indents lines properly and provides helpful programming documentation inside the editor.

Because Java programs are text files, you can open and edit them with any text editor. You could write a Java program with NetBeans, open it in Notepad or Text Edit and make changes, and then open it again later in NetBeans without any problems.

Creating the `Splash` Program

One of the funny quirks of Minecraft is the random message that displays in the game client when the program is run. It appears as yellow text across a corner of the Minecraft logo, as shown in Figure 4.1.

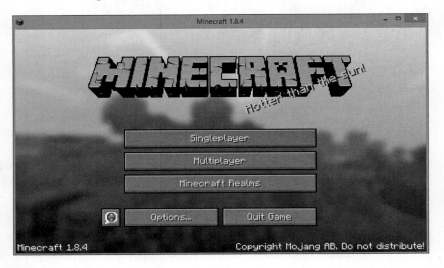

FIGURE 4.1

The Minecraft client displaying a splash message.

The splash in Figure 4.1 is "Hotter than the sun!" Mojang, the developer of Minecraft, uses the splash to crack jokes, make references to classic or obscure video games, and say other unusual things. Sometimes it even dispenses good advice.

The first Java program that you create will have its own simple splash message: "Blue warrior shot the food!"

To prepare for the first programming project in NetBeans, if you haven't already done so, create a new project called Minecraft by following these steps:

1. Select the menu command File, New Project. The New Project dialog opens.

2. Select the project category Java and the project type Java Application; then click Next.

3. Enter **Minecraft** as the project's name. (If you created a project with this name previously, you see the error message Project folder already exists and is not empty.)

4. Deselect the Create Main Class check box.

5. Click Finish.

The Minecraft project is created in its own folder. You can use this project for the Java programs you write as you progress through this book—at least as far as Chapter 17, "Read and Write Files." After that, you will be creating each Minecraft mod as its own project in NetBeans.

Beginning the Program

NetBeans groups related programs together into a project. If you don't have the Minecraft project open, here's how to retrieve it:

1. Select File, Open Project. A file dialog appears.

2. Find and select the folder where you installed the Spigot server (if necessary).

3. Open that folder.

4. Select Minecraft and click Open Project.

The Minecraft project appears in the Projects pane next to a coffee cup icon and a + sign that can be expanded to see the files and folders the project contains.

To add a new Java program to the currently open project, select File, New File. The New File Wizard opens, as shown in Figure 4.2.

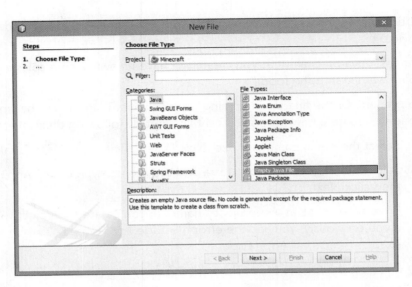

FIGURE 4.2

The New File Wizard.

The Categories pane lists the different kinds of Java programs you can create. Click the Java folder in this pane to see the file types that belong to this category. For this first project, select the Empty Java File type and click Next.

A New Empty Java File dialog opens. Follow these steps to begin writing the program:

1. In the Class Name field, enter `Splash`.

2. In the Package field, enter `com.javaminecraft`.

3. Click Finish.

So you can begin working right away on your program, an empty file named `Splash.java` opens in the source code editor. Using the editor, begin your Java programming career by entering each line from Listing 4.1. These statements are called the program's *source code*.

CAUTION   As you were warned in an earlier chapter, don't enter the line number and colon at the beginning of each line— these are used in this book to reference specific line numbers.

LISTING 4.1   The `Splash` Program

```
1: package com.javaminecraft;
2:
3: class Splash {
4:     public static void main(String[] arguments) {
5:         // My first Java program goes here
6:     }
7: }
```

Be sure to capitalize everything exactly as shown, and use your spacebar or Tab key to insert the blank spaces in front of Lines 4–6. When you're done, select File, Save to save the file.

At this point, `Splash.java` contains the bare-bones form of a Java program.

You will create many programs that start exactly like this one, except for the word `Splash` on Line 3. This word represents the name of your program and changes with each program you write. Line 5 should make sense to you because it's a sentence in actual English. The rest is probably new to you, aside from the sample Minecraft mod you wrote and tested in Chapter 3, "Create a Minecraft Mod."

The `class` Statement

The first line of the program is the following:

```
package com.javaminecraft;
```

A package is a way to group Java programs together. This line tells the computer to make `com.javaminecraft` the package name of the program.

After a blank line, the third line is this:

```
class Splash {
```

Translated into English, it means, "Computer, give my Java program the name `Splash`."

As you might recall from Chapter 3, each instruction you give a computer is called a *statement*. The `class` keyword is the way you give your computer program a name. It's also used to determine other things about the program, as you will see later. The significance of the term `class` is that Java programs also are called *classes*.

In this example, the program name `Splash` matches the document's filename, `Splash.java`. A Java program must have a name that matches the first part of its filename and should be capitalized the same way.

If the program name doesn't match the filename, you get an error when you try to compile some Java programs, depending on how the `class` statement is being used to configure the program.

What the `main` Statement Does

The next line of the program is the following:

```
public static void main(String[] arguments) {
```

This line tells the computer, "The main part of the program begins here." Java programs are organized into different sections, so there needs to be a way to identify the part of a program that is executed first when the program is run.

The `main` statement is the entry point to most Java programs. Mods are an exception because they are run by the Spigot server and cannot be run directly. When a player types a command that a mod supports, the server runs that mod.

Some other exceptions are applets, programs that are run on a web page by a web browser; servlets, programs run by a web server; and apps, programs run by a mobile device.

The Java programs you write during the next 13 chapters use `main` as their starting point. That's because you run them directly on your computer. Mods, applets, apps, and servlets are run indirectly by another program or device.

To differentiate programs with `main` from these other types, they are called *applications*.

Those Squiggly Bracket Marks

In the `Splash` program, Lines 3, 4, 6, and 7 contain a squiggly bracket mark of some kind—either a { or a }. These brackets are a way to group lines of your program (in the same way that parentheses are used in a sentence to group words). Everything between the opening bracket { and the closing bracket } is part of the same group.

These groupings are called *blocks*. In Listing 4.1, the opening bracket on Line 3 is associated with the closing bracket on Line 7, which makes your entire program a block. You use brackets in this way to show the beginning and end of a program.

Blocks can be located inside other blocks (just as parentheses are used in this sentence (and a second set is used here)). The `Splash` program has brackets on

Line 4 and Line 6 that establish another block. This block begins with the `main` statement. The lines inside the `main` statement's block will be run when the program begins.

 TIP NetBeans can help you figure out where a block begins and ends. Click one of the brackets in the source code of the `Splash` program. The bracket you clicked turns yellow along with its corresponding bracket. The Java statements enclosed within the two yellow brackets are a block. This tip is not that useful on a short program like `Splash`, but as you write much longer programs, it helps you avoid looking like a blockhead.

The following statement is the only thing located inside the block:

```
// My first Java program goes here
```

This line is a placeholder. The `//` at the beginning of the line tells the computer to ignore this line because it was put in the program solely for the benefit of humans who are looking at the source code. Lines that serve this purpose are called *comments*.

Right now, you have written a complete Java program. It can be compiled, but if you run it, nothing happens. The reason is that you haven't told the computer to do anything yet. The `main` statement block contains only a single comment, which is ignored by the computer. You must add some statements inside the opening and closing brackets of the `main` block.

 NOTE Semicolons are required at the end of each Java statement, but in the Splash program, the line `// My first Java program goes here` does not end with a semicolon.

The reason this is permitted is because comments are completely ignored by the compiler. If you put `//` on a line in your program, this tells the Java compiler to ignore everything to the right of the `//` on that line. The following example shows a comment on the same line as a statement:

```
System.out.println(greeting); // Exploding creepers!
```

Storing Information in a Variable

In the programs you write, you need a place to store information for a brief period of time. You can do this by using a variable, a storage place that can hold information such as integers, floating-point numbers, true-false values, characters, and lines of text. The information stored in a variable can change, which is how it gets the name *variable*.

In `Splash.java` file, replace Line 5 with the following:

```
String greeting = "Blue warrior shot the food!";
```

This statement tells the computer to store the text `Blue warrior shot the food!` in a variable called `greeting`.

In a Java program, you must tell the computer what type of information a variable will hold. In this program, `greeting` is a *string*—a line of text that can include letters, numbers, punctuation, and other characters. Putting `String` in the statement sets up the variable to hold string values.

When you enter this statement into the program, a semicolon must be included at the end of the line. Semicolons end each statement in a Java program. They're like the period at the end of a sentence. The computer uses them to determine when one statement ends and the next one begins.

Putting only one statement on each line makes a program more understandable (for us humans).

Displaying the Contents of a Variable

If you run the program at this point, it still seems like nothing happens. The command to store text in the `greeting` variable occurs behind the scenes. To make the computer show that it is doing something, you can display the contents of that variable.

Insert another blank line in the `Splash` program after the `String greeting = "Blue warrior shot the food!"` statement. Use that empty space to enter the following statement:

```
System.out.println(greeting);
```

This statement tells the computer to display the value stored in the `greeting` variable. The `System.out.println` statement makes the computer display information on the system output device—your monitor.

Now you're getting somewhere.

Saving the Finished Product

Your program should now resemble Listing 4.2, although you might have used slightly different spacing in Lines 5–6. Make any corrections that are needed and save the file (by selecting the menu command File, Save).

LISTING 4.2   The Finished Version of the `Splash` Program

```
1: package com.javaminecraft;
2:
3: class Splash {
4:     public static void main(String[] arguments) {
5:         String greeting = "Blue warrior shot the food!";
6:         System.out.println(greeting);
7:     }
8: }
```

When the computer runs this program, it runs each of the statements in the `main` statement block on Lines 5 and 6. Listing 4.3 shows what the program would look like if it was written in the English language instead of Java.

LISTING 4.3   A Line-by-Line Breakdown of the `Splash` Program

```
1: Put this program in the com.javaminecraft package.
2:
3: The Splash program begins here:
4:     The main part of the program begins here:
5:         Store the text "Blue warrior shot the food!" in a String
          ➥named greeting
6:         Display the contents of the variable greeting
7:     The main part of the program ends here.
8: The Splash program ends here.
```

Compiling the Program into a Class File

Before you can run a Java program, you must compile it. When you compile a program, the instructions given to the computer in the program are converted into a form the computer can better understand.

NetBeans compiles programs automatically as they are saved. If you typed everything as shown in Listing 4.2, the program compiles successfully.

A compiled version of the program, a new file called `Splash.class`, is created. All Java programs are compiled into class files, which are given the `.class` file extension. A Java program can be made up of several classes that work together, but in a simple program such as Splash only one class is needed.

The compiler turns Java source code into bytecode, a form that can be run by a Java Virtual Machine (JVM).

 NOTE   The Java compiler speaks up only when there's an error to complain about. If you compile a program successfully without any errors, nothing happens in response. This is disappointing. When I was starting out as a Java programmer, I was hoping successful compilation would be met with a grand flourish of celebratory horns.

Fixing Errors

As you compose a program in the NetBeans source editor, errors are flagged with a red alert icon to the left of the editor pane, as shown in Figure 4.3.

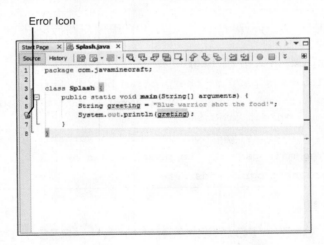

FIGURE 4.3

Spotting errors in the source editor.

The icon appears on the line that triggered the error. You can click this icon to display an error message that explains the compiler error with these details:

- The name of the Java program

- The type of error

- The line where the error was found

Here's an example of an error message you might see when compiling the `Splash` program:

```
cannot find symbol.
symbol  : variable greting
location: class Splash
```

The error is the first line of the message: `cannot find symbol`. These messages often can be confusing to new programmers. When the error message doesn't make sense to you, don't spend much time trying to figure it out. Instead, take a look at the line where the error occurred and look for the most obvious causes.

For instance, can you determine what's wrong with the following statement?

```
System.out.println(greting);
```

The error is a typo in the variable name, which should be `greeting` instead of `greting`. (Add this typo on purpose in NetBeans to see what happens.)

If you get error messages when creating the `Splash` program, double-check that your program matches Listing 4.2 and correct any differences you find. Make sure that everything is capitalized correctly and all punctuation marks such as {, }, and ; are included.

Often, a close look at the line identified by the error message is enough to reveal the error (or errors) that needs to be fixed.

Take note that the line number displayed with the error message isn't always the place where an error needs to be fixed. Examine the statements that are directly above the error message to see whether you can spot any typos or other bugs. The error usually is within the same programming block.

 TIP   This book's official website at www.javaminecraft.com includes source files for all programs you create. If you can't find any typos or other reasons for errors in the `Splash` program but there are still errors, go to the book's website and download `Splash.java` from the Downloads page. Try to run that file instead.

Running a Java Program

To see whether the `Splash` program does what you want, run the class with the JVM, the interpreter that runs all Java code. In NetBeans, select the menu command Run, Run File. An Output pane opens below the source code editor.

In this pane, if there are no errors, the program displays the output, as shown in Figure 4.4.

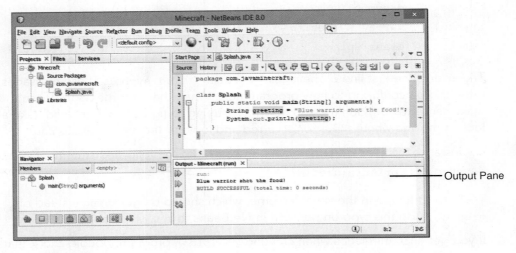

FIGURE 4.4

Running the Splash Java program.

If you see the text `Blue warrior shot the food!`, you have written, compiled, and run the Java program successfully.

 NOTE The message `Blue warrior shot the food!` is a splash message in Minecraft that pays homage to Gauntlet, a 1980s coin-operated videogame in which up to four players roamed through a dungeon killing monsters and accumulating treasure. Because players needed food to stay alive, accidentally shooting the food was a major faux pas.

You can find all of Minecraft's known splash messages and explanations for many of them on Minecraft Wiki. Visit the web page at http://minecraft.gamepedia.com/Splash.

Blank Spaces and Whitespace in a Java Program

As you typed in the Splash program in Listing 4.1, taking care to get the right number of spaces before each statement to make sure it all lined up properly, you might have asked yourself whether that's important.

Blank spaces and whitespace are completely unimportant as far as the computer is concerned. Spacing is strictly for the benefit of people looking at a computer program—the Java compiler doesn't care. You could have written the `Splash` program without using blank spaces or used the Tab key to indent lines, and it would compile successfully.

Although the number of spaces in front of lines isn't important, you should use consistent spacing and indentation in your Java programs. Why? Because spacing makes it easier for you to see how a program is organized and to which programming block a statement belongs.

The programs you write must be understandable to other programmers, including yourself when you look at the code weeks or months later to fix a bug or make an enhancement. Consistency in spacing and indentation are part of what's called a programming *style*. Good programmers adopt a style and practice it in all their work.

THE ABSOLUTE MINIMUM

During this chapter, you got an introduction to all the elements of a Java program. You learned that to develop a program, you need to complete these three basic steps:

1. Write the program with a text editor or a tool such as NetBeans.

2. Compile the program into a class file.

3. Tell the Java Virtual Machine to run the class.

Along the way, you were introduced to some basic computer programming concepts such as compilers, interpreters, blocks, statements, and variables. These will become clearer to you in successive chapters. As long as you got the `Splash` program to work during this chapter, you're ready to proceed.

IN THIS CHAPTER

- Learn how applications work
- Structure an application
- Send arguments to an application
- Learn how Java programs are organized
- Use the Java Class Library
- Create an object in an application

5

UNDERSTAND HOW JAVA PROGRAMS WORK

An important distinction to make in Java programming is where your program is supposed to be running. Some programs are intended to work on your computer. Other programs are intended to run as part of a web page.

Java programs that run locally on your own computer are called *applications*. Programs that run on web pages are called *applets*, programs that are run by web servers are called *servlets*, and programs that run on mobile devices are called *apps*.

The programs you create in this book are called *Minecraft mods*, and they are run by a Minecraft server. The server is written using Java, so they function as an extension of that server.

In this chapter, you will create an application and run it on your computer.

Creating an Application

The Minecraft mod you wrote during Chapter 3, "Create a Minecraft Mod," is an example of a Java application. The next application you create is simpler because it isn't a mod.

The Root application will calculate the square root of a number and display the value.

With the Minecraft project open in NetBeans, begin a new application:

1. Select File, New File. The New File Wizard opens.

2. Select the category Java and the file type Empty Java File, and then click Next.

3. Enter the class name **Root**.

4. Enter the package name **com.javaminecraft**.

5. Click Finish.

NetBeans creates the source code file Root.java and opens the empty file in the source editor so you can begin working on it. Enter everything from Listing 5.1, remembering not to enter the line numbers and colons along the left side of the listing (the numbers are used to make parts of programs easier to describe in the book). When you're done, save the file by clicking the Save All button on the toolbar.

LISTING 5.1 The Full Text of Root.java

```
 1: package com.javaminecraft;
 2:
 3: class Root {
 4:     public static void main(String[] arguments) {
 5:         int number = 17689;
 6:         System.out.println("The square root of "
 7:             + number
 8:             + " is "
 9:             + Math.sqrt(number)
10:         );
11:     }
12: }
```

The Root application accomplishes the following tasks:

- **Line 1:** The application is placed in the `com.javaminecraft` package.

- **Line 5:** An integer value of 17689 is stored in a variable named `number`.

- **Lines 6–10:** This integer and its square root are displayed. The `Math.sqrt(number)` statement in Line 9 displays the square root.

If you have entered Listing 5.1 without any typos, including all punctuation and every word capitalized as shown, you can run the file in NetBeans by selecting Run, Run File. The output of the program appears in the Output pane, as shown in Figure 5.1.

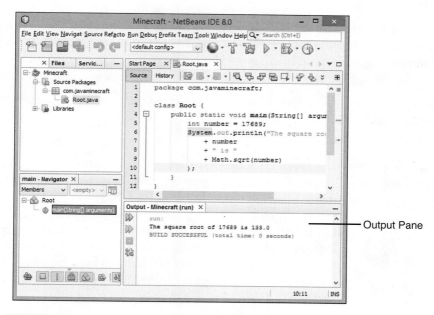

FIGURE 5.1

The output of the Root application.

When you run a Java application, the Java Virtual Machine (JVM) looks for a `main()` block and starts handling Java statements within that block. If your program does not have a `main()` block, the JVM responds with an error.

The statement `Math.sqrt(number)` in Line 9 demonstrates a built-in capability of the Java language—the ability to determine the square root of a number. A Java program named `Math` has a method called `sqrt()` to find a specified number's square root.

The Math program is part of the Java Class Library, which you explore later in this chapter.

Sending Arguments to Applications

You can run Java applications from a command line using java, a program that invokes the JVM. NetBeans uses this program behind the scenes when you run programs. When a Java program is run as a command, the JVM loads the application. The command can include extra items of information, as in this example:

```
java DataEditor game.dat delta
```

Any extra information sent to a program is called an *argument*. The first argument, if there is one, is provided one space after the name of the application. Each additional argument also is separated by a space. In the preceding example, the name of the application is DataEditor and the arguments are game.dat and delta.

If you want to include a space inside an argument, you must put quotation marks around it, as in the following:

```
java DataEditor game.dat delta "New Game"
```

This example runs the DataEditor program with three arguments: game.dat, delta, and "New Game". The quotation marks prevent New and Game from being treated as separate arguments.

 NOTE All arguments sent to a Java application are stored in strings, even when the argument is numeric. When you want to use one of these arguments as a number, you have to convert the value. Doing that is covered in Chapter 12, "Describe What Your Object Is Like."

You can send as many arguments as you want to a Java application (within reason). To do something with them, you must write statements in the application to handle them.

To see how arguments work in an application, create a new program in the Minecraft project:

1. Select File, New File.

2. In the New File Wizard, select the category Java and file type Empty Java File.

3. Give the class the name **Command**, give the package the name **com.javaminecraft**, and click Finish.

Enter the text of Listing 5.2 in the source code editor and save it when you're done. Compile the program, correcting any errors that are flagged by the editor as you type.

LISTING 5.2   The Full Text of `Command.java`

```
1: package com.javaminecraft;
2:
3: class Command {
4:     public static void main(String[] arguments) {
5:         System.out.println("You have summoned " + arguments[0]
6:             + " " + arguments[1] + " mobs."
7:         );
8:     }
9: }
```

This application compiles successfully and can be run, but if you try it with the menu command Run, Run File, you get a complicated-looking error:

```
Exception in thread "main" java.lang.ArrayIndexOutOfBoundsException:
    0 at Command.main(Command.java:5)
```

This error occurs because the program expects to receive two arguments when it is run. You can specify arguments by customizing the project in NetBeans:

1. Select the menu command Run, Set Project Configuration, Customize. The Project Properties dialog opens.

2. Enter `com.javaminecraft.Command` in the Main Class text field.

3. In the Arguments field, enter `13 Zombie` and click OK.

Because you've customized the project, you must run it a little differently. Select the menu command Run, Run Project. The application uses the arguments you specified in a sentence, as shown in Figure 5.2.

Return to the Project Properties dialog and change `13` to another number and `Zombie` to another type of mob in Minecraft; then run the project again.

Arguments are a simple way to customize the behavior of a program. The arguments are stored in a type of variable called an *array*. You learn about arrays during Chapter 10, "Store Information with Arrays."

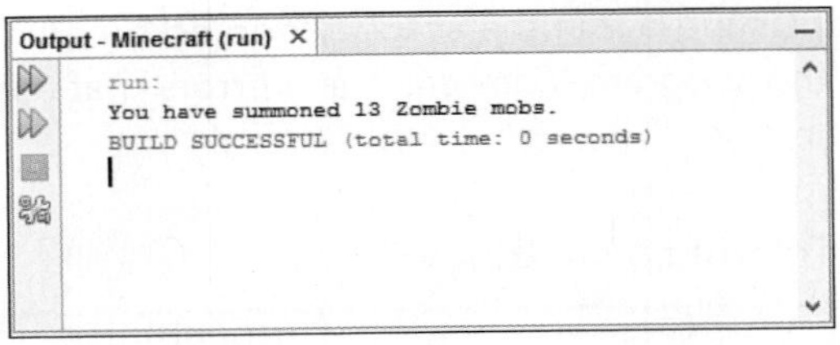

FIGURE 5.2

The output of the Command *application.*

Minecraft mods often take one or more arguments, so you will be seeing them again later. Players with operator privileges on a server can use the built-in Summon command to add a mob to the game. It takes three arguments: the type of mob; the x, y, and z coordinates where it should appear; and a data tag for additional configuration. Here's an example:

```
/Summon Bat 206 35 101
```

This summons a bat at the coordinates (206, 35, 101). The data tag argument has been omitted, which is okay because it is optional. All the arguments are optional except for the mob type, so here's another example that works:

```
/Summon PigZombie
```

This summons a zombie pigman at your own (x,y,z) coordinates.

These arguments are just like command-line arguments in a Java application.

The Java Class Library

The first half of this book explains how to use the Java language to create your own programs from scratch. You learn all the keywords and operators that form the language and then put them to work writing statements that make a computer do interesting and useful things.

Although this approach is the best way to learn Java, it's a bit like showing someone how to build a car by making her build every part of the car from scratch first.

A lot of work already is done for you as a Java programmer, provided you know where to look for it.

Java comes with an enormous collection of code you can utilize in your own programs called the Java Class Library. This library is a collection of thousands of classes, many of which can be used in the programs you write.

NOTE   There are many more class libraries provided by other companies and organizations. The Apache Project, the creators of the Apache web server, have more than a dozen Java open-source projects. One is HttpComponents, a set of classes for creating web servers, clients, and crawlers in Java.

For more information on the project, visit http://hc.apache.org. To see all of Apache's Java projects, visit http://projects.apache.org.

The classes can be put to work in your programs in a manner somewhat similar to using a variable.

A class is used to create an object, which is like a variable but far more sophisticated. An object can hold data, like a variable does, and also perform tasks, like a program.

Oracle offers comprehensive documentation for the Java Class Library on the web at http://docs.oracle.com/javase/8/docs/api. This page is shown in Figure 5.3.

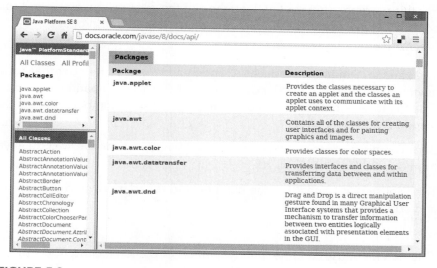

FIGURE 5.3

The Java Class Library documentation.

Java classes are organized into packages, which serve a similar function to a file folder on a computer. The programs you have created thus far belong to the com.javaminecraft package.

The home page for the documentation is divided into frames. The largest frame lists all the packages that compose the Java Class Library, along with a description of each one.

The names of the packages help describe their purposes. For instance, `java.io` is a set of classes for input and output from disk drives, Internet servers, and other data sources; `java.time` contains classes related to times and dates; and `java.util` collects helpful utility classes.

On the documentation home page, in the largest frame is a list of packages with a short description of each one. Click the name of a package to learn more about it. A page loads listing the classes in the package.

Each class in the Java Class Library has its own page of documentation on this reference site, which consists of more than 26,000 pages. (You don't have to read all of them now, or ever.)

For this chapter's final project, you will poke around the library and use an existing Java class to do some work for you.

The `Dice` program uses the `Math` class in the `java.lang` package, which can be used to create random numbers—a common requirement in Minecraft mods.

For this program, the `random()` method of the class will be employed to produce a random value from 1 to 20. Here's the first step in that process:

```
double roll = Math.random() * 20;
```

The `random()` method produces a randomly generated number that could be anything from 0.0 up to 1.0, not including 1.0. This is a floating-point number, so it needs to be stored in a variable that can hold such numbers—a `double` variable named `roll`.

Because this random number is multiplied by 20, the number will be anything from 0 to 20 (not including 20).

The final step in generating the number is to round it down to the nearest integer and add 1:

```
roll = Math.floor(roll) + 1;
```

This statement uses another handy method of the `Math` class. The `floor()` method takes a floating-point number and rounds it down, so if `roll` was equal to 17.38, it would be changed to 17.0. Because 1 is added, the final value of `roll` would be 18.0.

Without the `Math` class from the Java Class Library, you'd have to create your own program to produce random numbers, which is a highly complex task. Random numbers are useful in games, educational programs, and other programs that must do something randomly.

In NetBeans, create a new empty Java file, name it `Dice`, and put it in the package `com.javaminecraft`. When the source code editor opens, enter the text of Listing 5.3 into that window and then click the Save button (or select the menu command File, Save).

LISTING 5.3   The Full Text of `Dice.java`

```
 1: package com.javaminecraft;
 2:
 3: import java.util.*;
 4:
 5: class Dice {
 6:     public static void main(String[] arguments) {
 7:         double roll = Math.random() * 20;
 8:         roll = Math.floor(roll) + 1;
 9:         System.out.println("The random number is " + roll);
10:     }
11: }
```

Run the program by selecting Run, Run File. The output is shown in Figure 5.4, although your number probably will be different.

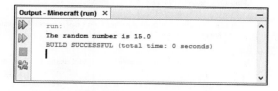

FIGURE 5.4

The output of the `Dice` *program.*

Run the program multiple times by using the keyboard shortcut Shift+F6 each time. You will see that the number always falls from 1 to 20. If you change 20 on Line 7 to 6, the number always will be from 1 to 6.

The `Math` class, like all classes in the Java Class Library, has extensive documentation you can read on Oracle's site. It describes the purpose of the class, the package to which it belongs, how to create an object of this class, and which methods it has that can be called to make it do something.

Follow these steps to see this documentation:

1. In your web browser, load the page http://docs.oracle.com/javase/8/docs/api.

2. In the main frame, scroll down until you see the link to the package `java.lang`. Click this link. Documentation for the package is displayed.

3. In the main frame, scroll down and click the Math link.

As a new Java programmer, you likely will find the documentation to be mind-bendingly tough to understand. Don't panic. It's written for experienced programmers.

But as you read this book and become curious about how Java's built-in classes are being used, you can get some value from looking at the official documentation for a class. One way to use it is to look up the methods in that class, each of which performs a job.

On the `Math` documentation page, you can scroll down to the explanation for the `random()` method. Figure 5.5 shows this section of the page.

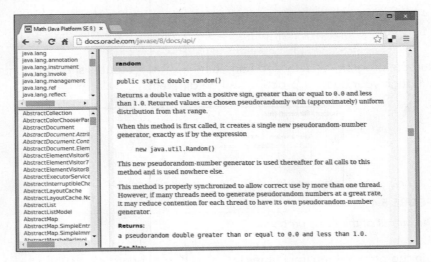

FIGURE 5.5

Oracle's documentation for the Math *class.*

NOTE   All the Java classes this book covers are described within its pages, so the online documentation is not required to progress through these chapters and become a Java programmer. Because the classes used in this book have many additional features beyond what an introductory book can cover, the Java Class Library documentation can supplement your learning.

Any Java class library that you use will have documentation organized the same way as the official Java Class Library. The set of classes in Spigot that enable Minecraft mods to be created has online documentation just like this.

You don't need it yet, but if you're curious and want to take a quick look, visit the website `http://hub.spigotmc.org/javadocs/spigot` and take a look at some of the packages.

THE ABSOLUTE MINIMUM

In this chapter, you had a chance to create a Java program, send arguments to a program, and make use of existing programs in the Java Class Library.

The next several chapters continue to focus on applications as you become more experienced as a Java programmer. Applications are quicker to test because they don't require you to do any extra work to run them, as you do for the other kinds of programs.

This chapter is the first of several that discuss how to make use of objects in a Java program. You will return to this subject in Chapter 11, "Create Your First Object."

STORE AND CHANGE INFORMATION IN A MOD

In Chapter 4, "Start Writing Java Programs," you used a variable, a special storage place designed to hold information. The information stored in variables can be changed as a program runs. Your first program stored a string of text in a variable. Strings are only one type of information that can be stored in variables. They also can hold characters, integers, floating-point numbers, and objects.

During this chapter, you learn more about using variables in your Java programs.

Statements and Expressions

A computer program is a set of instructions that tell the computer what to do. Each instruction is called a *statement*. The following example from a Java program is a statement:

```
int highScore = 450000;
```

You can use brackets to group a set of statements together in a program. These groupings are called *block* statements. Consider the following portion of a program:

```
1: public static void main(String[] arguments) {
2:     int a = 3;
3:     int b = 4;
4:     int c = 8 * 5;
5: }
```

Lines 2–4 of this example are a block statement. The opening bracket on Line 1 denotes the beginning of the block, and the closing bracket on Line 5 denotes the end of the block.

Some statements are called *expressions* because they involve a mathematical expression and produce a result. Line 4 in the preceding example is an expression because it sets the value of the c variable equal to 8 multiplied by 5. You work with expressions during this chapter.

Assigning Variable Types

Variables are the main way that a computer remembers something as it runs a program. The Splash program in Chapter 4 used the greeting variable to hold the text of a cryptic message like the ones on the Minecraft splash screen. The computer needed to remember that text so the message could be displayed later.

In a Java program, variables are created with a statement that must include two things:

- The name of the variable

- The type of information the variable will store

Variables also can include the value of the information being stored.

To see the different types of variables and how they are created, fire up NetBeans and create a new empty Java file in the package com.javaminecraft with the class name Variable.

Start writing the program by entering the following lines:

```
package com.javaminecraft;

class Variable {
    public static void main(String[] arguments) {
        // Coming soon: variables
    }
}
```

Go ahead and save these lines before making any changes.

Integers and Floating-Point Numbers

So far, the `Variable` program has a `main()` block with only one statement in it—the comment `// Coming soon: variables`. Delete the comment and enter the following statement in its place:

```
int tops;
```

This statement creates a variable named `tops`. It does not specify a value for `tops`, so for the moment this variable is an empty storage space. The `int` text at the beginning of the statement designates `tops` as a variable that is used to store integer numbers. You can use the `int` type to store most of the nondecimal numbers you need in your computer programs. It can hold any integer ranging from around −2.14 billion to 2.14 billion.

Add a blank line after the `int tops` statement and enter the following statement:

```
float radius;
```

This statement creates a variable with the name `radius`. The `float` text stands for floating-point numbers. Floating-point variables are used to store numbers that might contain a decimal point.

The `float` variable type holds decimal numbers of up to 38 figures. The larger `double` type holds decimal numbers up to 300 figures.

Characters and Strings

Because the variables you have dealt with so far are numeric, you might have the impression that all variables are used to store numbers. Think again. You also can use variables to store text. Two types of text can be stored as variables: characters and strings. A *character* is a single letter, number, punctuation mark, or symbol. A *string* is a group of characters.

Your next step in creating the Variable program is to create a char variable and a String variable. Add these two statements after the float radius line:

```
char key = 'C';
String playerName = "JeffStrongman";
```

When you are using character values in your program, you must put single quotation marks on both sides of the character value being assigned to a variable. For string values, you must surround them with double quotation marks.

Quotation marks prevent the character or string from being confused with a variable name or another part of a statement. Take a look at the following statement:

```
String playerName = JeffStrongman;
```

This statement might look like one telling the computer to create a string variable called playerName with the text value of JeffStrongman. However, because there are no quotation marks around JeffStrongman, the computer is being told to set the playerName value to the same value as a variable named JeffStrongman. (If there is no variable named JeffStrongman, the program fails to compile with an error.)

After adding the char and String statements, your program resembles Listing 6.1. Make any necessary changes, and be sure to save the file.

LISTING 6.1 The Full Text of Variable.java

```
 1: package com.javaminecraft;
 2:
 3: class Variable {
 4:     public static void main(String[] arguments) {
 5:         int tops;
 6:         float radius;
 7:         char key = 'C';
 8:         String playerName = "JeffStrongman";
 9:     }
10: }
```

The last two variables in the Variable program use the = sign to assign a starting value when the variables are created (Lines 7–8). You can use this option for any variables you create in a Java program, as you discover later in this chapter.

NOTE Although the other variable types are all lowercase letters (int, float, and char), the capital letter is required in the word String when creating string variables. A string in a Java program is different from the other types of information you use in variable statements. You learn about this distinction in Chapter 7, "Use Strings to Communicate."

This program can be run but produces no output.

Other Numeric Variable Types

The types of variables you have been introduced to thus far are the main ones you use for most of your Java programming. You can call on a few other types of variables in special circumstances.

You can use the first, byte, for integer numbers that range from –128 to 127. The following statement creates a variable called escapeKey with an initial value of 27:

```
byte escapeKey = 27;
```

The second, short, can be used for integers that are smaller in size than the int type. A short integer can range from –32,768 to 32,767, as in the following example:

```
short roomNumber = 222;
```

The last of the numeric variable types, long, is typically used for integers that are too big for the int type to hold. A long integer can be from –9.22 quintillion to 9.22 quintillion.

When working with large numbers in Java, it can be difficult to see at a glance the value of the number, as in this statement:

```
long salary = 264400000;
```

Unless you count the zeroes, you probably can't tell that it's $264.4 million. Java enables you to organize large numbers with underscore ("_") characters. Here's an example:

```
long salary = 264_400_000;
```

The underscores are ignored, so the variable still equals the same value. They're just a way to make numbers more human readable.

CAUTION These underscores are a new feature introduced in Java 8. Their use in numbers will be flagged as an error in the NetBeans source code editor if the IDE has been set up to use an older version of Java. To make sure this isn't happening, in the Projects pane, right-click the name of the current project (likely `Minecraft`) and select Properties. The Project Properties dialog opens with Sources chosen in the Categories pane. Check the Source/Binary Format drop-down to make sure it is the current version of Java.

Integers also can be specified using two other numbering systems: binary values and hexadecimal.

For binary values, put the characters "0b" in front of the number and follow it with the bits in the value. Because 1101 is the binary form for the number 13, the following statement sets an integer to 13:

```
int z = 0b0000_1101;
```

The underscore is just to make the number more readable. It's ignored by the Java compiler.

Hexadecimal values can be represented with numbers preceded by "0x", as in this statement:

```
int count = 0x30;
```

This sets the `count` variable equal to 48 using the equivalent hexadecimal value of 30.

The `boolean` Variable Type

Java has a type of variable called `boolean` that can be used only to store the value `true` or the value `false`. At first glance, a `boolean` variable might not seem particularly useful unless you plan to write a lot of true-or-false quizzes. However, `boolean` variables are used in a variety of situations in your programs. The following are some examples of questions that `boolean` variables can be used to answer:

- Has the user pressed a key?
- Is the game over?
- Is the mob riding a horse?
- Is the zombie angry?

Booleans are the place to hold the answer to yes/no and true/false questions.

The following statement creates a `boolean` variable called `gameOver`:

```
boolean gameOver = false;
```

This variable has the starting value of `false`, so a statement like this could indicate in a game program that the game isn't over yet. Later, when something happens to end the game, the `gameOver` variable can be set to `true`.

Although the two possible `boolean` values look like strings in a program, you should not surround them with quotation marks. Chapter 8, "Use Conditional Tests to Make Decisions," describes `boolean` variables more fully.

 NOTE   Boolean numbers are named for George Boole (1815–1864). Boole, a mathematician who was mostly self-taught until adulthood, invented Boolean algebra, which has become a fundamental part of computer programming, digital electronics, and logic. One imagines that he did pretty well on true/false tests as a child.

Naming Your Variables

Variable names in Java can begin with a letter, an underscore character (_), or a dollar sign ($). The rest of the name can be any letters or numbers. You can give your variables almost any name you like but should be consistent in how you name variables. This section outlines the generally recommended naming method for variables.

Java is case sensitive when it comes to variable names, so you must always capitalize variable names the same way. For example, if the `gameOver` variable is referred to as `GameOver` somewhere in the program, an error prevents the program from being compiled.

A variable's name should describe its purpose in some way. The first letter should be lowercase, and if the variable name has more than one word, make the first letter of each subsequent word a capital letter. For instance, if you want to create an integer variable to store the all-time high score in a game program, you can use the following statement:

```
int allTimeHighScore;
```

You can't use punctuation marks or spaces in a variable name, so neither of the following works:

```
int all-TimeHigh Score;
int all Time High Score;
```

If you try these variable names in a program, NetBeans responds by flagging the error with the red alert icon alongside the line in the source editor.

Variable names aren't the only aspect of Java that's case sensitive. Everything else you can give a name to in a program, including classes, packages, and methods, must be referred to using consistent capitalization.

> **NOTE** Some variable names represent multiple words, such as gameOver for the words "game over." Every letter in the variable name is lowercase except for the first letter of subsequent words, so the O in "over" is capitalized.
>
> This is not a requirement of the Java language. It's a naming convention that helps your programming in two ways. First, it makes variables easier to spot among the other elements of a Java program. Second, by following a consistent style in the naming of variables, you eliminate errors that can occur when you refer to a variable in several places in a program. The style of capitalization used in this book is the one that has been adopted by most Java programmers over the years.

Words that are used by the Java language, such as public, class, true, and false, cannot be the name of variables.

Storing Information in Variables

You can store a value in a variable at the same time that you create the variable in a Java program. You also can put a value in the variable at any time later in the program.

To set a starting value for a variable upon its creation, use the equal sign (=). Here's an example of creating a double floating-point variable called pi with the starting value of 3.14:

```
double pi = 3.14;
```

A value like 3.14 in a Java statement is called a *literal*.

All variables that store numbers can be set up in a similar fashion. If you're setting up a character or a string variable, quotation marks must be placed around the value as described earlier in this chapter.

You also can set one variable equal to the value of another variable if they both are of the same type. Consider the following example:

```
int distance = 300;
int totalDistance = distance;
```

First, an integer variable called `distance` is created with a starting value of 300. Next, an integer variable called `totalDistance` is created with the same value as `distance`. Both variables have the starting value of 300. In future chapters, you learn how to convert one variable's value to the type of another variable.

 CAUTION If you do not give a variable a starting value, you must give it a value before you use it in another statement. If you don't, when your program is compiled, you might get an error stating that the variable "may not have been initialized."

As you've learned, Java has similar numeric variables that hold values of different sizes. Both `int` and `long` hold integers, but `long` holds a larger range of possible values. Both `float` and `double` carry floating-point numbers, but `double` is bigger.

You can append a letter to a numeric value to indicate the value's type, as in this statement:

```
float pi = 3.14F;
```

The *F* after the value 3.14 indicates that it's a `float` value. If the letter was omitted, Java assumes that 3.14 is a `double` value.

The letter *L* is used for `long` integers and *D* for `double` floating-point values. Using `D` for `double` is optional because that's the default for floating-point values.

Another naming convention in Java is to capitalize every letter in the names of variables that do not change in value. These variables are called constants. The following creates three constants:

```
final int TOUCHDOWN = 6;
final int FIELDGOAL = 3;
final int PAT = 1;
```

Because constants never change in value, you might wonder why one ever should be used—you can just use the value assigned to the constant instead. One advantage of using constants is that they make a program easier to understand.

In the preceding three statements, the name of the constant was capitalized. This is not required in Java, but it has become a standard convention among programmers to distinguish constants from other variables.

All About Operators

Statements can use mathematical expressions by employing the operators +, -, *, /, and %. You use these operators to crunch numbers throughout your Java programs.

An addition expression in Java uses the + operator, as in these statements:

```
double power = 10;
power = power + 3;
```

The second statement uses the + operator to set the `power` variable equal to its current value plus 3. A subtraction expression uses the - operator:

```
power = power - 2;
```

This expression sets the `power` variable equal to its current value minus 2.

A division expression uses the / sign:

```
power = power / 3;
```

This sets the `power` variable to its current value divided by 3.

To find a remainder from a division expression, use the % operator (also called the modulo operator). The following statement finds the remainder of 245 divided by 3:

```
int remainder = 245 % 3;
```

A multiplication expression uses the * sign. Here's a statement that employs a multiplication expression as part of a more complicated statement:

```
int score = 20;
int total = 500 + (score * 12);
```

The `score * 12` part of the expression multiplies `score` by 12. The full statement multiples `score` by 12 and then adds 500 to the result. Because `score` equals 20, the result of the expression is that `total` equals 740: 500 + (20 * 12).

Incrementing and Decrementing a Variable

A common task in programs is changing the value of a variable by one. You can increase the value by one, which is called *incrementing* the variable, or decrease the value by one, which is *decrementing* the variable. There are operators to accomplish both of these tasks.

To increment the value of a variable by 1, use the ++ operator, as in the following statement:

```
health++;
```

This statement adds 1 to the value stored in the `health` variable.

To decrement the value of a variable by 1, use the -- operator:

```
health--;
```

This statement reduces `health` by 1.

You also can put the increment and decrement operators in front of the variable name, as in the following statements:

```
++health;
--health;
```

Putting the operator in front of the variable name is called *prefixing*, and putting it after the name is called *postfixing*.

 NOTE Confused yet? This is easier than it sounds, if you think back to school when you learned about prefixes. Just as a prefix such as *sub-* or *un-* goes at the start of a word like *suburban* or *unexpected*, a prefix operator goes at the start of a variable name. A postfix operator goes at the end.

The difference between prefixed and postfixed operators becomes important when you use the increment and decrement operators inside an expression.

Consider the following statements:

```
int x = 3;
int answer = x++ * 10;
```

What does the `answer` variable equal after these statements are handled? You might expect it to equal 40—which would be true if 3 was incremented by 1, which equals 4, and then 4 was multiplied by 10.

However, `answer` ends up with the value 30 because the postfixed operator was used instead of the prefixed operator.

When a postfixed operator is used on a variable inside an expression, the variable's value doesn't change until after the expression has been completely evaluated. The statement `int answer = x++ * 10` does the same thing in the same order, as the following two statements:

```
int answer = x * 10;
x++;
```

The opposite is true of prefixed operators. If they are used on a variable inside an expression, the variable's value changes before the expression is evaluated.

Consider the following statements:

```
int x = 3;
int answer = ++x * 10;
```

This does result in the `answer` variable being equal to 40. The prefixed operator causes the value of the `x` variable to be changed before the expression is evaluated. The statement `int answer = ++x * 10` does the same thing, in order, as these statements:

```
x++;
int answer = x * 10;
```

It's easy to become exasperated with the `++` and `--` operators because they're not as straightforward as many of the concepts you encounter in this book.

I hope I'm not breaking some unwritten code of Java programmers by telling you this, but you don't need to use the increment and decrement operators in your own programs. You can achieve the same results by using the `+` and `-` operators like this:

```
x = x + 1;
y = y - 1;
```

Incrementing and decrementing are useful shortcuts, but taking the longer route in an expression is fine, too.

Operator Precedence

When you are using an expression with more than one operator, you need to know what order the computer uses as it works out the expression. Consider the following statements:

```
int y = 10;
x = y * 3 + 5;
```

Unless you know what order the computer uses when working out the math in these statements, you cannot be sure what the `x` variable will be set to. It could be set to either 35 or 80, depending on whether `y * 3` is evaluated first or `3 + 5` is evaluated first.

The following evaluation order is used when working out an expression:

1. Incrementing and decrementing take place first.

2. Multiplication, division, and modulus division occur next.

3. Addition and subtraction follow.

4. Comparisons take place next.

5. The equal sign (=) is used to set a variable's value.

Because multiplication takes place before addition, you can revisit the previous example and come up with the answer: y is multiplied by 3 first, which equals 30, and then 5 is added. The x variable is set to 35.

Comparisons are discussed during Chapter 7. The rest has been described during this chapter, so you should be able to figure out the result of the following statements:

```
int x = 5;
int number = x++ * 6 + 4 * 10 / 2;
```

These statements set the number variable equal to 50.

How does the computer come up with this total? First, the increment operator is handled, and x++ sets the value of the x variable to 6. However, make note that the ++ operator is postfixed after x in the expression. This means that the expression is evaluated with the original value of x.

Because the original value of x is used before the variable is incremented, the expression becomes the following:

```
int number = 5 * 6 + 4 * 10 / 2;
```

Now, multiplication and division are handled from left to right. First, 5 is multiplied by 6, 4 is multiplied by 10, and that result is divided by 2 (4 * 10 / 2). The expression becomes the following:

```
int number = 30 + 20;
```

This expression results in the number variable being set to 50.

If you want an expression to be evaluated in a different order, you can use parentheses to group parts of an expression that should be handled first. For example, the expression x = 5 * 3 + 2; would normally cause x to equal 17 because multiplication is handled before addition. However, look at a modified form of that expression:

```
x = 5 * (3 + 2);
```

In this case, the expression within the parentheses is handled first, so the result equals 25. You can use parentheses as often as needed in a statement.

Using Expressions

As you worked on a particularly unpleasant math problem in school, did you ever complain to a higher power, protesting that you would never use this knowledge in your life? Sorry to break this to you, but your teachers were right—your math skills come in handy in your computer programming. That's the bad news.

The good news is that the computer does any math you ask it to do. Expressions are used frequently in your computer programs to accomplish tasks such as the following:

- Changing the value of a variable
- Counting the number of times something has happened in a program
- Using a mathematical formula in a program

As you write computer programs, you find yourself drawing on your old math lessons as you use expressions. Expressions can use addition, subtraction, multiplication, division, and modulus division.

To see expressions in action, return to NetBeans and create a new empty Java file in the com.javaminecraft package with the class name PlanetWeight. This program tracks a person's weight loss and gain as she travels to other bodies in the solar system. Enter the full text of Listing 6.2 in the source editor. Each part of the program is discussed in turn.

LISTING 6.2 The Full Text of PlanetWeight.java

```
 1: package com.javaminecraft;
 2:
 3: class PlanetWeight {
 4:     public static void main(String[] arguments) {
 5:         System.out.print("Your weight on Earth is ");
 6:         double weight = 178;
 7:         System.out.println(weight);
 8:
 9:         System.out.print("Your weight on Mercury is ");
10:         double mercury = weight * .378;
11:         System.out.println(mercury);
12:
13:         System.out.print("Your weight on the Moon is ");
14:         double moon = weight * .166;
15:         System.out.println(moon);
16:
17:         System.out.print("Your weight on Jupiter is ");
18:         double jupiter = weight * 2.364;
```

```
19:          System.out.println(jupiter);
20:      }
21: }
```

When you're done, save the file and it should compile automatically. Run the program with the menu command Run, Run File. The output is shown in the Output pane in Figure 6.1.

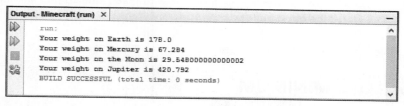

FIGURE 6.1

The output of the PlanetWeight *program.*

As in other programs you have created, the PlanetWeight program uses a main() block statement for all its work. This statement can be broken into the following four sections:

- **Lines 5–7:** The person's weight is set initially to 178.
- **Lines 9–11:** Mercury weight loss is calculated.
- **Lines 13–15:** Weight loss on the moon is determined.
- **Lines 17–19:** Jupiter weight gain is calculated.

Line 6 creates the weight variable and designates it as an integer variable with int. The variable is given the initial value 178 and used throughout the program to monitor the person's weight.

The next line is similar to several other statements in the program:

```
System.out.println(weight);
```

The System.out.println() command displays a string that is contained within its parentheses marks. On Line 5, the System.out.print() command displays the text "Your weight on Earth is". There are several System.out.print() and System.out.println() statements in the program.

The difference between them is that print() does not start a new line after displaying the text, whereas println() does.

NOTE   For the sample value, the `PlanetWeight` application used a weight of 178 pounds, which just happens to be the average weight of a person in North America according to a BMC Health Study. That compares to the average 164-pound Oceanian, 156-pound European, 150-pound Latin American, 134-pound African, and 127-pound Asian.

So if you're reading this in North America and someone asks you, "Would you like an apple pie with that?," the correct answer to the question is no.

THE ABSOLUTE MINIMUM

Now that you have been introduced to variables and expressions, you can give a wide range of instructions to your computer in a program.

With the skills you have developed during this chapter, you can write programs that accomplish many of the same tasks as a calculator, handling sophisticated mathematical equations with ease.

You've also learned that a trip to the moon is a particularly effective weight-loss plan.

Numbers are only one kind of thing that can be stored in a variable. You also can store characters, strings of characters, and special `true` or `false` values called `boolean` variables. The next chapter expands your knowledge of `String` variables and how they are stored and used.

IN THIS CHAPTER

- Use strings to store text
- Display strings in a program
- Include special characters in a string
- Paste two strings together
- Include variables in a string
- Compare two strings
- Determine the length of a string

7

USE STRINGS TO COMMUNICATE

In Minecraft, information often is presented to players as a line of text on the screen. A line of text in a Java program is called a *string*.

Strings are the simplest and most common means to communicate with users in any program. They are collections of text—letters, numbers, punctuation, and other characters. During this chapter, you learn all about working with strings.

Storing Text in Strings

Strings store text and present it to users. The most basic element of a string is a character. A *character* is a single letter, number, punctuation mark, or other symbol.

In Java programs, a character is one of the types of information that can be stored in a variable. Character variables are created with the `char` type in a statement such as the following:

```
char keyPressed;
```

This statement creates a variable named `keyPressed` that can store a character. When you create character variables, you can set them up with an initial value, as in the following:

```
char quitKey = '@';
```

The value of the character must be surrounded by single quotation marks.

A string is a collection of characters. You can set up a variable to hold a string value by following `String` with the name of the variable, as in this statement:

```
String fullName = "Markus Persson";
```

This statement creates a string variable called `fullName` containing the text "Markus Persson", the Swedish programmer who created Minecraft. A string is denoted with double quotation marks around the text in a Java statement. These quotation marks are not included in the string itself.

Unlike the other types of variables you have used—`int`, `float`, `char`, `boolean`, and so on—the name of the `String` type is capitalized.

Strings are a special kind of information called *objects*, and the types of all objects are capitalized in Java. You learn about objects during Chapter 11, "Create Your First Object." The important thing to note during this chapter is that strings are different from the other variable types, and because of this difference, `String` is capitalized.

Displaying Strings in Programs

The most basic way to display a string in a Java program is with the `System.out.println()` statement. This statement takes strings and other variables inside the parentheses and displays their values on the system output device, which is the computer's monitor. Here's an example:

```
System.out.println("Alfie has been killed by a Magma Cube.");
```

This statement causes the following text to be displayed:

```
Alfie has been killed by a Magma Cube.
```

Displaying text on the screen often is called *printing*, which is what `println()` stands for—print line. You can use the `System.out.println()` statement to display text within double quotation marks and also to display variables, as you see later. Put all the material you want to be displayed within the parentheses.

Another way to display text is to call `System.out.print()`. This statement displays strings and other variables inside the parentheses, but unlike `System.out.println()`, it enables subsequent statements to display text on the same line.

You can use `System.out.print()` several times in a row to display several things on the same line, as in this example:

```
System.out.print("Your ");
System.out.print("bed ");
System.out.print("is ");
System.out.print("missing ");
System.out.print("or ");
System.out.println("obstructed.");
```

These statements cause the following text to be displayed:

```
Your bed is missing or obstructed.
```

Using Special Characters in Strings

When a string is being created or displayed, its text must be enclosed within double quotation marks. These quotation marks are not displayed, which brings up a good question: What if you want to display double quotation marks?

To display them, Java has created a special code that can be put into a string: \". Whenever this code is encountered in a string, it is replaced with a double quotation mark. For example, examine the following:

```
System.out.println("Markus \"Notch\" Perrson");
```

This code is displayed as the following:

```
Markus "Notch" Persson
```

This special character also is called an escape sequence, and you can insert several such characters into a string in this manner. The following list shows these characters; note that each is preceded by a backslash (\).

Special Characters	Display
\'	Single quotation mark
\"	Double quotation mark
\\	Backslash
\t	Tab
\b	Backspace
\r	Carriage return
\f	Formfeed
\n	Newline

The newline character causes the text following the newline character to be displayed at the beginning of the next line. Look at this example:

```
System.out.println("Starting server\nLoading properties");
```

This statement would be displayed like this:

```
Starting server
Loading properties
```

Pasting Strings Together

When you use `System.out.println()` and work with strings in other ways, you can paste two strings together by using +, the same operator that is used to add numbers.

The + operator has a different meaning in relation to strings. Instead of performing some math, it pastes two strings together. This action can cause strings to be displayed together or make one big string out of two smaller ones.

Concatenation is the word used to describe this action because it means to link two things together.

The following statement uses the + operator to display a long string:

```
System.out.println("\"\'Minecraft\' is a towering achievement \n"
    + "in the very possibilities of gaming.\"\n"
    + "\t-- Alec Meer, EuroGamer.Net");
```

Instead of putting this entire string on a single line, which would make it harder to understand when you look at the program later, the + operator is used to break the text over three lines of the program's source code. When this statement is displayed, it appears as the following:

```
"'Minecraft' is a towering achievement
in the very possibilities of gaming."
    -- Alec Meer, EuroGamer.Net
```

Several special characters are used in the string: \", \', \n, and \t. To better familiarize yourself with these characters, compare the output with the System.out.println() statement that produced it.

Using Other Variables with Strings

Although you can use the + operator to paste two strings together, you use it more often to link strings and other variables. Take a look at the following:

```
double version = 1.8;
char rating = 'G';
System.out.println("Minecraft version: " + version);
System.out.println("Rated " + rating);
```

This code will be displayed as the following:

```
Minecraft version: 1.8
Rated G
```

This example displays a unique facet about how the + operator works with strings. It can cause variables that are not strings to be treated just like strings when they are displayed. The variable version is an integer set to the value 1.8. It is displayed after the string "Minecraft version:". The System.out.println() statement is being asked to display a string plus an integer. This statement works because at least one part of the group is a string. The Java language offers this functionality to make displaying information easier.

One thing you might want to do with a string is paste something to it several times, as in the following example:

```
String mobNames = "";
mobNames = mobNames + "Ocelot ";
mobNames = mobNames + "Silverfish ";
mobNames = mobNames + "Blaze";
```

This code would result in the mobNames variable being set to "Ocelot Silverfish Blaze". The first line creates the mobNames variable and sets it to be an empty string because there's nothing between the double quotation marks. The second line sets the `mobNames` variable equal to its current string plus the string "Ocelot" added to the end. The next two lines add "Silverfish" and "Blaze" in the same way.

As you can see, when you are pasting more text at the end of a variable, the name of the variable has to be listed twice. Java offers a shortcut to simplify this process: the += operator. The += operator combines the functions of the = and + operators. With strings, it is used to add something to the end of an existing string. The `mobNames` example can be shortened by using +=, as shown in the following statements:

```
String mobNames = "";
mobNames += "Ocelot ";
mobNames += "Silverfish ";
mobNames += "Blaze";
```

This code produces the same result: `mobNames` is set to "Ocelot Silverfish Blaze".

Advanced String Handling

There are several other ways you can examine a string variable and change its value. These advanced features are possible because strings are objects in the Java language. Working with strings develops skills you'll use on other objects later.

Comparing Two Strings

One thing you are testing often in your programs is whether one string is equal to another. You do this by using `equals()` in a statement with both of the strings, as in this example:

```
String favorite = "TNT";
String guess = "cow cannon";
System.out.println("Is Kat's favorite weapon a " + guess + "?");
System.out.println("Answer: " + favorite.equals(guess));
```

This example uses two different string variables. One, `favorite`, stores the name of Kat's favorite mob-hunting instrument: a cow cannon. The other, `guess`, stores a guess as to what her favorite might be. The guess is that Kat prefers TNT.

The third line displays the text "Is Kat's favorite weapon a" followed by the value of the `guess` variable, and then a question mark. The fourth line displays the text "Answer:" and then contains something new:

```
favorite.equals(guess)
```

This part of the statement is known as a method. A method is a way to accomplish a task in a Java program. This method's task is to determine whether one string has the same value as another. If the two string variables have the same values, the text `true` is displayed. If not, the text `false` is displayed. The following is the output of this example:

```
Is Kat's favorite weapon a cow cannon?
Answer: false
```

Determining the Length of a String

It also can be useful to determine the length of a string in characters. You do this with the `length()` method. This method works in the same fashion as the `equals()` method, except that only one string variable is involved. Look at the following example:

```
String developer = "Jens Bergensten";
int nameLength = developer.length();
```

This example sets `nameLength`, an integer variable, equal to 15. The `developer.length()` method counts the number of characters in the string variable called `developer` and stores this count in the `nameLength` integer variable.

Changing a String's Case

Because computers take everything literally, it's easy to confuse them. Although a human would recognize that the text *Notch* and the text *NOTCH* refer to the same thing, most computers would disagree. The `equals()` method discussed previously in this chapter would state authoritatively that `Notch` is not equal to `NOTCH`.

To get around some of these obstacles, Java has methods that display a string variable as all uppercase letters or all lowercase letters—`toUpperCase()` and `toLowerCase()`, respectively. The following example shows the `toUpperCase()` method in action:

```
String name = "Notch";
String change = name.toUpperCase();
```

This code sets the string variable `change` equal to the `name` string variable converted to all uppercase letters—"NOTCH". The `toLowerCase()` method works in the same fashion but returns an all-lowercase string value.

Note that the `toUpperCase()` method does not change the case of the string variable it is called on. In the preceding example, the `name` variable is still equal to `Notch`. An important concept to remember in Java is that strings do not change in value in Java after they are created. Later, you will see how to create an object for something similar to a string that does change in value.

 NOTE   Another way to get around this particular obstacle is to call the `equalsIgnoreCase()` method, which compares two strings irrespective of capitalization. Calling that method to compare the string `Notch` to `NOTCH` would return the value `true` to indicate they match.

Looking for a String

Another common task when handling strings is to see whether one string can be found inside another. To look inside a string, use its `indexOf()` method. Put the string you are looking for inside the parentheses. If the string is not found, `indexOf()` produces the value -1. If the string is found, `indexOf()` produces an integer that represents the position where the string begins. Positions in a string are numbered upward from 0, beginning with the first character in the string. In the string `Minecraft`, the text `craft` begins at position 4.

One possible use of the `indexOf()` method would be to search the server properties file of Minecraft for the place where the world's seed is set. The seed is a random number that determines what the world looks like when it is generated before a player enters it for the first time. Two worlds created from the same seed will always look the same.

If the text of the server properties file was stored in a string called `file`, you could search it for the text `level-seed=` with the following statement.

```
int position = file.indexOf("level-seed=");
```

If that text can be found in the `file` string, `position` equals the position at which the text `level-seed=` begins. Otherwise, it will equal -1.

If you are looking for one string inside another but don't care about the position, a string's `contains()` method returns a boolean value. It is `true` if the looked-for string is found and `false` otherwise. Here's an example:

```
if (file.contains("level-seed=") == false) {
    System.out.println("Level seed not found");
}
```

CAUTION The `indexOf()` and `contains()` methods are case sensitive, which means they look only for text capitalized exactly like the search string. If the string contains the same text capitalized differently, `indexOf()` produces the value -1 and `contains()` returns false.

Presenting Credits

Next, to reinforce the string-handling features that have been covered, you write a Java program to display credits for a game. You can probably guess which one.

Return to the `Minecraft` project in NetBeans and create a new empty Java file in the `com.javaminecraft` project called `Credits`. Enter the text of Listing 7.1 into the source editor, and save the file when you're done.

LISTING 7.1 The `Credits` Program

```
 1: package com.javaminecraft;
 2:
 3: class Credits {
 4:     public static void main(String[] arguments) {
 5:         // set up game information
 6:         String title = "Minecraft";
 7:         int year = 2009;
 8:         String creator = "Markus 'Notch' Persson";
 9:         String developer = "Jens 'Jeb' Bergensten";
10:         String music = "Daniel 'C418' Rosenfeld";
11:         String art = "Kristoffer Zetterstrand";
12:         // display information
13:         System.out.println(title + " (" + year + ")\n" +
14:             "A " + creator + " game.\n\n" +
15:             "Developer\t" + developer + "\n" +
16:             "Music\t\t" + music + "\n" +
17:             "Art\t\t" + art);
18:     }
19: }
```

Look over the program and see whether you can figure out what it's doing at each stage. Here's a breakdown of what's taking place:

- Line 3 gives the Java program the name `Credits`.

- Line 4 begins the `main()` method in which all the program's work gets done.

- Lines 6–11 set up variables to hold information about the game, its creator, and its contributors. One of the variables, `year`, is an integer. The rest are string variables.

- Lines 13–17 are one long `System.out.println()` statement. Everything between the first parenthesis on Line 13 and the last parenthesis on Line 17 is displayed onscreen. The newline character (\n) causes the text after it to be displayed at the beginning of a new line. The tab character (\t) inserts tab spacing in the output. The rest are either text or string variables that should be shown.

- Line 18 ends the `main()` block statement.

- Line 19 ends the program.

If you do encounter error messages, correct any typos you find in your version of the `Credits` program and save it again. NetBeans compiles the program automatically. When you run the program, you see an output window like the Output pane in Figure 7.1.

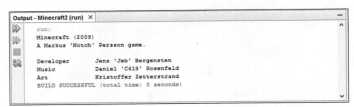

FIGURE 7.1

The output of the `Credits` *program.*

THE ABSOLUTE MINIMUM

When your version of `Credits` looks like Figure 7.1, give yourself some credit. Seven chapters into this book, you're writing longer Java programs and dealing with more sophisticated issues. Strings are something you use every time you sit down to write a program. In your mods, you'll be using strings in many ways to communicate with players.

IN THIS CHAPTER

- Use the `if` statement for basic conditional tests
- Test whether one value is greater than or less than another
- Test whether two values are equal or unequal
- Use `else` statements as the opposite of `if` statements
- Chain several conditional tests together
- Use the `switch` statement for complicated conditional tests

8

USE CONDITIONAL TESTS TO MAKE DECISIONS

When you write a computer program, you provide the computer with a list of instructions called *statements*, and these instructions are followed to the letter. You can tell the computer to work out some unpleasant mathematical formulas, and it works them out. Tell it to display some information, and it dutifully responds.

There are times when you need the computer to be more selective about what it does. For example, if you have written a Minecraft mod that makes creepers afraid of the player, you want to check whether a mob is a creeper before scaring it off. Otherwise, it will make all mobs afraid.

The way to accomplish this task in a Java program is to use a *conditional*, a statement that causes something to happen in a program only if a specific condition is met. During this chapter, you learn how to use the conditionals `if`, `else`, and `switch`.

When a Java program makes a decision, it does so by employing a conditional statement. During this chapter, you are checking the condition of several things in your Java programs using the conditional keywords `if`, `else`, `switch`, `case`, and `break`. You also use the conditional operators `==`, `!=`, `<`, `>`, `<=`, `>=`, and `?`, along with `boolean` variables.

`if` Statements

The most basic way to test a condition in Java is by using an `if` statement. The `if` statement tests whether a condition is true or false and takes action only if the condition is true.

You use `if` along with the condition to test, as in the following statement:

```
long account = -17_000_000_000_000L;
if (account < 0) {
    System.out.println("Account overdrawn; you need a bailout");
}
```

The `if` statement checks whether the `account` variable is below 0 by using the less than operator, `<`. If it is, the block within the `if` statement is run, displaying text.

The block runs only if the condition is true. In the preceding example, if the `account` variable has a value of `0` or higher, the `println` statement is ignored. Note that the condition you test must be surrounded by parentheses, as in `(account < 0)`.

The less-than operator, `<`, is one of several operators you can use with conditional statements.

Less-Than and Greater-Than Comparisons

In the preceding section, the `<` operator is used the same way as in math class: as a less-than sign. There also is a greater-than conditional operator, `>`, which is used in the following statements:

```
int elephantWeight = 900;
int elephantTotal = 13;
```

```
int cleaningExpense = 200;

if (elephantWeight > 780) {
    System.out.println("Elephant too big for tightrope act");
}

if (elephantTotal > 12) {
    cleaningExpense = cleaningExpense + 150;
}
```

The first `if` statement tests whether the value of the `elephantWeight` variable is greater than 780. The second `if` statement tests whether the `elephantTotal` variable is greater than 12.

If the two preceding statements are used in a program where `elephantWeight` is equal to 600 and `elephantTotal` is equal to 10, the statements within each `if` block are ignored.

You can determine whether something is less than or equal to something else with the `<=` operator. Here's an example:

```
if (account <= 0) {
    System.out.println("You are flat broke");
}
```

There's also a `>=` operator for greater-than-or-equal-to tests.

Equal and Not Equal Comparisons

Another condition to check in a program is equality. Is a variable equal to a specific value? Is one variable equal to the value of another? These questions can be answered with the `==` operator, as in the following statements:

```
if (answer == rightAnswer) {
    studentGrade = studentGrade + 10;
}

if (studentGrade == 100) {
    System.out.println("Show off!");
}
```

CAUTION The operator used to conduct equality tests has two equal signs: ==. It's easy to confuse this operator with the = operator, which is used to give a value to a variable. Always use two equal signs in a conditional statement.

You also can test inequality, whether something is not equal to something else, with the != operator, as follows:

```
if (answer != rightAnswer) {
    score = score - 5;
}
```

You can use the == and != operators with every type of variable except for strings because strings are objects.

Organizing a Program with Block Statements

Up to this point, the `if` statements in this chapter have been accompanied by a block contained within the { and } brackets. (I believe the technical term for these characters is "squiggly bracket marks.")

Previously, you have seen how block statements are used to mark the beginning and end of the `main()` block of a Java program. Each statement within the `main()` block is handled when the program is run.

An `if` statement does not require a block statement. It can occupy a single line, as in this example:

```
if (account <= 0) System.out.println("No more money");
```

The statement that follows the `if` conditional is executed only if the conditional is true. When there's more than one statement inside the `if`, a block statement is required.

Listing 8.1 is an example of a Java program with a block statement used to denote the `main()` block. The block statement begins with the opening bracket, {, on Line 4 and ends with the closing bracket, }, on Line 15. Create a new empty Java file called Game in NetBeans in the `com.javaminecraft` package, and enter the text in Listing 8.1.

LISTING 8.1 The Full Text of Game.java

```
1: package com.javaminecraft;
2:
3: class Game {
```

```
 4:     public static void main(String[] arguments) {
 5:         int total = 0;
 6:         int score = 7;
 7:         if (score == 7) {
 8:             System.out.println("You score a touchdown!");
 9:         }
10:         if (score == 3) {
11:             System.out.println("You kick a field goal!");
12:         }
13:         total = total + score;
14:         System.out.println("Total score: " + total);
15:     }
16: }
```

When you run the program, the output should resemble Figure 8.1.

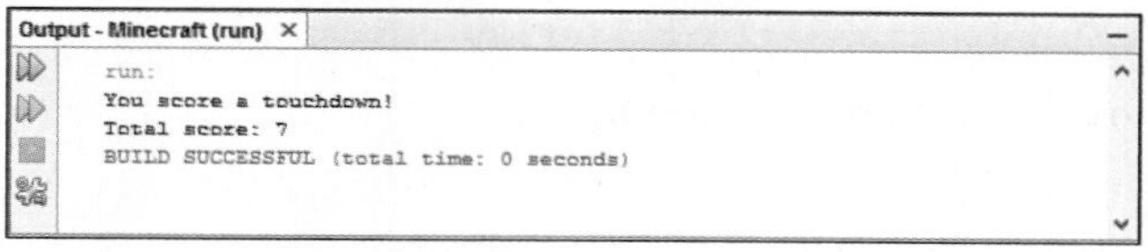

FIGURE 8.1

The output of the Game *program.*

You can use block statements in if statements to make the computer do more than one thing if a condition is true. The following is an example of an if statement that includes a block statement:

```
int playerScore = 12000;
int playerLives = 3;
int difficultyLevel = 10;


if (playerScore > 9999) {
    playerLives++;
    System.out.println("Extra life!");
    difficultyLevel = difficultyLevel + 5;
}
```

The brackets are used to group all statements that are part of the if statement. If the variable playerScore is greater than 9,999, three things happen:

- The value of the `playerLives` variable increases by one (because the increment operator ++ is used).

- The text "Extra life!" is displayed.

- The value of the `difficultyLevel` variable is increased by 5.

If the variable `playerScore` is not greater than 9,999, nothing happens. All three statements inside the `if` statement block are ignored.

if-else Statements

There are times when you want to do something if a condition is true and something else if the condition is false. You can do this by using the `else` statement in addition to the `if` statement, as in the following example:

```
int score = 30;
int answer = 17;
int correctAnswer = 13;


if (answer == correctAnswer) {
    score += 10;
    System.out.println("That's right. You get 10 points");
} else {
    score -= 5;
    System.out.println("Sorry, that's wrong. You lose 5 points");
}
```

The `else` statement does not have a condition listed alongside it, unlike the `if` statement. The `else` statement is matched with the `if` statement that immediately precedes it. You also can use `else` to chain several `if` statements together, as in the following example:

```
if (grade == 'A') {
    System.out.println("You got an A. Awesome!");
} else if (grade == 'B') {
    System.out.println("You got a B. Beautiful!");
} else if (grade == 'C') {
    System.out.println("You got a C. Concerning!");
} else {
    System.out.println("You got an F. Flabbergasting!");
}
```

By putting together several `if` and `else` statements in this way, you can handle a variety of conditions. The preceding example sends a specific message to A students, B students, C students, and students who will lose all Minecraft privileges until their grades improve.

`switch` Statements

The `if` and `else` statements are good for situations with two possible conditions, but there are times when you have more than two conditions.

With the preceding grade example, you saw that `if` and `else` statements can be chained to handle several different conditions.

Another way to do this is with the `switch` statement, which can test for a variety of conditions and respond accordingly. In the following code, the grading example has been rewritten with a `switch` statement:

```
switch (grade) {
    case 'A':
        System.out.println("You got an A. Awesome!");
        break;
    case 'B':
        System.out.println("You got a B. Beautiful!");
        break;
    case 'C':
        System.out.println("You got a C. Concerning!");
        break;
    default:
        System.out.println("You got an F. Flabbergasting!");
}
```

The first line of the `switch` statement specifies the variable that is tested—in this example, `grade`. Then, the `switch` statement uses the { and } brackets to form a block statement.

 NOTE You might be wondering whether `break` has to be used at the end of each block that follows a `case` statement. The answer is no. You can omit the `break`, which causes the statements in the next case to be executed as well regardless of their `case` conditional. In most cases, you're likely to want a `break` statement at the end of each group.

Each case statement checks the test variable in the switch statement against a specific value. The value used in a case statement can be a character, an integer, or a string. In the preceding example, there are case statements for the characters A, B, and C. Each has one or two statements that follow it. When one of these case statements matches the variable in switch, the computer handles the statements after the case statement until it encounters a break statement.

For example, if the grade variable has the value of B, the text "You got a B. Beautiful!" is displayed. The next statement is break, so nothing else in the switch statement is executed. The break statement tells the computer to break out of the switch statement.

Forgetting to use break statements in a switch statement can lead to undesired results. If there were no break statements in this grading example, the first three "You got a" messages would be displayed whether the grade variable equals A, B, or C.

The default statement is used as a catch-all if none of the preceding case statements is true. In this example, it occurs if the grade variable does not equal A, B, or C. You do not have to use a default statement with every switch block statement you use in your programs. If it is omitted, nothing happens if none of the case statements has the correct value.

The Commodity class in Listing 8.2 uses switch to either buy or sell an unspecified commodity. The commodity costs $20 when purchased and earns $15 when sold.

A switch-case statement tests the value of a string named command, running one block if it equals BUY and another if it equals SELL. Create this class as an empty Java file in the com.javaminecraft package.

LISTING 8.2 The Full Text of Commodity.java

```
 1: package com.javaminecraft;
 2:
 3: class Commodity {
 4:     public static void main(String[] arguments) {
 5:         String command = "BUY";
 6:         int balance = 550;
 7:         int quantity = 42;
 8:
 9:         switch (command) {
10:             case "BUY":
11:                 quantity += 5;
```

```
12:                        balance -= 20;
13:                        break;
14:                   case "SELL":
15:                        quantity -= 5;
16:                        balance += 15;
17:                }
18:            System.out.println("Balance: " + balance + "\n"
19:                + "Quantity: " + quantity);
20:        }
21: }
```

This application sets the command string to BUY in Line 5. When the switch is tested, the case block in Lines 11–13 is run. The quantity of the commodity increases by 5 and the balance is lowered by $20.

When the Commodity program is run, it produces the output shown in Figure 8.2.

FIGURE 8.2

The output of the Commodity *program.*

The Ternary Operator

The most complicated conditional statement in Java is the ternary operator: ?.

You can use the ternary operator when you want to assign a value or display a value based on a condition. For example, consider a video game that sets the numberOfMobs variable based on whether the skillLevel variable is greater than 5. One way you can do this is an if-else statement:

```
if (skillLevel > 5) {
    numberOfMobs = 20;
} else {
    numberOfMobs = 10;
}
```

A shorter way to do this is to use the ternary operator. A ternary expression has five parts:

- The condition to test, surrounded by parentheses, as in `(skillLevel > 5)`
- A question mark (?)
- The value to use if the condition is true
- A colon (:)
- The value to use if the condition is false

To use the ternary operator to set `numberOfMobs` based on `skillLevel`, you could use the following statement:

```
int numberOfMobs = (skillLevel > 5) ? 20 : 10;
```

You also can use the ternary operator to determine what information to display. Consider the example of a program that displays the text "Mr." or "Ms." depending on the value of the `gender` variable. Here's a statement that accomplishes this:

```
System.out.print( (gender.equals("male")) ? "Mr." : "Ms." );
```

The ternary operator can be useful, but it's also the hardest conditional in Java to understand. As you learn Java, you don't encounter any situations where the ternary operator must be used instead of `if-else` statements.

Watching the Clock

This chapter's final project gives you another look at each of the conditional tests you can use in your programs. For this project, you use Java's built-in timekeeping feature, which keeps track of the current date and time, and present this information in sentence form.

Load NetBeans or another development tool you're using to create Java programs, give a new document the name `Clock.java`, and put it in the package `com.javaminecraft`. This program is long, but most of it consists of long conditional statements. Type the full text of Listing 8.3 into the editor, and save the file as `Clock.java` when you're done.

LISTING 8.3   The Full Text of `Clock.java`

```
1: package com.javaminecraft;
2:
3: import java.time.*;
```

```
 4: import java.time.temporal.*;
 5:
 6: class Clock {
 7:     public static void main(String[] arguments) {
 8:         // get current time and date
 9:         LocalDateTime now = LocalDateTime.now();
10:         int hour = now.get(ChronoField.HOUR_OF_DAY);
11:         int minute = now.get(ChronoField.MINUTE_OF_HOUR);
12:         int month = now.get(ChronoField.MONTH_OF_YEAR);
13:         int day = now.get(ChronoField.DAY_OF_MONTH);
14:         int year = now.get(ChronoField.YEAR);
15:
16:         // display greeting
17:         if (hour < 12) {
18:             System.out.println("Good morning.\n");
19:         } else if (hour < 17) {
20:             System.out.println("Good afternoon.\n");
21:         } else {
22:             System.out.println("Good evening.\n");
23:         }
24:
25:         // begin time message by showing the minutes
26:         System.out.print("It's");
27:         if (minute != 0) {
28:             System.out.print(" " + minute + " ");
29:             System.out.print( (minute != 1) ? "minutes" :
30:                 "minute");
31:             System.out.print(" past");
32:         }
33:
34:         // display the hour
35:         System.out.print(" ");
36:         System.out.print( (hour > 12) ? (hour - 12) : hour );
37:         System.out.print(" o'clock on ");
38:
39:         // display the name of the month
```

```
40:        switch (month) {
41:            case 1:
42:                System.out.print("January");
43:                break;
44:            case 2:
45:                System.out.print("February");
46:                break;
47:            case 3:
48:                System.out.print("March");
49:                break;
50:            case 4:
51:                System.out.print("April");
52:                break;
53:            case 5:
54:                System.out.print("May");
55:                break;
56:            case 6:
57:                System.out.print("June");
58:                break;
59:            case 7:
60:                System.out.print("July");
61:                break;
62:            case 8:
63:                System.out.print("August");
64:                break;
65:            case 9:
66:                System.out.print("September");
67:                break;
68:            case 10:
69:                System.out.print("October");
70:                break;
71:            case 11:
72:                System.out.print("November");
73:                break;
```

```
74:                    case 12:
75:                        System.out.print("December");
76:                }
77:
78:                // display the date and year
79:                System.out.println(" " + day + ", " + year + ".");
80:        }
81: }
```

After the program is saved, look it over to get a good idea about how the conditional tests are being used.

 CAUTION   Because this program uses new features of Java 8, it won't compile if the current NetBeans project is set to use an earlier version of the language. To make sure the correct setting has been chosen, select File, Project Properties. In the Project Properties dialog, look for the Source/Binary Format value. It should be JDK 8.

With the exception of Lines 3–4 and Lines 8–14, the Clock program contains material that has been covered up to this point. After a series of variables are set up to hold the current date and time, a series of if or switch conditionals are used to determine what information should be displayed.

This program contains several uses of System.out.println() and System.out.print() to display strings.

Lines 8–14 refer to a LocalDateTime variable called now. The LocalDateTime variable type is capitalized because LocalDateTime is an object.

You learn how to create and work with objects during Chapter 11, "Create Your First Object." For this chapter, focus on what's taking place in those lines rather than how it's happening.

The Clock program is made up of the following sections:

- Line 3 enables your program to use a class that is needed to track the current date and time: java.time.LocalDateTime.

- Line 4 enables the program to use the class java.time.temporalfield.ChronoField, which sounds like something from a time travel movie.

- Lines 6–7 begin the Clock program and its main() statement block.

- Line 9 creates a `LocalDateTime` object called `now` that contains the current date and time of your system. The `now` object changes each time you run this program. (Unless the physical laws of the universe are altered and time stands still.)

- Lines 10–14 create variables to hold the `hour`, `minute`, `month`, `day`, and `year`. The values for these variables are pulled from the `LocalDateTime` object, which is the storehouse for all this information. The information within the parentheses, such as `ChronoField.DAY_OF_MONTH`, indicates which part of the date and time to pull.

- Lines 17–23 display one of three possible greetings: "Good morning.", "Good afternoon.", or "Good evening." The greeting to display is selected based on the value of the `hour` variable.

- Lines 26–32 display the current minute along with some accompanying text. First, the text "It's" is displayed in Line 26. If the value of `minute` is equal to 0, Lines 28–31 are ignored because of the `if` statement in Line 27. This statement is necessary because it would not make sense for the program to tell someone that it's 0 minutes past an hour. Line 28 displays the current value of the `minute` variable. A ternary operator is used in Lines 29–30 to display either the text "minutes" or "minute," depending on whether `minute` is equal to 1. Finally, in Line 31 the text "past" is displayed.

- Lines 35–37 display the current hour by using another ternary operator. This ternary conditional statement in Line 36 causes the hour to be displayed differently if it is larger than 12, which prevents the computer from stating times like "15 o'clock."

- Lines 40–76, almost half of the program, are a long `switch` statement that displays a different name of the month based on the integer value stored in the `month` variable.

- Line 79 finishes off the display by showing the current date and the year.

- Lines 80–81 close out the `main()` statement block and then the entire `Clock` program.

When you run this program, the output should display a sentence based on the current date and time. The output of the application is shown in the Output pane in Figure 8.3.

Run the program several times to see how it keeps up with the clock.

```
Output - Minecraft2 (run)  ×
    run:
    Good evening.

    It's 50 minutes past 11 o'clock on May 20, 2015.
    BUILD SUCCESSFUL (total time: 0 seconds)
```

FIGURE 8.3

The output of the Clock *program.*

NOTE   The Clock application uses the new Date/Time API introduced in Java 8. Earlier versions of Java used a different set of classes to work with dates and times. As you might recall from Chapter 5, "Understand How Java Programs Work," the Java Class Library includes thousands of classes that perform useful tasks. The java.time and java.time.temporalfield packages used in this program are part of the Date/Time API.

THE ABSOLUTE MINIMUM

Now that you can use conditional statements, the overall intelligence of your Java programs has improved greatly. Your programs can evaluate information and use it to react differently in different situations, even if information changes as the program is running. They can decide between two or more alternatives based on specific conditions.

Programming a computer forces you to break down a task into a logical set of steps to undertake and decisions that must be made. This will be used often in your Minecraft mods to make specific things happen in response to conditions.

IN THIS CHAPTER

- Use the `for` loop
- Use the `while` loop
- Use the `do-while` loop
- Exit a loop prematurely
- Name a loop

REPEAT AN ACTION WITH LOOPS

A computer program can repeat a task with ease. Programs are ideally suited to do the same thing over and over because of loops. A *loop* is a statement or block that is repeated in a program. Some loops run a fixed number of times. Others run indefinitely.

There are three loop statements in Java: `for`, `do`, and `while`. Each can work like the others, but it's beneficial to learn how all three operate. You often can simplify a loop section of a program by choosing the right statement.

for Loops

In your programming, you find many circumstances in which a loop is useful. You can use them to keep doing something several times, such as when Minecraft draws flames flickering on a furnace. You also can use loops to cause the computer to do nothing for a brief period, such as an animated clock that displays the current time once per minute.

A loop statement causes a computer program to return to the same place more than once, like a stunt plane completing an acrobatic loop.

Java's most complex loop statement is `for`. A `for` loop repeats a section of a program a fixed number of times. The following is an example:

```
for (int dex = 0; dex < 1000; dex++) {
    if (dex % 12 == 0) {
        System.out.println("#: " + dex);
    }
}
```

This loop displays every number from 0 to 999 that is evenly divisible by 12.

Every `for` loop has a variable that determines when the loop should begin and end. This variable is called the *counter* (or index). The counter in the preceding loop is the variable `dex`.

The example illustrates the three parts of a `for` statement:

- **The initialization section:** In the first part, the `dex` variable is given an initial value of 0.

- **The conditional section:** In the second part, there is a conditional test like one you might use in an `if` statement: `dex < 1000`.

- **The change section:** The third part is a statement that changes the value of the `dex` variable, in this example by using the increment operator.

In the initialization section, you set up the counter variable. The word *initialize* means to give something an initial value and set it up.

You can create the initialization variable in the `for` statement, as the preceding example does with the integer variable `dex`. You also can create the variable elsewhere in the program. In either case, you should give the variable a starting value in this section of the `for` statement. The variable has this value when the loop starts.

The conditional section contains a test that must remain `true` for the loop to continue looping. When the test is `false`, the loop ends. In this example, the loop ends when the `dex` variable is equal to or greater than 1,000.

The last section of the `for` statement contains a statement that changes the value of the counter variable. This statement is handled each time the loop goes around. The counter variable has to change in some way or the loop never ends. In the example, `dex` is incremented by 1 in the change section. If `dex` was not changed, it would stay at its original value of 0 and the conditional `dex < 1000` always would be true.

The `for` statement's block is executed during each trip through the loop.

The preceding example had the following statements inside the `for` block:

```
if (dex % 12 == 0) {
    System.out.println("#: " + dex);
}
```

These statements are executed 1,000 times. The loop starts by setting the `dex` variable equal to 0. During each pass through the loop, it adds 1 to `dex`. When `dex` is no longer less than 1,000, the loop stops looping.

 NOTE An unusual term you might hear in connection with loops is iteration. An iteration is a single trip (or step) through a loop. The counter variable that is used to control the loop is called an iterator.

As you have seen with `if` statements, a `for` loop does not require brackets if it contains only a single statement. This is shown in the following example:

```
for (int p = 0; p < 500; p++)
    System.out.println("Never befriend a creeper");
```

This loop displays the text "Never befriend a creeper" 500 times. Although brackets are not required around a single statement inside a loop, you can use them to make the block easier to spot, like so:

```
for (int p = 0; p < 500; p++) {
    System.out.println("Never befriend a creeper");
}
```

The first program you create during this chapter displays the first 200 multiples of 9: 9, 18, 27, and so on, up to 1,800 (9 × 200). In NetBeans, create a new empty Java file named `Nines` in the `com.javaminecraft` package and enter the text of Listing 9.1. When you save the file, it is stored as `Nines.java`.

LISTING 9.1 The Full Text of `Nines.java`

```
 1: package com.javaminecraft;
 2:
 3: class Nines {
 4:     public static void main(String[] arguments) {
 5:         for (int dex = 1; dex <= 200; dex++) {
 6:             int multiple = 9 * dex;
 7:             System.out.print(multiple + " ");
 8:         }
 9:     System.out.println();
10:     }
11: }
```

The `Nines` program contains a `for` statement in Line 5. This statement has three sections:

- **Initialization section:** `int dex = 1`, which creates an integer variable called `dex` and gives it an initial value of 1.

- **Conditional section:** `dex <= 200`, which must be true during each trip through the loop. When it is not true, the loop ends.

- **Change section:** `dex++`, which increments the `dex` variable by one during each trip through the loop.

Run the program by selecting Run, Run File in NetBeans. The program produces the output shown in Figure 9.1.

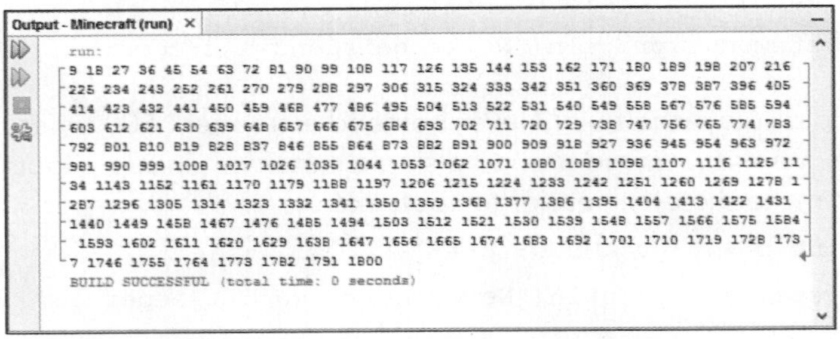

FIGURE 9.1

The output of the `Nines` *program.*

The output window in NetBeans does not wrap text, so all the numbers appear on a single line. To make the text wrap, right-click the Output pane and select Wrap Text from the pop-up menu. (Figure 9.1 shows the text wrapped.)

while Loops

The while loop does not have as many different sections as a for loop does. The only thing it needs is a conditional test, which accompanies the while statement. The following is an example of a while loop:

```
while (gameLives > 0) {
    // the statements inside the loop go here
}
```

This loop continues repeating until the gameLives variable is no longer greater than 0.

The while statement tests the condition at the beginning of the loop before any statements in the loop have been handled. If the tested condition is false when a program reaches the while statement for the first time, the statements inside the loop are ignored.

If the while condition is true, the loop goes around once and tests the while condition again. If the tested condition never changes inside the loop, the loop keeps looping forever.

The following statements cause a while loop to display the same line of text several times:

```
int limit = 5;
int count = 1;
while (count < limit) {
    System.out.println("Mooshroom!");
    count++;
}
```

A while loop uses one or more variables set up before the loop statement. In this example, two integer variables are created: limit, which has a value of 5, and count, which has a value of 1.

The while loop displays the text "Mooshroom!" four times. If you gave the count variable an initial value of 6 instead of 1, the text never would be displayed.

CAUTION   A loop will loop for as long as the tested condition remains true. Usually in a program where a loop does not end, something else in the program is set up to stop execution in some way. For example, a loop in a game program could continue indefinitely while the player still has lives left.

One bug that crops up often as you work on programs is an infinite loop, a loop that never stops because of a programming mistake. If one of the Java programs you run in NetBeans gets stuck in an infinite loop, press the red-and-white box icon to the left of the Output pane. This stops execution of the program.

do-while Loops

The do-while loop is similar to the while loop, but the conditional test goes in a different place. The following is an example of a do-while loop:

```
do {
    // the statements inside the loop go here
} while (gameLives > 0);
```

Like the while loop, this loop continues looping until the gameLives variable is no longer greater than 0. The do-while loop is different because the conditional test is conducted after the statements inside the loop, instead of before them.

When the do loop is reached for the first time as a program runs, the statements between the do and while are handled automatically, and then the while condition is tested to determine whether the loop should be repeated. If the while condition is true, the loop goes around one more time. If the condition is false, the loop ends. Something must happen inside the do and while statements that changes the condition tested with while; otherwise, the loop continues indefinitely. The statements inside a do-while loop always are handled at least once.

The following statements cause a do-while loop to display the same line of text several times:

```
int limit = 5;
int count = 1;
do {
    System.out.println("Don't eat that spider eye");
    count++;
} while (count < limit);
```

Like a `while` loop, a do-while loop uses one or more variables that are set up before the loop statement.

The loop displays the text "Don't eat that spider eye" four times. If you gave the count variable an initial value of 6 instead of 1, the text would be displayed once, even though count is never less than `limit`.

In a `do-while` loop, the statements inside the loop are executed at least once even if the loop condition is `false` the first time around.

Exiting a Loop

The normal way to exit a loop is for the tested condition to become `false`. This is true of all three types of loops in Java. Sometimes you might want a loop to end immediately, even if the condition being tested is still `true`. You can accomplish this with a `break` statement, as shown in the following code:

```
int index = 0;
while (index <= 1000) {
    index = index + 5;
    if (index == 400) {
        break;
    }
}
```

A `break` statement ends the loop that contains the statement.

In this example, the `while` loop loops until the `index` variable is greater than 1,000. However, a special case causes the loop to end earlier than that: If index equals 400, the `break` statement is executed, ending the loop immediately.

Another special-circumstance statement you can use inside a loop is `continue`. The `continue` statement causes the loop to exit its current trip through the loop and start over at the first statement of the loop. Consider the following loop:

```
int index = 0;
while (index <= 1000) {
    index = index + 5;
    if (index == 400) {
        continue;
    }
    System.out.println("The index is " + index);
}
```

In this loop, the statements are handled normally unless the value of `index` equals 400. In that case, the `continue` statement causes the loop to go back to the `while` statement instead of proceeding normally to the `System.out.println()` statement. Because of the `continue` statement, the loop never displays the following text:

```
The index is 400
```

You can use the `break` and `continue` statements with all three kinds of loops.

The `break` statement lets you create a loop in your program that's designed to run forever, as in this example:

```
while (true) {
    if (quitKeyPressed == true) {
        break;
    }
}
```

Naming a Loop

Like other statements in Java programs, you can place loops inside each other. The following shows a `for` loop inside a `while` loop:

```
int points = 0;
int target = 100;
while (target <= 100) {
    for (int i = 0; i < target; i++) {
        if (points > 50) [
            break;
        ]
        points = points + i;
    }
}
```

In this example, the `break` statement causes the `for` loop to end if the `points` variable is greater than 50. However, the `while` loop never ends because `target` is never greater than 100.

In some cases, you might want to `break` out of both loops. To make this possible, you have to give the outer loop—in this example, the `while` statement—a name. To name a loop, put the name on the line before the beginning of the loop and follow it with a colon (:).

When the loop has a name, use the name after the `break` or `continue` statement to indicate the loop to which the `break` or `continue` statement applies. The following example repeats the previous one with the exception of one thing: If the `points` variable is greater than 50, both loops end.

```
int points = 0;
int target = 100;
targetLoop:
while (target <= 100) {
    for (int i = 0; i < target; i++) {
        if (points > 50) {
            break targetLoop;
        }
        points = points + i;
    }
}
```

When a loop's name is used in a `break` or `continue` statement, the name does not include a colon.

Complex `for` Loops

A `for` loop can be more complex, including more than one variable in its initialization, conditional, and change sections. Each section of a `for` loop is set off from the other sections with a semicolon (;). A `for` loop can have more than one variable set up during the initialization section and more than one statement in the change section, as in the following code:

```
int i, j;
for (i = 0, j = 0; i * j < 1000; i++, j += 2) {
    System.out.println(i + " * " + j + " = " + (i * j));
}
```

In each section of the `for` loop, commas are used to separate the variables, as in `i = 0, j = 0`. The sample loop displays a list of equations where the `i` and `j` variables are multiplied together. The `i` variable increases by 1, and the `j` variable increases by 2 during each trip through the loop. When `i` multiplied by `j` is equal to or greater than 1,000, the loop ends.

Sections of a `for` loop also can be empty. An example of this is when a loop's counter variable already has been created with an initial value in another part of the program, as in the following:

```
for ( ; displayCount < endValue; displayCount++) {
    // loop statements would be here
}
```

Testing Your Computer Speed

This chapter's next project is a Java program that performs a benchmark, a test that measures how fast computer hardware or software is operating. The `Benchmark` program uses a loop statement to repeatedly perform the following mathematical expression:

```
double x = Math.sqrt(index);
```

This statement calls the `Math.sqrt()` method to find the square root of a number. You learn how methods work during Chapter 12, "Describe What Your Object Is Like."

The benchmark you're creating sees how many times a Java program can calculate a square root in one minute.

Use NetBeans to create a new empty Java file called `Benchmark`. Enter the text of Listing 9.2 and save the program when you're done.

LISTING 9.2 The Full Text of `Benchmark.java`

```
 1: package com.javaminecraft;
 2:
 3: class Benchmark {
 4:     public static void main(String[] arguments) {
 5:         long startTime = System.currentTimeMillis();
 6:         long endTime = startTime + 60000;
 7:         long index = 0;
 8:         while (true) {
 9:             double x = Math.sqrt(index);
10:             long now = System.currentTimeMillis();
11:             if (now > endTime) {
12:                 break;
13:             }
14:             index++;
```

```
15:            }
16:            System.out.println(index + " loops in one minute.");
17:        }
18: }
```

The following things take place in the program:

- In Lines 3–4, the Benchmark class is declared and the main() block of the program begins.

- On Line 5, the startTime variable is created with the current time in milliseconds as its value, measured by calling the currentTimeMillis() method of Java's System class.

- On Line 6, the endTime variable is created with a value 60,000 higher than startTime. Because 1 minute equals 60,000 milliseconds, this sets the variable one minute past startTime.

- On Line 7, a long named index is set up with an initial value of 0.

- On Line 8, the while statement begins a loop using true as the conditional, which causes the loop to continue forever (in other words, until something else stops it).

- On Line 9, the square root of index is calculated and stored in the x variable.

- On Line 10, currentTimeMillis() is used to create the now variable with the current time.

- On Lines 11–13, if now is greater than endTime, this signifies that the loop has been running for one minute and break ends the while loop. Otherwise, it keeps looping.

- On Line 14, the index variable is incremented by 1 with each trip through the loop.

- On Line 16, outside the loop, the program displays the number of times it performed the square root calculation.

The output of the application is shown in the Output pane in Figure 9.2.

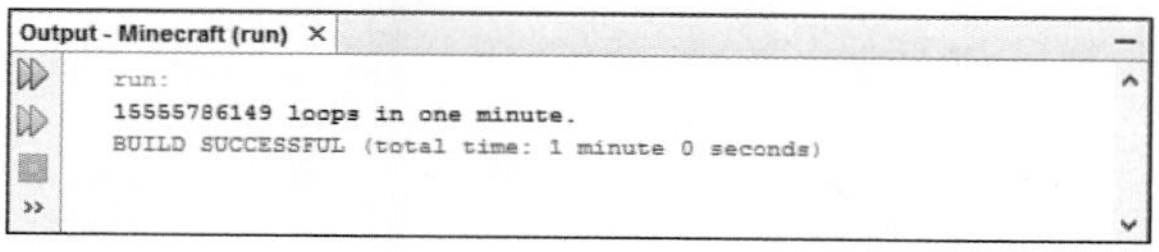

FIGURE 9.2

The output of the Benchmark *program.*

The `Benchmark` program is an excellent way to see whether your computer is faster than mine. During the testing of this program, my PC performed around 15.5 billion calculations. People with faster computers sometimes contact me on Twitter at @rcade to let me know I need to upgrade my PC.

THE ABSOLUTE MINIMUM

Loops are a fundamental part of most programming languages. Animation created by displaying several graphics in sequence is one of many tasks you could not accomplish in Java or any other programming language without loops.

One common use of loops in a Minecraft mod is to load all the mobs in the vicinity of the player and loop through them to find mobs of a specific type, such as chickens, zombies, or zombies riding chickens.

IN THIS CHAPTER

- Create an array
- Set the size of an array
- Give a value to an array element
- Change the information in an array
- Make multidimensional arrays
- Sort an array

10

STORE INFORMATION WITH ARRAYS

Computers are ideal for the storage, categorization, and study of information.

The most basic way that information is stored in a computer program is by putting it into a variable. So far, all the variables you've worked with have been a single item of information, such as a floating-point number or a string.

A list of Minecraft mobs near the player is an example of a larger collection of similar information. To keep track of a list of this kind, you can use arrays.

An array is a group of related variables that share the same type. Any type of information that can be stored as a variable can become the items stored in an array. Arrays can be used to keep track of more sophisticated types of information than a single variable, but they are almost as easy to create and manipulate.

Creating Arrays

Arrays are variables grouped together under a common name. The term *array* should be familiar to you—think of a store with an array of products or a warrior with an array of weapons. Like variables, arrays are created by stating the type of variable being organized into the array and the name of the array. A pair of square brackets ([]) follows the type to distinguish arrays from variables.

You can create arrays for any type of information that can be stored as a variable. For example, the following statement creates a variable that can hold an array of strings:

```
String[] monthNames;
```

Here are two more examples:

```
int[] itemWeights;
boolean[] answers;
```

 NOTE   Java is flexible about where the square brackets are placed when an array is being created. You can put them after the variable name instead of the variable type, as in the following:

```
String monthNames[];
```

To make arrays easier for humans to spot in your programs, you should stick to one style rather than switching back and forth. Programs that use arrays in this book always place the brackets after the variable or class type.

The previous examples create arrays, but they do not store any values in them. To do this, you can use the `new` keyword along with the variable type or store values in the array within { and } marks. When using `new`, you must specify how many different items are stored in the array. Each item in an array is called an *element*. The following statement creates an array and sets aside space for the values it holds:

```
int[] seniority = new int[250];
```

This example creates an array of integers called `seniority`. The array has 250 elements that could each hold the months that an individual worker has been employed.

When you create an array with the `new` statement, you must specify the number of elements. Each element of the array is given an initial value that depends on the type of the array. All numeric arrays have the initial value 0, `char` arrays equal `'\0'`, and `boolean` arrays have the value `false`. A `String` array and all other objects are created with the initial value of `null`.

For arrays that are not extremely large, you can set up their initial values at the same time you create them. The following example creates an array of strings and gives them initial values:

```
String[] reindeerNames = { "Dasher", "Dancer", "Prancer", "Vixen",
    "Comet", "Cupid", "Donner", "Blitzen" };
```

The information that should be stored in elements of the array is placed between { and } brackets with commas separating each element. The number of elements in the array is set to the number of elements in the comma-separated list.

Array elements are numbered, beginning with 0 for the first element. A specific element can be accessed by referring to this number within [and] brackets. The preceding statement accomplishes the same thing as the following code:

```
String[] reindeerNames = new String[8];
reindeerNames[0] = "Dasher";
reindeerNames[1] = "Dancer";
reindeerNames[2] = "Prancer";
reindeerNames[3] = "Vixen";
reindeerNames[4] = "Comet";
reindeerNames[5] = "Cupid";
reindeerNames[6] = "Donner";
reindeerNames[7] = "Blitzen";
```

Each element of the array must be of the same type. Here, a string is used to hold each of the reindeer names.

After the array is created, you cannot make room for more elements. Sorry, Rudolph!

Using Arrays

You use arrays in a program as you would any variable, with one difference: The element number of the array item must be provided between the square brackets next to the array's name. You can use an array element anywhere a variable could be used. The following statements all use arrays that have already been defined in this chapter's examples:

```
seniority[193] += 1;
monthNames[2] = "February";
int currentReindeer = 4;
System.out.println(reindeerNames[currentReindeer]);
```

Because the first element of an array is numbered 0 instead of 1, this means that the highest number is one less than you might expect. Consider the following statement:

```
String[] gifts = new String[10];
```

This statement creates an array of string variables numbered from 0 to 9. If you referred to `gifts[10]` somewhere else in the program, you would get an error message referring to an `ArrayIndexOutOfBoundsException`.

Exceptions is another word for errors in Java programs. This exception is an "array index out of bounds" error, which means that a program tried to use an array element that doesn't exist within its defined boundaries. You learn more about exceptions during Chapter 15, "Handle Errors in a Mod."

If you want to check the upper limit of an array so you can avoid going beyond that limit, a variable called `length` is associated with each array that is created. The `length` variable is an integer that contains the number of elements an array holds. The following example creates an array and then reports its length:

```
String[] reindeerNames = { "Dasher", "Dancer", "Prancer", "Vixen",
    "Comet", "Cupid", "Donner", "Blitzen", "Rudolph" };
System.out.println("There are "
    + reindeerNames.length + " reindeer.");
```

In this example, the value of `reindeerNames.length` is 9, which means that the highest element number you can specify is 8.

 NOTE You might be curious why an error would be called an exception because the words don't seem like synonyms. A program normally runs without any problems, so the exception signals an exceptional circumstance that must be dealt with. Exceptions are warning messages that are sent from within a Java program. In the Java language, the term *error* is sometimes confined to describe error conditions that take place within the Java Virtual Machine running a program. You learn more about errors and exceptions during Chapter 15.

You can work with text in Java as a string or an array of characters. When you're working with strings, one useful technique is to put each character in a string into its own element of a character array. To do this, call the string's `toCharArray()` method, which produces a `char` array with the same number of elements as the length of the string.

This chapter's first project uses both of the techniques introduced in this section. The `SpaceRemover` program displays a string with all space characters replaced with periods (.).

To get started, open the Minecraft project in NetBeans; select File, New File; and create a new Empty Java File in the `com.javaminecraft` package called `SpaceRemover`. Enter Listing 10.1 in the source editor and save it when you're done.

LISTING 10.1   The Full Text of `SpaceRemover.java`

```
 1: package com.javaminecraft;
 2:
 3: class SpaceRemover {
 4:     public static void main(String[] arguments) {
 5:         String mostFamous = "Rudolph the Red-Nosed Reindeer";
 6:         char[] mfl = mostFamous.toCharArray();
 7:         for (int dex = 0; dex < mfl.length; dex++) {
 8:             char current = mfl[dex];
 9:             if (current != ' ') {
10:                 System.out.print(current);
11:             } else {
12:                 System.out.print('.');
13:             }
14:         }
15:         System.out.println();
16:     }
17: }
```

Run the program with the command Run, Run File to see the output shown in Figure 10.1.

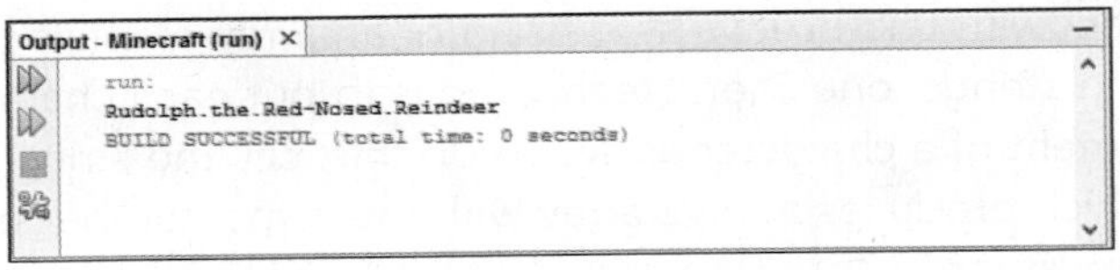

FIGURE 10.1

The output of the `SpaceRemover` *program.*

The `SpaceRemover` application stores the text "Rudolph the Red-Nosed Reindeer" in two places—a string called `mostFamous` and a `char` array called `mf1`. The array is created in Line 6 by calling the `toCharArray()` method of `mostFamous`, which fills an array with one element for each character in the text. The character "R" goes into element 0, "u" into element 1, and so on, up to "r" in element 29.

The `for` loop in Lines 7–14 looks at each character in the `mf1` array. If the character is not a space, it is displayed. If it is a space, a . character is displayed instead.

Multidimensional Arrays

The arrays thus far in the chapter all have one dimension, so you can retrieve an element using a single number. Some types of information require more dimensions to store adequately as arrays, such as points in an (x,y) coordinate system. One dimension of the array could store the x coordinate, and the other dimension could store the y coordinate.

To create an array that has two dimensions, you must use an additional set of square brackets when creating and using the array, as in these statements:

```
boolean[][] selectedPoint = new boolean[50][50];
selectedPoint[4][29] = true;
selectedPoint[6][1]  = true;
selectedPoint[11][22] = true;
```

This example creates an array of Boolean values called `selectedPoint`. The array has 50 elements in its first dimension and 50 elements in its second dimension, so there are 2,500 individual array elements (50 multiplied by 50). When the array is created, each element is given the default value of `false`. Three elements are given the value `true`: a point at the (x,y) position of 4,29; one at 6,1; and one at 11,22.

Arrays can have as many dimensions as you need, but keep in mind that they take up a lot of memory if they're extremely large. Creating the 50-by-50 `selectedPoint` array was equivalent to creating 2,500 individual variables.

The `length` variable can be used to find the size of any dimension in a multidimensional array.

For the first dimension, use `length` with the name of the array, as in `selectedPoint.length`. Subsequent dimensions can be measured by using `length` with the `[0]` element of that dimension. Consider an array called `data` that was created with the following statement:

```
int [] [] [] data = new int [12] [8] [14];
```

The dimensions of this array can be measured by using the `data.length` variable for the first dimension, `data[0].length` for the second, and `data[0][0].length` for the third.

Sorting an Array

When you have grouped a bunch of similar items together into an array, one thing you can do is rearrange items. The following statements swap the values of two elements in an integer array called `numbers`:

```
int temporary = numbers[5];
numbers[5] = numbers[6];
numbers[6] = temporary;
```

These statements result in `numbers[5]` and `numbers[6]` trading values with each other. The integer variable called `temporary` is used as a temporary storage place for one of the values being swapped. Sorting is the process of arranging a list of related items into a set order, such as when a list of numbers is sorted from lowest to highest.

Sorting an array is easy in Java because the `Arrays` class does all the work. `Arrays`, which is part of the `java.util` group of classes, can rearrange arrays of all variable types.

To use the `Arrays` class in a program, use the following steps:

1. Use the `import java.util.*` statement to make all the classes in the `java.util` package available in the program.

2. Create the array.

3. Use the `sort()` method of the `Arrays` class to rearrange an array.

An array of variables that is sorted by the `Arrays` class is rearranged into ascending numerical order. Characters and strings are arranged in alphabetical order.

To see this in action, create a new Empty Java File named `NameSorter` in the `com.javaminecraft` package and enter the text of Listing 10.2 in the source editor.

LISTING 10.2 The Full Text of `NameSorter.java`

```
 1: package com.javaminecraft;
 2:
 3: import java.util.*;
 4:
 5: class NameSorter {
 6:     public static void main(String[] arguments) {
 7:         String names[] = { "Glimmer", "Marvel", "Rue", "Clove",
 8:             "Thresh", "Foxface", "Cato", "Peeta", "Katniss" };
 9:         System.out.println("The original order:");
10:         for (int i = 0; i < names.length; i++) {
11:             System.out.println(i + ": " + names[i]);
12:         }
13:         System.out.println();
14:         Arrays.sort(names);
15:         System.out.println("The new order:");
16:         for (int i = 0; i < names.length; i++) {
17:             System.out.println(i + ": " + names[i]);
18:         }
19:         System.out.println();
20:     }
21: }
```

When you run this Java program, it displays a list of nine names in their original order, sorts the names, and then redisplays the list. Figure 10.2 shows the output.

When you're working with strings and the basic types of variables such as integers and floating-point numbers, the `Arrays` class can sort them only by ascending order. You can write code to do your own sorts by hand if you desire a different arrangement of elements during a sort or want better efficiency than the `Arrays` class provides.

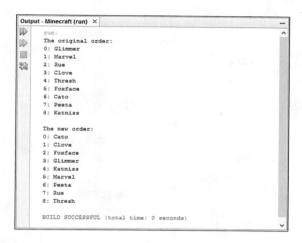

FIGURE 10.2

The output of the `NameSorter` *program.*

Counting Characters in Strings

The letters that appear most often in English are *e, t, a, o, i, n, s, r, h,* and *t,* in that order. This is a fact worth knowing if you ever find yourself on the syndicated game show *Wheel of Fortune*.

NOTE   If you're unfamiliar with the show, *Wheel of Fortune* is a game in which three contestants guess the letters of a phrase, name, or quote. If they get a letter right and it's a consonant, they win the amount of money spun on a big wheel. To re-create the experience, play hangman with your friends in front of a studio audience, hand out random amounts of money when someone guesses a letter correctly, and give the winner a new refrigerator.

Your final project during this chapter counts letter frequency in as many different phrases and expressions as you care to type. An array is used to count the number of times that each letter appears. When you're done, the program presents the number of times each letter appeared in the phrases.

Create a new Empty Java File in NetBeans called `Wheel.java` in the `com.javaminecraft` package, fill it with the contents of Listing 10.3, and save the file when you're finished. Feel free to add phrases between Lines 17 and 18, formatting them exactly like Line 17.

LISTING 10.3 The Full Text of `Wheel.java`

```
 1: package com.javaminecraft;
 2:
 3: class Wheel {
 4:     public static void main(String[] arguments) {
 5:         String phrase[] = {
 6:             "A STITCH IN TIME SAVES NINE",
 7:             "THE TRIBE HAS SPOKEN",
 8:             "JUST DO IT",
 9:             "EVERY GOOD BOY DOES FINE",
10:             "YOU ONLY LIVE ONCE",
11:             "I LIKE IKE",
12:             "PLAY IT AGAIN, SAM",
13:             "FROSTY THE SNOWMAN",
14:             "THERE'S AN APP FOR THAT",
15:             "HOME FIELD ADVANTAGE",
16:             "VALENTINE'S DAY MASSACRE",
17:             "GROVER CLEVELAND OHIO",
18:             "SPAGHETTI WESTERN",
19:             "BEKARTON GUARDS THE GATE",
20:             "IT'S A WONDERFUL LIFE"
21:         };
22:         int[] letterCount = new int[26];
23:         for (int count = 0; count < phrase.length; count++) {
24:             String current = phrase[count];
25:             char[] letters = current.toCharArray();
26:             for (int count2 = 0;  count2 < letters.length;
                 ➥count2++) {
27:                 char lett = letters[count2];
28:                 if ( (lett >= 'A') & (lett <= 'Z') ) {
29:                     letterCount[lett - 'A']++;
30:                 }
31:             }
32:         }
33:         for (char count = 'A'; count <= 'Z'; count++) {
34:             System.out.print(count + ": " +
35:                 letterCount[count - 'A'] +
36:                 " ");
```

```
37:                    if (count == 'M') {
38:                        System.out.println();
39:                    }
40:                }
41:            System.out.println();
42:        }
43: }
```

If you run the program without adding your own phrases, the output should resemble Figure 10.3.

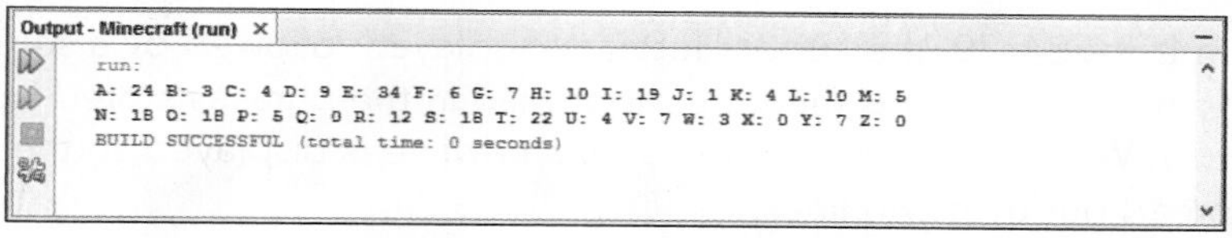

FIGURE 10.3

The output of the Wheel *program.*

The following things are taking place in the Wheel program:

- On Lines 5–21, phrases are stored in a string array called phrase.

- On Line 22, an integer array called letterCount is created with 26 elements. This array is used to store the number of times each letter appears. The order of the elements is from A to Z. letterCount[0] stores the count for letter *a*, letterCount[1] stores the count for *b*, and so on, up to letterCount[25] for *z*.

- On Line 23, a for loop cycles through the phrases stored in the phrase array. The phrase.length variable is used to end the loop after the last phrase is reached.

- On Line 24, a string variable named current is set with the value of the current element of the phrase array.

- On Line 25, a character array is created and stores all the characters in the current phrase.

- On Line 26, a for loop cycles through the letters of the current phrase. The letters.length variable is used to end the loop after the last letter is reached.

- On Line 27, a character variable called lett is created with the value of the current letter. In addition to its text value, each character has a numeric value. Because elements of an array are numbered, the numeric value of each character is used to determine its element number.

- On Lines 28–30, an `if` statement weeds out all characters that are not part of the alphabet, such as punctuation and spaces. An element of the `letterCount` array is increased by 1 depending on the numeric value of the current character, which is stored in `lett`. The numeric values of the alphabet range from 65 for `'A'` to 90 for `'Z'`. Because the `letterCount` array begins at 0 and ends at 25, `'A'` (65) is subtracted from `lett` to determine which array element to increase.

- On Line 33, a `for` loop cycles through the alphabet from *a* to *z*.

- On Lines 34–39, the current letter is displayed followed by a semicolon and the number of times the letter appeared in the phrases stored in the `phrase` array. When the current letter is *m*, a newline is displayed so the output is spread out over two lines.

This project shows how two nested `for` loops can be used to cycle through a group of phrases one letter at a time. Java attaches a numeric value to each character; this value is easier to use than the character inside arrays.

 NOTE   The numeric values associated with each of the characters from *a* to *z* are those used by the ASCII character set. The ASCII character set is part of Unicode, the full character set supported by the Java language. Unicode includes support for more than 60,000 different characters used in the world's written languages. ASCII is limited to just 256.

THE ABSOLUTE MINIMUM

Arrays make it possible to store complicated types of information in a program and manipulate that information. They're ideal for anything that can be arranged in a list and can be accessed easily using the loop statements you learned about during Chapter 9, "Repeat an Action with Loops."

Your programs are likely to use arrays to store information that is unwieldy to work with using variables. When arrays aren't getting the job done either, you learn about more sophisticated ways to store information in Chapter 14, "Store Objects in Data Structures."

IN THIS CHAPTER

- Create an object
- Describe an object with attributes
- Determine how objects behave
- Combine objects
- Inherit from other objects
- Convert objects and other types of information

11

CREATE YOUR FIRST OBJECT

One of the more fearsome examples of jargon that you encounter is this book is *object-oriented programming (OOP)*. This complicated term describes, in an elegant way, what a computer program is and how it works.

Before OOP, a computer program was usually described as a set of instructions listed in a file and handled in some kind of reliable order.

By thinking of a program as a collection of objects, you can figure out the tasks a program must accomplish and assign the tasks to the objects where they best belong.

How Object-Oriented Programming Works

You can think of the Java programs you create as objects, just like physical objects that exist in the real world. Objects exist independently of other objects, interact in specific ways, and can be combined with other objects to form something bigger. If you think of a computer program as a group of objects that interact with each other, you can design a program that's more reliable, easier to understand, and reusable in other projects.

The game Minecraft is full of objects. One of them is a `Location` object, which represents a location in the game. Another is `World`, which represents the entire world that players explore. `World` is an object that is made up of smaller objects—individual locations, the blocks at each location, the mobs in the world, and more.

Each object has things that make it different from other objects. In OOP, an object contains two things: attributes and behavior. *Attributes* are things that describe the object and show how it is different from other objects. *Behavior* is what an object does.

You create objects in Java by using a class as a template. A *class* is a master copy of the object that determines the attributes and behavior an object should have. The term *class* should be familiar to you because Java programs are called classes.

Every program you create with Java is a class that you can use as a template for the creation of new objects. As an example, any Java program that uses strings is using objects created from the `String` class. This class contains attributes that determine what a `String` object is and behavior that controls what `String` objects can do.

With OOP, a computer program is a group of objects that work together to get something done. Some simple programs might seem as though they consist of only one object: the class file. However, even those programs are using other objects to get work done.

Objects in Action

The developers of Minecraft needed an object that represented a spot in the game world, so they created a `Location` class for this purpose. A `Location` object could consist of the following:

- Attributes to store the x, y, and z coordinates at that spot

- Behavior to find out what block is at that spot, such as dirt, stone, water, or air

- Behavior to calculate the distance between two spots

Objects in OOP work for themselves whenever possible. This capability makes it easier to incorporate them in other programs. If a Location object did not know how to figure out what block it holds, for instance, every time you used that Location object in another program, you would have to create behavior to determine that information.

For another example of OOP, consider an Internet router that offers wireless Internet connectivity to a house.

The router, like any computer program, can be thought of as a group of objects that work together. It could be broken down into the following:

- A Modem object, which knows its attributes such as connection speed and has behavior—for example, it can make the router accept a wireless connection and connect to websites and Internet servers

- A Network object, which keeps track of which devices are connected to the router and blocks unauthorized access

Each object exists independently of the other.

One advantage of designing a completely independent Modem object is that it could be used in other programs that need that functionality.

Another reason to use self-contained objects is that they are easier to debug. Computer programs quickly become unwieldy in size. If you're debugging something like a Modem object and you know it's not dependent on anything else, you can focus on making sure the Modem object does the job it's supposed to do and holds the information that it needs to do its job.

Learning an object-oriented language such as Java as your first programming language can be advantageous because you're not unlearning the habits of other styles of programming.

What Objects Are

Objects are created by using a class of objects as a template. The following statements create a class:

```
public class Modem {
 }
```

An object created from this class can't do anything because it doesn't have any attributes or behavior. You need to add those to make the class useful, as in the following statements:

```
public class Modem {
    int speed;

    public void displaySpeed() {
        System.out.println("Speed: " + speed);
    }
}
```

The Modem class now should be starting to look like programs you've written during the previous chapters. The Modem class begins with a class statement, except that it has the word public in it. This means that the class is available for use by the public—in other words, by any program that wants to use Modem objects.

NOTE Making a class or method public raises the question of when you would want to create one that isn't public. The main time is when the class is strictly for the use of one program you're writing. For instance, if you're creating a game program and your drawWorld() method is highly specific to the game you're writing, it could be a private method. To keep a method from being public, leave off the public statement in front of the method's name.

The first part of the Modem class creates an integer variable called speed. This variable is an attribute of the object.

The second part of the Modem class is a method called displaySpeed(). This method is part of the object's behavior. It contains one statement, System.out.println(), which reveals the modem's speed value.

An object's variables are called *instance* variables or *member* variables.

If you want to use a Modem object in a program, you create the object with the following statement:

```
Modem device = new Modem();
```

This statement creates a Modem object called device. After you have created an object, you can set its variables and call its methods. Here's how to set the value of the speed variable of the device object:

```
device.speed = 3.77;
```

To make this modem display its speed by calling the `displaySpeed()` method, you call the method:

```
device.displaySpeed();
```

The `Modem` object named `device` would respond to this statement by displaying the text "Speed: 3.77."

Understanding Inheritance

A big advantage to OOP is inheritance, which enables one object to inherit behavior and attributes from another object.

When you start creating objects, you sometimes find that a new object you want is a lot like an object you already have.

For instance, what if faster Internet service is developed after the `Modem` class has been designed? A new `HighSpeedModem` object could be created by copying the statements of the `Modem` object and revising them. However, if most of the behavior and attributes of `HighSpeedModem` are the same as those of `Modem`, this is a lot of unnecessary work. It also means that the programmer would have two separate programs to update if something needed to be changed later.

Through inheritance, a programmer can create a new class of objects by defining how they are different from an existing class. The `HighSpeedModem` could inherit from `Modem`, and all that must be written are things that make high-speed modems different from regular modems.

A class of objects inherits from another class by using the `extends` statement. The following is a skeleton of a `HighSpeedModem` class that inherits from the `Modem` class:

```
public class HighSpeedModem extends Modem {
    // program goes here
}
```

Building an Inheritance Hierarchy

Inheritance, which enables a variety of related classes to be developed without redundant work, makes it possible for code to be passed down from one class to another class to another class. This grouping of classes is called a *class hierarchy*, and all the standard classes you can use in your Java programs are part of a hierarchy.

Understanding a hierarchy is easier if you understand subclasses and superclasses. A class that inherits from another class is called a *subclass*. The class that is inherited from is called a *superclass*.

In the preceding example, the Modem class is the superclass of the HighSpeedModem class, and HighSpeedModem is the subclass of Modem.

A class can have more than one class that inherits from it in the hierarchy—another subclass of Modem could be PhoneModem because phone modems have behavior and attributes that make them different from high-speed modems. If there was a subclass of HighSpeedModem such as CableModem, it would inherit from all classes above it in the hierarchy—both HighSpeedModem and Modem.

The classes that make up the standard Java language make full use of inheritance, so understanding it is essential. You learn more about inheritance during Chapter 13, "Make the Most of Existing Objects."

 CAUTION Although a superclass can have more than one subclass, a subclass can have only one superclass. In Java, a class can inherit from only one class.

Multiple inheritance is possible in other programming languages, but Java's developers decided to limit inheritance to one super-class for any class. One way to compensate for this limitation is to inherit methods from a special type of class called an *interface*. You learn more about interfaces during Chapter 16, "Create a Threaded Mod."

Converting Objects and Simple Variables

One of the most common tasks you need to accomplish in Java is to convert information from one form into another. Several types of conversions you can do include the following:

- Converting an object into another object
- Converting a simple variable into another type of variable
- Using an object to create a simple variable
- Using a simple variable to create an object

Simple variables are the basic data types you learned about during Chapter 6, "Store and Change Information in a Mod." These types are int, float, char, long, double, byte, and short.

When using a method or an expression in a program, you must use the right type of information that's expected by these methods and expressions. A method that expects a `Location` object must receive a `Location` object, for instance. If you used a method that takes a single integer argument and you sent it a floating-point number instead, an error would occur when you attempted to compile the program.

 NOTE When a method such as `System.out.println()` requires a string argument, you can use the + operator to combine several types of information in that argument. As long as one of the things being combined is a string, the combined argument is converted into a string.

Converting information to a new form is called *casting*. Casting produces a new value that is a different type of variable or object from its source. You don't actually change the value when casting. Instead, a new variable or object is created in the format you need.

The terms *source* and *destination* are useful when discussing the concept of casting. The source is some kind of information in its original form—whether it's a variable or an object. The destination is the converted version of the source in a new form.

Casting Simple Variables

With simple variables, casting occurs most commonly between numeric variables such as integers and floating-point numbers. One type of variable that cannot be used in any casting is a Boolean value.

To cast information into a new format, you precede it with the new format surrounded by parentheses. For example, if you want to cast something into a `long` variable, you precede it with `(long)`. The following two statements cast a `float` value into an `int`:

```
// create a float variable
float source = 7.06F;
// cast it to an integer
int destination = (int) source;
```

In variable casting where the destination holds larger values than the source, the value is converted easily, such as when a `byte` is cast into an `int`. A `byte` holds values from –128 to 127, whereas an `int` holds values from –2.1 billion to

2.1 billion. No matter what value the `byte` variable holds, the new `int` variable has plenty of room for it.

You sometimes can use a variable in a different format without casting it at all. For example, you can use `char` variables as if they were `int` variables. Also, you can use `int` variables as if they were `long` variables, and anything can be used as a `double`.

In most cases, because the destination provides more room than the source, the information is converted without changing its value. The main exceptions occur when an `int` or `long` variable is cast to a `float`, or a `long` is cast into a `double`.

When you are converting information from a larger variable type into a smaller type, you must explicitly cast it, as in the following statements:

```
// create an integer variable
int xNum = 103;
// cast it to a byte
byte val = (byte) xNum;
```

Here, casting converts an integer value called `xNum` into a `byte` variable called `val`. This is an example where the destination variable holds a smaller range of values than the source variable. A `byte` holds integer values ranging from –128 to 127, and an `int` holds a much larger range of integer values.

When the source variable in a casting operation has a value that isn't possible in the destination variable, Java changes the value to make the cast fit successfully. This can produce unexpected results if you're not expecting the change.

 NOTE   A character can be used as an `int` variable because each character has a corresponding numeric code that represents its position in the character set. If you have a variable named `key` with the value 67, the cast `(char) key` produces the character value 'C' because the numeric code associated with a capital *C* is 67, according to the ASCII character set. The ASCII character set is part of the Unicode character standard adopted by the Java language.

Casting Objects

You can cast objects into other objects when the source and destination are related by inheritance. One class must be a subclass of the other.

Some objects do not require casting at all. You can use an object where any of its superclasses are expected. All objects in Java are subclasses of the `Object` class, so you can use any object as an argument when an `Object` is expected.

You also can use an object where one of its subclasses is expected. However, because subclasses usually contain more information than their superclasses, you might lose some of this information. If the object doesn't have a method that the subclass would contain, an error results if that missing method is used in the program.

To use an object in place of one of its subclasses, you must cast it explicitly with statements such as the one inside this method:

```
public void paintComponent(Graphics comp) {
    // the casting takes place below
    Graphics2D comp2D = (Graphics2D) comp;
}
```

This casts a `Graphics` object called `comp` into a `Graphics2D` object. You don't lose any information in the cast, but you gain all the methods and variables the subclass defines.

Converting Simple Variables to Objects and Back

One thing you can't do is cast an object to a simple variable or a simple variable to an object. There are classes in Java for each of the simple variable types including `Boolean`, `Byte`, `Character`, `Double`, `Float`, `Integer`, `Long`, and `Short`. All these classes are capitalized because they are objects, not simple variable types.

Using methods defined in each of these classes, you can create an object using a variable's value as an argument. The following statement creates an `Integer` object with the value 5309:

```
Integer suffix = new Integer(5309);
```

After you have created an object like this, you can use it like any other object. When you want to use that value again as a simple variable, the class has methods to perform that conversion. To get an `int` value from the preceding `suffix` object, the following statement could be used:

```
int newSuffix = suffix.intValue();
```

This statement causes the `newSuffix` variable to have the value 5309, expressed as an `int` value. One common casting from an object to a variable is to use a string in a numeric expression. When the string's value could become an integer, this can be done using the `parseInt()` method of the `Integer` class, as in this example:

```
String count = "25";
int myCount = Integer.parseInt(count);
```

This converts a string with the text "25" into an integer with the value 25. If the string value was not a valid integer, the conversion would not work.

The next project you create is an application that converts a string value in a command-line argument to a numeric value, a common technique when you're taking input from a user at the command line.

Return to your `Minecraft` project in NetBeans; select File, New File; and then create a new Empty Java File in the `com.javaminecraft` package named `NewRoot`. Enter Listing 11.1 in the source editor and remember to save the file.

LISTING 11.1 The Full Text of `NewRoot.java`

```
 1: package com.javaminecraft;
 2:
 3: class NewRoot {
 4:     public static void main(String[] arguments) {
 5:         int number = 100;
 6:         if (arguments.length > 0) {
 7:             number = Integer.parseInt(arguments[0]);
 8:         }
 9:         System.out.println("The square root of "
10:             + number
11:             + " is "
12:             + Math.sqrt(number)
13:         );
14:     }
15: }
```

Before you run the program, you must configure NetBeans to run it with a command-line argument. Select the menu command Run, Set Project Configuration, Customize. The Project Properties window opens. Enter **com.javaminecraft.NewRoot** as the Main Class and **19474569** in the Arguments field. Click OK to close the dialog.

To run the program, select Run, Run Main Project (instead of Run, Run File). The program displays the number and its square root, as shown in Figure 11.1.

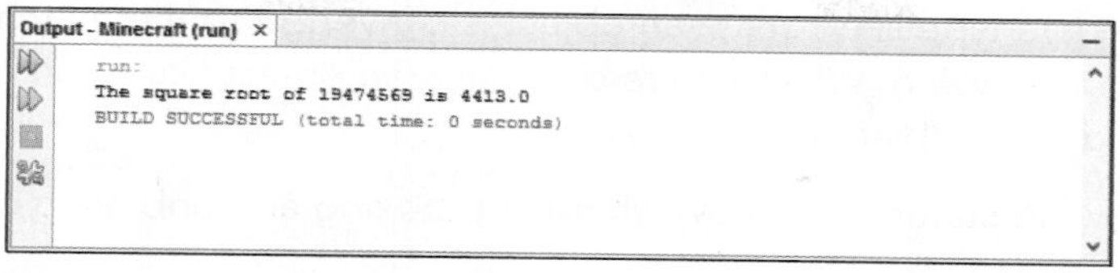

FIGURE 11.1

The output of the NewRoot *program.*

The NewRoot application is an expansion of an earlier tutorial from Chapter 5, "Understand How Java Programs Work," that displayed the square root of the integer 17,689.

That program would have been more useful if it took a number submitted by a user and displayed its square root. This requires conversion from a string to an integer. All command-line arguments are stored as elements of a String array, so you must cast them to numbers before using them in mathematical expressions.

To create an integer value based on the contents of a string, the Integer. parseInt() method is called with the string as the only argument, as in Line 7:

```
number = Integer.parseInt(arguments[0]);
```

The arguments[0] array element holds the first command-line argument submitted when the application is run. When the program was run with "19474569" as an argument, the string "19474569" was converted to the int 19,474,569.

Autoboxing and Unboxing

Every one of the basic data types in Java has a corresponding object class: boolean (Boolean class), byte (Byte), char (Character), double (Double), float (Float), int (Integer), long (Long), and short (Short).

For each of these pairs, the information has identical values. The only difference between them is the format the value takes. An integer value such as 413 could be represented by either an int or an object of the Integer class.

Java's autoboxing and unboxing capabilities enable you to use the basic data type and object forms of a value interchangeably.

Autoboxing casts a simple variable value to the corresponding class.

Unboxing casts an object to the corresponding simple value.

These features work behind the scenes, ensuring that when you are expecting a simple data type like `float`, an object is converted to the matching data type with the same value. When you're expecting an object like `Float`, a data type is converted to an object as necessary.

The following statements show where autoboxing and unboxing come in handy:

```
Float total = 1.3F;
float sum = total / 5;
```

In early versions of Java, this code would fail with two errors. The first statement assigns a literal `float` value of 1.3 to a `Float` object (not allowed), and the second statement divides a `Float` object and assigns it to a `float` type (not allowed). It works perfectly in Java now because the first statement boxes the literal into an object and the second unboxes an object to a primitive type. Java automatically makes the statements work, resulting in `sum` being equal to 0.26.

Earlier in this chapter, you saw an example of how to create an `Integer` object:

```
Integer suffix = new Integer(5309);
```

Because of autoboxing and unboxing, the following statement also does the same thing:

```
Integer suffix = 5309;
```

Java recognizes that the `int` value 5,309 is being stored in an `Integer` object, so it is converted automatically.

Creating an Object

To see a working example of classes and inheritance, you will create classes that represent two types of objects for specific kinds of modems: cable modems, which are implemented as the `CableModem` class, and DSL modems, which are implemented as the `DslModem` class. The project focuses on simple attributes and behavior for these objects:

- Each object should have a speed that it can display.

- Each object should be able to connect to the Internet.

One thing that cable modems and DSL modems have in common is that they both have a speed. Because this is something they share, it can be put into a class that is the superclass of both the `CableModem` and `DslModem` classes. Call this class Modem. In NetBeans, create a new empty Java class called Modem in the com.javaminecraft package. Enter Listing 11.2 in the source editor and save the file.

LISTING 11.2 The Full Text of Modem.java

```
1: package com.javaminecraft;
2:
3: public class Modem {
4:     double speed;
5:
6:     public void displaySpeed() {
7:         System.out.println("Speed: " + speed + " Mbps");
8:     }
9: }
```

This file is compiled automatically as Modem.class. You cannot run this program directly, but you can use it in other classes. The Modem class can handle one of the things that the CableModem and DslModem classes have in common. By using the extends statement when you are creating the CableModem and DslModem classes, you can make each of them a subclass of Modem.

Start a new empty Java file in NetBeans with the class name CableModem in the com.javaminecraft package. Enter Listing 11.3 and save the file.

LISTING 11.3 The Full Text of CableModem.java

```
1: package com.javaminecraft;
2:
3: public class CableModem extends Modem {
4:     String method = "cable connection";
5:
6:     public void connect() {
7:         System.out.println("Connecting to the Internet ...");
8:         System.out.println("Using a " + method);
9:     }
10: }
```

Create a third file in NetBeans named DslModem in com.javaminecraft. Enter Listing 11.4 and save the file.

LISTING 11.4   The Full Text of `DslModem.java`

```
 1: package com.javaminecraft;
 2:
 3: public class DslModem extends Modem {
 4:     String method = "DSL phone connection";
 5:
 6:     public void connect() {
 7:         System.out.println("Connecting to the Internet ...");
 8:         System.out.println("Using a " + method);
 9:     }
10: }
```

If there were no errors, you now have three class files: `Modem.class`, `CableModem.class`, and `DslModem.class`. However, you cannot run any of these class files because they do not have `main()` blocks like the ones in other programs you've created. You need to create a short application to test the class hierarchy you have just built.

Return to NetBeans and create a new empty Java file with the class name `ModemTester` and the package name `com.javaminecraft`. Enter Listing 11.5 in the source editor, and save the file.

LISTING 11.5   The Full Text of `ModemTester.java`

```
 1: package com.javaminecraft;
 2:
 3: public class ModemTester {
 4:     public static void main(String[] arguments) {
 5:         CableModem alpha = new CableModem();
 6:         DslModem beta = new DslModem();
 7:         alpha.speed = 3.77;
 8:         beta.speed = 5.25;
 9:         System.out.println("\nTrying the cable modem:");
10:         alpha.displaySpeed();
11:         alpha.connect();
12:         System.out.println("\nTrying the DSL modem:");
```

```
13:              beta.displaySpeed();
14:              beta.connect();
15:       }
16: }
```

When you run the program, you should see output matching Figure 11.2.

FIGURE 11.2

The output of the ModemTester *program.*

The following things are taking place in Listing 11.5:

- On Lines 5–6, two new objects are created—a CableModem object called alpha and a DslModem object called beta.

- On Line 7, the speed variable of the CableModem object named alpha is set to 3.77.

- On Line 8, the speed variable of the DslModem object named beta is set to 5.25.

- On Line 10, the displaySpeed() method of the alpha object is called. This method is inherited from Modem—even though it isn't present in the CableModem class, you can call it.

- On Line 11, the connect() method of the alpha object is called.

- On Line 13, the displaySpeed() method of the beta object is called.

- On Line 14, the connect() method of the beta object is called.

THE ABSOLUTE MINIMUM

After creating your first class of objects and arranging several classes into a hierarchy, you ought to be more comfortable with the term *object-oriented programming (OOP)*. You learn more about object behavior and attributes in the next two chapters as you start creating more sophisticated objects.

Terms such as *program*, *class*, and *object* make more sense as you become more experienced with this style of development. OOP is a concept that takes some time to get used to. When you have mastered it, you find that it's an effective way to design, develop, and debug computer programs.

12

DESCRIBE WHAT YOUR OBJECT IS LIKE

As you learned during the past chapter's introduction to object-oriented programming (OOP), an *object* is a way of organizing a program so it has everything it needs to accomplish a task. Objects consist of attributes and behavior.

Attributes are the information stored within an object. They can be variables such as integers, characters, and Boolean values or objects such as `String` and `Calendar` objects. *Behavior* consists of the groups of statements used to handle specific jobs within the object. Each of these groups is called a *method*.

Up to this point, you have been working with methods and variables of objects without knowing it. Any time your statement had a period in it that wasn't a decimal point or part of a string, an object was involved.

Creating Variables

In this chapter, you are looking at an example class of objects called `Virus` whose sole purpose is to be a computer nuisance. A `Virus` has several different things it needs to do its work, and these are implemented as the behavior of the class. The information that's needed for the methods is stored as attributes.

The attributes of an object represent variables needed for the object to function. These variables could be simple data types such as integers, characters, and floating-point numbers, or they could be arrays or objects of classes such as `String` or `Calendar`. You can use an object's variables throughout its class in any of the methods the object contains. By convention, you create variables immediately after the `class` statement that creates the class and before any methods.

One of the things that a `Virus` object needs is a unique code that differentiates it from other computer viruses.

The `Virus` object uses the code 8603 in an integer variable called `identifier`. The following statements begin a class called `Virus` with an attribute called `identifier` and two other attributes:

```
public class Virus {
    public int identifier = 8603;
    public String author = "Sam Snett";
    int maxFileSize = 30000;
}
```

All three variables are attributes for the class: `identifier`, `maxFileSize`, and `author`.

Putting a statement such as `public` in a variable declaration statement is called *access control* because it determines how other objects made from other classes can use that variable—or if they can use it at all.

Making a variable `public` makes it possible to modify the variable from another program that is using the `Virus` object.

If the other program attaches special significance to the number 9201, for instance, it can change `identifier` to that value. The following statements create a `Virus` object called `influenza` and set its `identifier` variable:

```
Virus influenza = new Virus();
influenza.identifier = 9201;
```

In the `Virus` class, the `author` variable also is `public`, so it can be changed freely from other programs. The other variable, `maxFileSize`, can be used only within the class itself.

When you make a variable in a class `public`, the class loses control over how that variable is used by other programs. In many cases, this might not be a problem. For example, the `author` variable can be changed to any name or pseudonym that identifies the author of the program.

Restricting access to a variable keeps errors from occurring if the variable is set incorrectly by another program. With the `Virus` class, a sample restriction could be to require that the `identifier` be a number greater than 999. This could be accomplished by doing these two things:

- Switch the variable from `public` to `protected` or `private`—two other statements that provide more restrictive access.

- Add behavior to change the value of the variable (if it is higher than 999), and report the value of the variable to other programs.

You can use a `protected` variable only in the same class as the variable, any subclasses of that class, or by classes in the same package. A package is used to group related classes together that serve a common purpose. An example is the `java.util` package, which contains classes that offer useful utilities such as date and time programming and file archiving. When you use the `import` statement in a Java program with an asterisk, as in `import java.util.*`, you are making it easier to refer to the classes of that package in a program.

A `private` variable is restricted even further than a `protected` variable—you can use it only in the same class. Unless you know that a variable can be changed to anything without affecting how its class functions, you should make the variable `private` or `protected`.

The following statement makes `identifier` a `private` variable:

```
private int identifier = 8603;
```

If you want other programs to use the `identifier` variable in some way, you have to create behavior that makes it possible. This task is covered later in the chapter.

There also is another type of access control: the lack of any `public`, `private`, or `protected` statement when the variable is created.

In most of the programs you have developed prior to this chapter, you didn't specify any access control. When no access control is set, the variable is available only to classes in the same package. This is called *default* or *package access*.

Creating Class Variables

When you create an object, it has its own version of all variables that are part of the object's class. Each object created from the `Virus` class of objects has its own version of the `identifier`, `maxFileSize`, and `author` variables. If you modified one of these variables in an object, it would not affect the same variable in another `Virus` object.

Sometimes an attribute should describe an entire class of objects instead of a specific object itself. These are called *class* variables.

If you want to keep track of how many `Virus` objects are being used in a program, you could use a class variable to store this information. Only one copy of the variable exists for the whole class. The variables you have been creating for objects thus far can be called *object* variables because they are associated with a specific object.

Both types of variables are created and used in the same way, but `static` is part of the statement that creates class variables. The following statement creates a class variable for the `Virus` example:

```
static int virusCount = 0;
```

Changing the value of a class variable is no different from changing an object's variables. If you have a `Virus` object called `tuberculosis`, you could change the class variable `virusCount` with the following statement:

```
tuberculosis.virusCount++;
```

Because class variables apply to an entire class, you can use the name of the class instead:

```
Virus.virusCount++;
```

Both statements accomplish the same thing, but an advantage to using the name of the class when working with class variables is that it shows immediately that `virusCount` is a class variable instead of an object variable. If you always use object names when working with class variables, you aren't able to tell whether they are class or object variables without looking carefully at the source code.

Class variables also are called *static* variables.

 CAUTION   Although class variables are useful, you must take care not to overuse them. These variables exist for as long as the class is running. If a large array of objects is stored in class variables, it will take up a sizable chunk of memory and never release it.

Creating Behavior with Methods

Attributes are the way to keep track of information about a class of objects, but for a class to do the things it was created to do, you must create behavior. Behavior describes the parts of a class that accomplish specific tasks. Each of these sections is called a *method*.

You have been using methods throughout your programs up to this point without knowing it, including one in particular: `println()`. This method displays text onscreen. Like variables, methods are used in connection with an object or a class. The name of the object or class is followed by a period and the name of the method, as in `robot.move()` or `Integer.parseInt()`.

 NOTE The `System.out.println()` method might seem confusing because it has two periods instead of one. This is because two classes are involved in the statement—the `System` class and the `PrintStream` class. The `System` class has a variable called `out` that is a `PrintStream` object. `println()` is a method of the `PrintStream` class. The `System.out.println()` statement means, in effect, "Use the `println()` method of the `out` instance variable of the `System` class." You can chain together references in this way.

Declaring a Method

You create methods with a statement that looks similar to the statement that begins a class. Both can take arguments between parentheses after their names, and both use { and } marks at the beginning and end. The difference is that methods can send back a value after they are handled. The value can be one of the simple types such as integers or Boolean values, or it can be a class of objects.

The following is an example of a method the `Virus` class can use to change the `maxFileSize` variable:

```
public boolean changeMaxFileSize(int newSize) {
    if (newSize > 0) {
        maxFileSize = newSize;
        return true;
    }
    return false;
}
```

This method takes a single argument: an int variable called newSize, which represents the new value for maxFileSize. If this value is greater than 0, maxFileSize is set to it. Otherwise, the method does not change maxFileSize.

In the statement that begins the method, boolean precedes the name of the method, changeMaxFileSize. This statement signifies that a boolean value is sent back after the method is handled. The return statement is what actually sends a value back. In this method, the value of true is returned if maxFileSize is set to the specified value; false is returned otherwise.

If a method should not return a value, use the keyword void.

When a method returns a value, you can use the method as part of an expression. For example, if you created a Virus object called malaria, you could use statements such as these:

```
if (malaria.changeMaxFileSize(100000)) {
    System.out.println("New size set!");
} else {
    System.out.println("Curses! Foiled again!");
}
```

You can use a method that returns a value at any place in the program where you could have used a variable.

Earlier in the chapter, you switched the identifier variable to private to prevent it from being read or modified by other programs.

When an instance variable is private, there's still a way to make it possible for identifier to be used elsewhere: Create public methods in the Virus class that get the value of identifier and set identifier to a new value. These new methods should be public, unlike the identifier variable itself, so they can be called in other programs.

Consider the following two methods:

```
public int getIdentifier() {
    return identifier;
}

public void setIdentifier(int newValue) {
    if (newValue > 999) {
        identifier = newValue;
    }
}
```

These methods are called *accessor* methods because they enable the `identifier` variable to be accessed from other objects.

The `getIdentifier()` method is used to retrieve the current value of `identifier`. The `getIdentifier()` method does not have any arguments, but it still must have parentheses after the method name. The `setIdentifier()` method takes one argument, an integer called `newValue`. This argument is the new value of `identifier`. If `newValue` is greater than 60, the change will be made.

In this example, the `Virus` class controls how the `identifier` variable can be used by other classes. This process is called *encapsulation*, and it's a fundamental concept of OOP. The better your objects are able to protect themselves against misuse, the more useful they are when you put them to work in other programs.

Although `identifier` is private, the new methods `getIdentifier()` and `setIdentifier()` are able to work with `identifier` because they are in the same class.

Similar Methods with Different Arguments

As you have seen with the `setIdentifier()` method, you can send arguments to a method to affect what it does. Different methods in a class can have different names, but methods also can have the same name if they have different arguments.

Two methods can have the same name if they have a different number of arguments or the arguments are of different variable types. For example, it might be useful for the `Virus` class of objects to have two `alert()` methods. One could have no arguments and would deliver a generic message. The other could specify the message as a string argument. The following statements implement these methods:

```
void alert() {
    System.out.println("Danger! Danger!");
}


void alert(String message) {
    System.out.println("Danger: " + message);
}
```

The methods have the same name, but the arguments differ—one has no argument, and the other has a single `string` argument. The arguments to a method are called the method's *signature*. A class can have different methods with the same name as long as each method has a different signature.

Constructor Methods

When you want to create an object in a program, the new statement is used, as in the following example:

```
Virus typhoid = new Virus();
```

This statement creates a new Virus object called typhoid. When you use the new statement, a special method of that object's class is called. This method is called a *constructor* because it handles the work required to create the object. The purpose of a constructor is to set up any variables and call the methods that must take place for the object to function properly.

Constructors are defined like other methods, except they cannot return a value. The following are two constructors for the Virus class of objects:

```
public Virus() {
    author = "Ignoto"; // author is a string
    maxFileSize = 30000; // maxFileSize is an int
}


public Virus(String name, int size) {
    author = name;
    maxFileSize = size;
}
```

Like other methods, constructors can use the arguments they are sent as a way to define more than one constructor in a class. In this example, the first constructor would be called when a new statement such as the following is used:

```
Virus mumps = new Virus();
```

The other constructor could be called only if a string and an integer are sent as arguments with the new statement, as in this example:

```
Virus rubella = new Virus("April Mayhem", 60000);
```

If you don't include any constructor methods in a class, it inherits a single constructor with no arguments from its superclass. There also might be other constructor methods that it inherits, depending on the superclass used.

In any class, there must be a constructor that has the same number and type of arguments as the new statement that's used to create objects of that class. In the example of the Virus class, which has Virus() and Virus(String name, int size) constructors, you could create Virus objects with only two different types of new statements: one without arguments and one with a string and an integer as the only two arguments.

CAUTION If your subclass defines a constructor with one or more arguments, the class will no longer inherit a constructor with no arguments from its superclass. For this reason, you must always define a no-argument constructor when your class has other constructors.

Class Methods

Like class variables, class methods are a way to provide functionality associated with an entire class instead of a specific object. Use a class method when the method does nothing that affects an individual object of the class. In the previous chapter, "Create Your First Object," you used the `parseInt()` method of the `Integer` class to convert a string to a variable of the type `int`:

```
String count = "25";
int myCount = Integer.parseInt(count);
```

This is a class method. To make a method into a class method, use `static` in front of the method name, as in the following code:

```
static void showVirusCount() {
    System.out.println("There are " + virusCount + " viruses");
}
```

The `virusCount` class variable was used earlier to keep track of how many `Virus` objects have been created by a program. The `showVirusCount()` method is a class method that displays this total, and you can call it with a statement such as the following:

```
Virus.showVirusCount();
```

Because class variables and methods aren't associated with a specific object, you don't need to create an object solely for the purpose of using them. The use of the `Integer.parseInt()` method is an example of this because you don't have to create a new `Integer` object just to convert a string to an `int` value.

Variable Scope Within Methods

When you create a variable or an object inside a method in one of your classes, it is usable only inside that method. The reason for this is the concept of variable scope. *Scope* is the block in which a variable exists in a program. If you go outside of the part of the program defined by the scope, you can no longer use the variable.

The { and } statements in a program define the boundaries for a variable's scope. Any variable created within these marks cannot be used outside of them. For example, consider the following statements:

```
if (numFiles < 1) {
    String warning = "No files remaining.";
}
System.out.println(warning);
```

This code does not work—and does not compile in NetBeans—because the warning variable was created inside the brackets of the if block. Those brackets define the scope of the variable. The warning variable does not exist outside of the brackets, so the System.out.println() method cannot use it as an argument.

When you use a set of brackets inside another set of brackets, you need to pay attention to the scope of the enclosed variables. Take a look at the following example:

```
if (infectedFiles < 5) {
    int status = 1;
    if (infectedFiles < 1) {
        boolean firstVirus = true;
        status = 0;
    } else {
        firstVirus = false;
    }
}
```

See any problems? In this example, the status variable can be used anywhere, but the statement that assigns a value of false to the firstVirus variable causes a compiler error. Because firstVirus is created within the scope of the if (infectedFiles < 1) statement, it doesn't exist inside the scope of the else statement that follows.

To fix the problem, firstVirus must be created outside both of these blocks so that its scope includes both of them. One solution is to create firstVirus one line after status is created.

Rules that enforce scope make programs easier to debug because scope limits the area in which you can use a variable. This reduces one of the most common errors that can crop up in programming—using the same variable two different ways in different parts of a program.

The concept of scope also applies to methods because they are defined by an opening bracket and closing bracket. A variable created inside a method cannot be used in other methods. You can use a variable in more than one method only if it was created as an object variable or class variable.

Putting One Class Inside Another

Although a Java program is called a class, there are many occasions when a program requires more than one class to get its work done. These programs consist of a main class and any helper classes that are needed.

When you divide a program into multiple classes, there are two ways to define the helper classes. One way is to define each class separately, as in the following example:

```java
public class Wrecker {
    String author = "Ignoto";

    public void infectFile() {
        VirusCode vic = new VirusCode(1024);
    }
}


class VirusCode {
    int vSize;

    VirusCode(int size) {
        vSize = size;
    }
}
```

In this example, the VirusCode class is a helper class for the Wrecker class. Helper classes often are defined in the same source code file as the class they're assisting. When the source file is compiled, multiple class files are produced. The preceding example produces the files Wrecker.class and VirusCode.class when compiled.

CAUTION If more than one class is defined in the same source file, only one of the classes can be public. The other classes cannot have public in their class statements. The name of the source code file must match the public class it defines.

Using the `this` Keyword

Because you can refer to variables and methods in other classes along with variables and methods in your own classes, the variable you're referring to can become confusing in some circumstances. One way to make things more clear is with the `this` statement—a way to refer within a program to the program's own object.

When you are using an object's methods or variables, you put the name of the object in front of the method or variable name, separated by a period. Consider these examples:

```
Virus chickenpox = new Virus();
chickenpox.author = "Sneezy";
chickenpox.setIdentifier(7513);
```

These statements create a new `Virus` object called `chickenpox`, set the `author` variable of `chickenpox`, and then call the `setIdentifier()` method of `chickenpox`.

Sometimes in a program you need to refer to the current object—in other words, the object represented by the program itself. For example, inside the `Virus` class, you might have a method that has its own variable called `author`:

```
public void checkAuthor() {
    String author = null;

}
```

In this example, a variable called `author` exists within the scope of the `checkAuthor()` method, but it isn't the same variable as the object variable called `author`. If you want to refer to the current object's `author` variable, you have to use the `this` statement, as in the following:

```
System.out.println(this.author);
```

By using `this`, you make it clear to which variable or method you are referring. You can use `this` anywhere in a class that you would refer to an object by name. If you want to send the current object as an argument to a method, for example, you could use a statement such as the following:

```
verifyData(this);
```

In many cases, the `this` statement is not needed to make it clear that you're referring to an object's variables and methods. However, there's no detriment to using `this` any time you want to be sure you're referring to the right thing.

The `this` keyword comes in handy in a constructor when setting the value of an object's instance variables. Consider a `Virus` object that has `author` and `maxFileSize` variables. This constructor sets them:

```
public Virus(String author, int maxFileSize) {
    this.author = author;
    this.maxFileSize = maxFileSize;
}
```

Using Class Methods and Variables

For this chapter's first programming project, you create a simple `Virus` object that can count the number of `Virus` objects that a program has created and report the total.

You know the drill: Select File, New File in NetBeans and create a new Empty Java File called `Virus` in the `com.javaminecraft` package. Enter Listing 12.1 in the source editor; then click Save.

LISTING 12.1 The Full Text of `Virus.java`

```
 1: package com.javaminecraft;
 2:
 3: public class Virus {
 4:     static int virusCount = 0;
 5:
 6:     public Virus() {
 7:         virusCount++;
 8:     }
 9:
10:     static int getVirusCount() {
11:         return virusCount;
12:     }
13: }
```

Save the file, which NetBeans compiles automatically. This class lacks a `main()` method and thus cannot be run directly. To test this new `Virus` class, you need to create a second class that can create `Virus` objects.

The `VirusLab` class is a simple application that creates `Virus` objects and then counts the number of objects that have been created with the `getVirusCount()` class method of the `Virus` class.

Open a new file with NetBeans and enter Listing 12.2. Save the file as `VirusLab.java` when you're done.

LISTING 12.2   The Full Text of `VirusLab.java`

```
 1: package com.javaminecraft;
 2:
 3: public class VirusLab {
 4:     public static void main(String[] arguments) {
 5:         int numViruses = Integer.parseInt(arguments[0]);
 6:         if (numViruses > 0) {
 7:             Virus[] virii = new Virus[numViruses];
 8:             for (int i = 0; i < numViruses; i++) {
 9:                 virii[i] = new Virus();
10:             }
11:             System.out.println("There are "
12:                 Virus.getVirusCount() + " viruses.");
13:         }
14:     }
15: }
```

The `VirusLab` class is an application that takes one argument when you run it at the command line: the number of `Virus` objects to create. To specify the command-line argument in NetBeans, do the following:

1. Select Run, Set Project Configuration, Customize. The Project Properties dialog opens.

2. Enter `VirusLab` in the Main Class field, and enter the number of `Virus` objects you'd like the program to create in the Arguments field.

3. Click OK to close the dialog.

To run a program you've configured in this manner, select Run, Run Project in NetBeans.

Arguments are read into an application using a string array that's sent to the `main()` method. In the `VirusLab` class, this occurs in Line 4.

To work with an argument as an integer, it must be converted from a `String` object to an integer. This requires the use of the `parseInt()` class method of the `Integer` class. In Line 5, an `int` variable named `numViruses` is created from the first argument sent to the program on the command line.

If the `numViruses` variable is greater than 0, the following things take place in the `VirusLab` application:

- On Line 7, an array of `Virus` objects is created with the `numViruses` variable determining the number of objects in the array.

- On Lines 8–10, a `for` loop is used to call the constructor method for each `Virus` object in the array.

- On Lines 11–12, after all the `Virus` objects have been constructed, the `getVirusCount()` class method of the `Virus` class is used to count the number of its objects that have been created. This should match the argument that was set when you ran the `VirusLab` application.

If the `numViruses` variable is not greater than 0, nothing happens in the `VirusLab` application.

After the `VirusLab.java` file has been compiled, test it with any command-line argument you'd like to try. The number of `Virus` objects that can be created depends on the memory that's available on your system when you run the `VirusLab` application. On the author's system, anything greater than 128 million viruses causes the program to crash after displaying an `OutOfMemoryError` message.

If you don't specify more `Virus` objects than your system can handle, the output should be something like Figure 12.1.

FIGURE 12.1

The output of the `VirusLab` *program.*

 CAUTION   The `VirusLab` project raises the issue of how to control how much memory a Java program uses.

The memory available to the Java Virtual Machine (JVM) when it runs an application is controlled by two things: the total physical memory available on the computer and the amount the JVM is configured to use. The default memory allocation is 256MB. A different amount can be set with the -Xmx command-line argument.

To set this in NetBeans, select Run, Set Project Configuration, Customize. The Project Properties dialog opens with the Run settings at the front. In the VM Options field, enter -Xmx1024M to allocate 1024MB of memory to the JVM. Alter that number for more or less memory. Also fill out the Main Class and Arguments fields and run the program by selecting Run, Run Project.

THE ABSOLUTE MINIMUM

You now have completed two of the three chapters devoted to object-oriented concepts in this book. You've learned how to create an object, give behavior and attributes to the object and its class of objects, and convert objects and variables into other forms by using casting.

Thinking in terms of objects is one of the tougher challenges of the Java programming language. After you start to understand it, however, you realize that the entire language makes use of objects and classes.

During the next chapter, you learn how to give your objects parents and children.

IN THIS CHAPTER

- Design superclasses and subclasses
- Form an inheritance hierarchy
- Override methods

13

MAKE THE MOST OF EXISTING OBJECTS

Java objects can have kids. When you create an object—a set of attributes and behavior—you have designed something that's ready to pass these qualities on to offspring. These child objects take on a lot of the same attributes and behaviors as their parents. They also can do some things differently from their parents.

This system is called *inheritance*, and it's something every superclass (parent) gives to its subclasses (children). Inheritance is one of the most useful aspects of object-oriented programming (OOP), and you learn about it during this chapter.

Another useful aspect of OOP is the capability to create an object you can use with different programs. Reusability makes it easier to develop error-free, reliable programs.

The Power of Inheritance

You have used inheritance every time you worked with one of the standard Java classes such as `String` or `Integer`. Java classes are organized into a pyramid-shaped hierarchy of classes in which all classes descend from the `Object` class.

A class of objects inherits from all superclasses that are above it. To get a working idea of how this operates, consider the `JApplet` class. This class is a superclass of all applets and Java programs that run in a web browser. The `JApplet` class is a subclass of `Applet`.

A partial family tree of `JApplet` is shown in Figure 13.1. Each of the boxes is a class, and the lines connect a superclass to any subclasses below it.

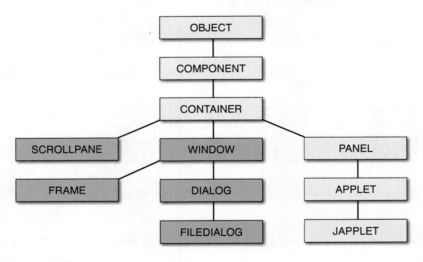

FIGURE 13.1

The family tree of the `JApplet` class.

At the top is the `Object` class. `JApplet` has five superclasses above it in the hierarchy: `Applet`, `Panel`, `Container`, `Component`, and `Object`.

The `JApplet` class inherits attributes and behaviors from each of these classes because each is directly above it in the hierarchy of superclasses. `JApplet` does not inherit anything from the five green classes in Figure 13.1, which include `Dialog` and `Frame`, because they are not above it in the hierarchy.

If this seems confusing, think of the hierarchy as a family tree. `JApplet` inherits from its parent, the parent's parent, and on upward. It even might inherit some things from its great-great-great-grandparent, `Object`. The `JApplet` class doesn't inherit from its siblings or its cousins, however.

Creating a new class boils down to the following task: You only have to define the ways in which it is different from an existing class. The rest of the work is done for you.

Inheriting Behavior and Attributes

The behavior and attributes of a class are a combination of two things: its own behavior and attributes and all the behavior and attributes it inherits from its superclasses.

The following are some of the behavior and attributes of `JApplet`:

- The `equals()` method determines whether a `JApplet` object has the same value as another object.

- The `setBackground()` method sets the background color of the applet window.

- The `add()` method adds user interface components such as buttons and text fields to the applet.

- The `setLayout()` method defines how the applet's graphical user interface is organized.

The `JApplet` class can use all these methods, even though `setLayout()` is the only one it didn't inherit from another class. The `equals()` method is defined in `Object`, `setBackground()` comes from `Component`, and `add()` comes from `Container`.

Overriding Methods

Some methods defined in the `JApplet` class of objects also are defined in one of its superclasses. As an example, the `update()` method is part of both the `JApplet` class and the `Component` class. When a method is defined in a subclass and its superclass, the subclass method is used. This enables a subclass to change, replace, or completely wipe out some of the behavior or attributes of its superclasses. In the case of `update()`, the purpose is to wipe out some behavior present in a superclass.

Creating a new method in a subclass to change behavior inherited from a superclass is called *overriding* the method. You need to override a method any time the inherited behavior produces an undesired result.

Establishing Inheritance

A class is defined as the subclass of another class using the `extends` statement, as in the following:

```
class AnimatedLogo extends JApplet {
    // behavior and attributes go here
}
```

The `extends` keyword establishes the `AnimatedLogo` class of objects as a subclass of `JApplet`. All applets that use the Swing graphical user interface in Java must be subclasses of `JApplet`. They need the functionality this class provides to run when presented on a web page.

One method that `AnimatedLogo` must override is the `paint()` method, which is used to draw everything within the program's window. The `paint()` method, implemented by the `Component` class, is passed all the way down to `AnimatedLogo`. However, the `paint()` method does not do anything. It exists so that subclasses of `Component` have a method they can use when something must be displayed.

To override a method, you must declare the method in the same way it was declared in the superclass from which it was inherited. A `public` method must remain public, the value sent back by the method must be the same, and the number and type of arguments to the method must not change.

 NOTE   All but one of the programs created in the previous 12 chapters did not use the `extends` keyword. For this reason, you might be thinking that they must exist outside of the Java class hierarchy. That's not possible.

All classes you create in Java are part of the hierarchy because they have a default superclass, `Object`, when no other superclass is specified with `extends`. `Object` includes behavior required in all objects, such as the `equals()` and `toString()` methods.

The `paint()` method of the `Component` class begins as follows:

```
public void paint(Graphics g) {
```

When `AnimatedLogo` overrides this method, it must begin with a statement like this:

```
public void paint(Graphics screen) {
```

The only difference lies in the name of the Graphics object, which does not matter when determining whether the methods are created in the same way. These two statements match because the following things match:

- Both paint() methods are public.

- Both methods return no value, as declared by the use of the void keyword.

- Both have a Graphics object as their only argument.

Using **this** and **super** in a Subclass

Two keywords that are extremely useful in a subclass are this and super.

As you learned during the previous chapter, the this keyword is used to refer to the current object. When you're creating a class and you need to refer to the specific object created from that class, you can use this, as in the following statement:

```
this.title = "Mordecai";
```

This statement sets the object's title variable to the text "Mordecai."

The super keyword serves a similar purpose: It refers to the immediate superclass of the object. You can use super in several ways:

- To refer to a constructor method of the superclass, as in super("Rigby");

- To refer to a variable of the superclass, as in super.skips = 250;

- To refer to a method of the superclass, as in super.show();

One way you use the super keyword is in the constructor method of a subclass. Because a subclass inherits the behaviors and attributes of its superclass, you have to associate each constructor of that subclass with a constructor of its superclass. Otherwise, some of the behaviors and attributes might not be set up correctly, and the subclass won't be able to function properly.

To associate the constructors, the first statement of a subclass constructor must be a call to a constructor of the superclass. This requires the super keyword, as in the following statements:

```
public FileLoader(String name, int length) {
    super(name, length);
}
```

This example is the constructor of a subclass that is using the statement super(name, length) to call a comparable constructor in its superclass.

If you don't use `super` to call a constructor in the superclass, Java automatically calls `super()` with no arguments when the subclass constructor begins. If this superclass constructor doesn't exist or provides unexpected behavior, errors will result, so it's better to call a superclass constructor yourself.

Working with Existing Objects

OOP encourages reuse. If you develop an object for use with one Java programming project, you should be able to incorporate that object into another project without modification.

If a Java class is well-designed, it's possible to make that class available for use in other programs. The more objects available for use in your programs, the less work you have to do when creating your own software. If there's an excellent map-drawing object that suits your needs, you can use it instead of writing your own.

When Java was first introduced, the system of sharing objects was largely an informal one. Programmers developed their objects to be as independent as possible and protected them against misuse through the use of private variables and public methods to read and write those variables.

Sharing objects becomes more powerful when there's a standard approach to developing reusable objects.

The benefits of a standard include the following:

- There's less need to document how an object works because anyone who knows the standard already knows a lot about how it functions.

- You can design development tools that follow the standard, making it possible to work more easily with these objects.

- Two objects that follow the standard are able to interact with each other without special programming to make them compatible.

Storing Objects of the Same Class in Array Lists

An important decision to make when writing a computer program is where to store data. In the first half of this book, you've discovered three useful places to keep information:

- Basic data types such as `int` and `char`

- Arrays

- `String` objects

There are many more places to store information because any Java class can hold data. One of the most useful is `ArrayList`, a data structure that holds objects of the same class.

As the class name suggests, array lists are like arrays, which also hold elements of related data, but they can grow or shrink in size at any time.

The `ArrayList` class belongs to the `java.util` package of classes, one of the most useful in the Java Class Library. An `import` statement makes it available in your program:

```
import java.util.ArrayList;
```

An array list holds objects that either belong to the same class or share the same superclass. They are created by referencing two classes—the `ArrayList` class and the class the list holds.

The name of the class held by the list is placed within < and > characters, as in this statement:

```
ArrayList<String> structure = new ArrayList<String>();
```

The preceding statement creates a list that holds strings. Identifying a list's class in this manner utilizes generics, a way to indicate the type of objects a data structure such as an array list holds. If you were using lists with an older version of Java, you would have written a constructor like this:

```
ArrayList structure = new ArrayList();
```

Although you can still do this, generics make your code more reliable because they give the Java compiler a way to prevent more errors. Here, they stop you from misusing an array list by putting the wrong class of objects in it. If you attempt to put an `Integer` object in a list that's supposed to hold `String` objects, the compiler fails with an error.

Unlike arrays, array lists aren't created with a fixed number of elements they hold. The list is created with 10 elements. If you know you're storing a lot more objects than that, you can specify a size as an argument to the constructor. Here's a statement that creates a 300-element list:

```
ArrayList<String> structure = new ArrayList<String>(300);
```

You can add an object to a list by calling its `add()` method, using the object as the only argument:

```
structure.add("Fin");
structure.add("Jake");
structure.add("Bubblegum");
```

You add objects in order, so if these are the first three objects added to `structure`, element 0 is "Fin", element 1 is "Jake", and element 2 is "Bubblegum".

You retrieve elements from lists by calling their `get()` method with the element's index number as the argument:

```
String name = structure.get(1);
```

This statement stores "Jake" in the `name` string.

To see whether a list contains an object in one of its elements, call its `contains()` method with that object as an argument:

```
if (structure.contains("Marceline")) {
    System.out.println("Marceline found");
}
```

You can remove an object from a list using itself or an index number:

```
structure.remove(0);
structure.remove("Bubblegum");
```

These two statements leave "Jake" as the only string in the list.

Looping Through an Array List

Java includes a special `for` loop that makes it easy to load an array list and examine each of its elements in turn.

This loop has just two parts, which is one less than the `for` loops you learned about in Chapter 9, "Repeat an Action with Loops."

The first part is the initialization section: the class and name of a variable that holds each object retrieved from the list. This object should belong to the same class that holds the list.

The second part identifies the list.

Here's code that loops through the `structure` list, displaying each name to the screen:

```
for (String name : structure) {
    System.out.println(name);
}
```

The chapter's first project takes array lists and the special `for` loop for a spin, presenting a list of strings in alphabetical order. The list comes from an array and command-line arguments.

With your Minecraft project open within NetBeans, select File, New File; then create a new Empty Java File named StringLister in the com.javaminecraft package. Enter Listing 13.1 in the source editor, and save the file.

LISTING 13.1 The Full Text of StringLister.java

```
 1: package com.javaminecraft;
 2:
 3: import java.util.*;
 4:
 5: public class StringLister {
 6:     String[] names = { "Harry", "Dudley", "Ginny", "Ron",
 7:     "Hermione", "Draco", "Neville", "Vincent", "Gregory" };
 8:
 9:     public StringLister(String[] moreNames) {
10:         ArrayList<String> list = new ArrayList<String>();
11:         for (int i = 0; i < names.length; i++) {
12:             list.add(names[i]);
13:         }
14:         for (int i = 0; i < moreNames.length; i++) {
15:             list.add(moreNames[i]);
16:         }
17:         Collections.sort(list);
18:         for (String name : list) {
19:             System.out.println(name);
20:         }
21:     }
22:
23:     public static void main(String[] arguments) {
24:         StringLister lister = new StringLister(arguments);
25:     }
26: }
```

Before you run the application, you should use the Run, Set Project Configuration, Customize command to set the main class to com.minecraft.StringLister and the argument to one or more names separated by spaces, such as Percy Fred George. Then select Run, Run Project to see the result.

The names specified at the command line are added to the names stored in an array in Lines 6–7. Because the total number of names is not known until the program runs, an array list serves as a better storage place for these strings than an array.

The list's strings are sorted in alphabetical order using a method of the `Collections` class:

```
Collections.sort(list);
```

This class, like `ArrayList`, belongs to the `java.util` package. Array lists and other useful data structures are called *collections* in Java.

When you run the program, the output should be a list of names in alphabetical order (see Figure 13.2). The flexible size of array lists enables your additional names to be added to the data structure and sorted along with the others.

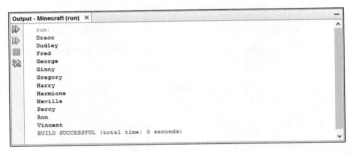

FIGURE 13.2

The output of the `StringLister` *program.*

Creating a Subclass

To see an example of inheritance at work, in the next project you create a class called `Point3D` that represents a point in three-dimensional space—a purpose similar to what the `Location` class does in Minecraft.

You can express a two-dimensional point with an (x,y) coordinate. Three-dimensional space adds a third coordinate, which can be called z.

The `Point3D` class of objects can do three things:

- Keep track of an object's (x,y,z) coordinate
- Move an object to a new (x,y,z) coordinate
- Move an object by a specified amount of x, y, and z values

Java already has a standard class that represents two-dimensional points called Point.

That class has two integer variables called x and y that store a Point object's (x,y) location. It also has a move() method to place a point at the specified location and a translate() method to move an object by an amount of x and y values.

In the Minecraft projects in NetBeans, create a new empty file called Point3D in the com.javaminecraft package and enter the text of Listing 13.2 into the file. Save it when you're done.

LISTING 13.2 The Full Text of Point3D.java

```
1: package com.javaminecraft;
2:
3: import java.awt.*;
4:
5: public class Point3D extends Point {
6:     public int z;
7:
8:     public Point3D(int x, int y, int z) {
9:         super(x,y);
10:        this.z = z;
11:    }
12:
13:    public void move(int x, int y, int z) {
14:        this.z = z;
15:        super.move(x, y);
16:    }
17:
18:    public void translate(int x, int y, int z) {
19:        this.z += z;
20:        super.translate(x, y);
21:    }
22: }
```

The Point3D class does not have a main() method, so you cannot run it as an application, but you can use it in Java programs anywhere a three-dimensional point is needed.

The `Point3D` class only has to do work that isn't being done by its superclass, `Point`. This primarily involves keeping track of the integer variable `z` and receiving it as an argument to the `move()` method, `translate()` method, and `Point3D()` constructor method.

All the methods use the keywords `super` and `this`. The `this` statement is used to refer to the current `Point3D` object, so `this.z = z;` in Line 10 sets the object variable `z` equal to the `z` value that is sent as an argument to the method in Line 8.

The `super` statement refers to the current object's superclass, `Point`. It is used to set variables and call methods that are inherited by `Point3D`. The statement `super(x,y)` in Line 9 calls the `Point(x,y)` constructor in the superclass, which then sets the (x,y) coordinates of the `Point3D` object. Because `Point` already is equipped to handle the x and y axes, it would be redundant for the `Point3D` class of objects to do the same thing.

To test the new `Point3D` class, create a program that uses `Point` and `Point3D` objects and moves them around. Create a new file in NetBeans called `PointTester` in the `com.javaminecraft` package, and enter Listing 13.3 into it. The file compiles automatically when it is saved.

LISTING 13.3   The Full Text of `PointTester.java`

```
1: package com.javaminecraft;

2:

3: import java.awt.*;

4:

5: class PointTester {

6:     public static void main(String[] arguments) {

7:         Point location1 = new Point(11,22);

8:         Point3D location2 = new Point3D(7,6,64);

9:

10:        System.out.println("The 2D point is at (" + location1.x

11:            + ", " + location1.y + ")");

12:        System.out.println("It's being moved to (4, 13)");

13:        location1.move(4,13);

14:        System.out.println("The 2D point is now at (" +
           location1.x

15:            + ", " + location1.y + ")");
```

```
16:            System.out.println("It's being moved -10 units on both
the x "
17:                + "and y axes");
18:            location1.translate(-10,-10);
19:            System.out.println("The 2D point ends up at (" +
            ➥location1.x
20:                + ", " + location1.y + ")\n");
21:

22:            System.out.println("The 3D point is at (" + location2.x
23:                + ", " + location2.y + ", " + location2.z + ")");
24:            System.out.println("It's being moved to (10, 22, 71)");
25:        .   location2.move(10,22,71);
26:            System.out.println("The 3D point is now at (" +
            ➥location2.x
27:                + ", " + location2.y + ", " + location2.z + ")");
28:            System.out.println("It's being moved -20 units on the
            ➥x, y "
29:                + "and z axes");
30:            location2.translate(-20,-20,-20);
31:            System.out.println("The 3D point ends up at (" +
            ➥location2.x
32:                + ", " + location2.y + ", " + location2.z + ")");
33:        }
34: }
```

When you run the file by selecting Run, Run File, you see the output shown in Figure 13.3 if the program compiled properly. If not, look for the red alert icon alongside the source editor that indicates the line that triggered an error.

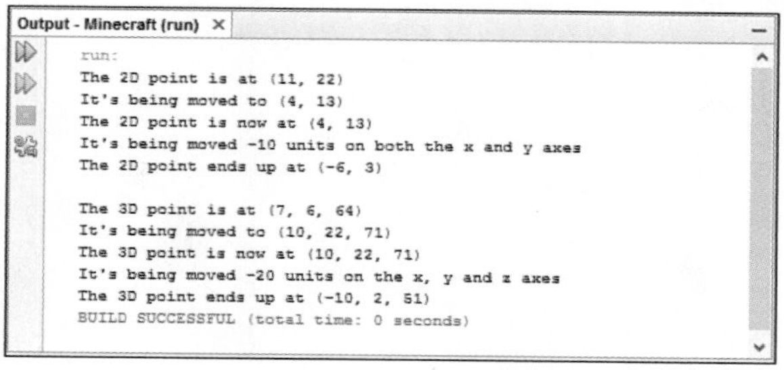

FIGURE 13.3

The output of the PointTester *program.*

THE ABSOLUTE MINIMUM

When people talk about the miracle of birth, they're probably not speaking of the way a superclass in Java can give birth to subclasses or the way behavior and attributes are inherited in a hierarchy of classes.

If the real world worked the same way that OOP does, every descendant of Mozart could choose to be a brilliant composer. All descendants of J. K. Rowling could write epic tales of heroic babies with odd birthmarks. Every skill your ancestors worked to achieve would be handed to you without an ounce of toil.

On the scale of miracles, inheritance isn't quite up to par with continuing the existence of a species or defeating a Wither Skull. However, it's an effective way to design software with a minimum of redundant work.

14

IN THIS CHAPTER

- Create an array list
- Add and remove items from the list
- Search a list for an object
- Loop through the contents of a list
- Create a hash map of keys and values
- Add and remove items from the map
- Loop through the keys and values of a map

STORE OBJECTS IN DATA STRUCTURES

Programmers are hoarders.

In computer programming, you spend a lot of time collecting information and looking for a place to store it. The information can come in the form of a primitive data type, such as a `float`, or as an object of a particular class. It can be read from disk, retrieved from an Internet server, entered by a user, or gathered through other means.

After you have the information, you must decide where to put it while a program is running in the Java Virtual Machine. Several items that are related to each other by data type or class can be stored in an array.

This is sufficient for many purposes, but as your programs grow in sophistication, your needs as a hoarder will increase.

During this chapter, you learn about some classes in Java that are designed for information hoarders: array lists and hash maps.

Array Lists

In Chapter 10, "Store Information with Arrays," you were introduced to arrays, an extremely handy way to work with groups of variables and objects in programs. Arrays are so essential to Java that they are a built-in data type like integers and characters. An array packages together elements of the same data type or class.

As useful as arrays can be, they are limited by the fact that the size of an array does not change. After an array is created to hold 90 elements, it can't be altered to hold more or fewer. The size is fixed.

There's a class in the `java.util` package that does everything an array can do without that limitation: `ArrayList`.

An array list is a data structure that holds objects of the same class or a common superclass. The list can grow or shrink as needed as a program is running.

The simplest way to create an array list is by calling its constructor with no arguments:

```
ArrayList servants = new ArrayList();
```

Array lists can be created by specifying an initial capacity, which provides some guidance on how many elements the list might hold. The capacity is set as an integer argument to the constructor:

```
ArrayList servants = new ArrayList(30);
```

Although this looks like creating an array and determining its exact size, the capacity is just a hint. If the capacity is exceeded, the array list will be adjusted accordingly and continue to function properly. (The better you estimate the capacity, the more efficient the program will be.)

The list holds objects that belong to the same class or share a superclass.

When you create an array list, you know the class or superclass the list is intended to hold. This can be specified in the constructor within < and > signs, a feature of the language called *generics*. Here's an improvement on the constructor for a list that holds `String` objects:

```
ArrayList<String> servants = new ArrayList<String>();
```

To add an object, call the array list's `add(Object)` method with that object as the argument. Here are statements that add five strings:

```
servants.add("Bates");
servants.add("Anna");
servants.add("Thomas");
```

```
servants.add("Mrs. O'Brien");
servants.add("Daisy");
```

Each element is added to the end of the list, so the first string in `servants` is "Bates" and the last is "Daisy".

NOTE If you have some experience with earlier versions of Java, you might have heard of vectors and wonder why they're so much like array lists. They are another data structure that functions almost identically to the `ArrayList` class, and they are in the same package and named `java.util.Vector`. The difference between the two is that vectors require synchronization, so any class that makes use of vectors will run more slowly. For this reason, array lists are generally the preferred choice.

There's a corresponding `remove(Object)` method that takes the object out of the list:

```
servants.remove("Mrs. O'Brien");
```

The size of an array list is the number of elements it currently holds. Retrieve this information by calling the list's `size()` method, which returns an integer:

```
int servantCount = servants.size();
```

When you have used generics to specify the class the list contains, it's simple to use a `for` loop to iterate through each element of the list:

```
for (String servant : servants) {
    System.out.println(servant);
}
```

The first argument to `for` is a variable where an element should be stored. The second is the array list. Other data structures can employ the same loop.

The `add(Object)` method stores the object at the end of the list. Objects also can be added to a list by specifying the position within the list where the object should be stored. This requires the `add(int, Object)` method, which takes the position as the first argument:

```
ArrayList<String> aristocrats = new ArrayList<String>();
aristocrats.add(0, "Lord Robert");
aristocrats.add(1, "Lady Mary");
aristocrats.add(2, "Lady Edith");
```

```
aristocrats.add(3, "Lady Sybil");
aristocrats.add(0, "Lady Grantham");
```

The last statement in the preceding example adds "Lady Grantham" at the top of the list instead of the bottom, putting her above "Lord Robert" and the others.

The position specified as the first argument must be no greater than the size() of the list. If "Lord Robert" had been added with 1 as the position instead of 0, the program would fail with an IndexOutOfBoundsException.

An element can be removed from a list by specifying its position as the argument to remove(int):

```
aristocrats.remove(4);
```

The element at a specified position in a list can be retrieved by calling get(int) with that position. Here's a for loop that pulls each string out of a list and displays it:

```
for (int i = 0; i < aristocrats.size(); i++) {
    String aristocrat = aristocrats.get(i);
    System.out.println(aristocrat);
}
```

Often it is necessary to find out whether an array list contains a specific object. This can be determined by calling the list's indexOf(Object) method with that object as the argument. The method returns the position of the object or –1 if it cannot be found in the list:

```
int hasCarson = servants.indexOf("Carson");
```

The chapter's first project employs these techniques on a simple game in which shots are fired at (x,y) points on a 10-by-10 grid. Some points contain a target; others do not.

The targets are represented by the Point class in the java.awt package. A point is created by calling the Point(int, int) constructor with the x and y coordinates as the two arguments.

This statement creates a point at (9,2):

```
Point p1 = new Point(9,2);
```

Here's a 10-by-10 grid with that point marked by an *X* and empty spaces marked by a period character (.):

```
    1   2   3   4   5   6   7   8   9

1   .   .   .   .   .   .   .   .

2   .   .   .   .   .   .   .   X

3   .   .   .   .   .   .   .   .

4   .   .   .   .   .   .   .   .

5   .   .   .   .   .   .   .   .

6   .   .   .   .   .   .   .   .

7   .   .   .   .   .   .   .   .

8   .   .   .   .   .   .   .   .

9   .   .   .   .   .   .   .   .
```

Columns go from left to right and represent the x coordinate. Rows extend from top to bottom and mark the y coordinate.

Before this project, you saw how array lists could hold strings. They can hold Point or any other class of objects. This statement creates a list of points:

```
ArrayList<Point> targets = new ArrayList<Point>();
```

The Java compiler won't allow any class other than `Point` or its subclasses to be added to the array list.

In NetBeans, create an empty Java file named `Battlepoint` and designate `com.javaminecraft` as its package. Enter the text of Listing 14.1 into the file.

LISTING 14.1   The Full Text of `Battlepoint.java`

```
 1: package com.javaminecraft;
 2:
 3: import java.awt.*;
 4: import java.util.*;
 5:
 6: public class Battlepoint {
 7:     ArrayList<Point> targets = new ArrayList<Point>();
 8:
 9:     public Battlepoint() {
10:         // create targets to shoot at
11:         createTargets();
```

```
12:          // display the game map
13:          showMap();
14:          // shoot at three points
15:          shoot(7,4);
16:          shoot(3,3);
17:          shoot(9,2);
18:          // display the map again
19:          showMap();
20:      }
21:
22:      private void showMap() {
23:          System.out.println("\n    1  2  3  4  5  6  7  8  9");
24:          for (int column = 1; column < 10; column++) {
25:              for (int row = 1; row < 10; row++) {
26:                  if (row == 1) {
27:                      System.out.print(column + " ");
28:                  }
29:                  System.out.print(" ");
30:                  Point cell = new Point(row, column);
31:                  if (targets.indexOf(cell) > -1) {
32:                      // a target is at this position
33:                      System.out.print("X");
34:                  } else {
35:                      // no target is here
36:                      System.out.print(".");
37:                  }
38:                  System.out.print(" ");
39:              }
40:              System.out.println();
41:          }
42:          System.out.println();
43:      }
44:
45:      private void createTargets() {
```

```
46:              Point p1 = new Point(5,9);
47:              targets.add(p1);
48:              Point p2 = new Point(4,5);
49:              targets.add(p2);
50:              Point p3 = new Point(9,2);
51:              targets.add(p3);
52:          }
53:
54:      private void shoot(int x, int y) {
55:              Point shot = new Point(x,y);
56:              System.out.print("Firing at (" + x + "," + y + ") ...
");
57:              if (targets.indexOf(shot) > -1) {
58:                  System.out.println("you sank my battlepoint!");
59:                  // delete the destroyed target
60:                  targets.remove(shot);
61:              } else {
62:                  System.out.println("miss.");
63:              }
64:      }
65:
66:      public static void main(String[] arguments) {
67:          new Battlepoint();
68:      }
69: }
```

Comments in the `Battlepoint` application describe each part of the constructor and important parts of the conditional logic in the program.

The application creates targets as three `Point` objects and adds them to an array (Lines 45–52). A map is displayed showing these targets (Lines 22–43).

Next, shots are taken at three points by calling the `shoot(int, int)` method (Lines 54–64). Each time, the application reports back whether the shot hit one of the targets. If it does, the target is removed from the array list.

Finally, the map is displayed again and the application terminates.

The output is shown in Figure 14.1.

FIGURE 14.1

Putting Point *objects in an array list and shooting at them.*

The three targets are shown in the top map of Figure 14.1. One target is removed after it is hit. The bottom map in the output reflects this change.

When a target is hit by a shot, it is removed from the targets array list by calling the remove(Object) method with the shot's point as the argument.

 NOTE   In the shoot() method of the Battlepoint application, the Point object that will be removed from the array list is the one that represents the shot. This has the same (x,y) coordinates as the target that was hit.

Hash Maps

The ability to use one piece of information to access another is common in programming. An array list is the simplest example of this among the data structures, where an index number can be used to retrieve one object from the list. Here's an example that pulls the first string from the aristocrats array list:

```
String first = aristocrats.get(0);
```

Arrays also use index numbers to retrieve each item in the array.

Hash maps are data structures in Java that use an object to retrieve another object. The first object is the key and the second is the value. They are implemented as the `HashMap` class in the `java.util` package.

The name refers to how keys are mapped to values. An example of this kind of structured data is a phone book. A person's name (a string) can be used to retrieve the person's phone number.

 NOTE   Just as array lists have another class called `Vector` that does the same thing in a more resource-intensive way, hash maps have `Hashtable`. Hash tables are synchronized and hash maps are not, so any class that makes use of hash tables takes longer to run. Hash maps generally are preferred.

A hash map can be created by calling its constructor with no arguments:

```
HashMap phonebook = new HashMap();
```

Two things can be specified in a new hash map that control how efficient it is: the initial capacity and the load factor. These are set with two arguments, in that order:

```
HashMap phonebook = new HashMap(30, 0.7F);
```

The capacity is the number of buckets in which hash map values can be stored. The load factor is the amount of buckets that can be used before the capacity automatically is increased. The value is a floating-point number from 0 (empty) to 1.0 (full), so a 0.7 means that when the buckets are 70 percent full, the capacity increases. The defaults are a capacity of 16 and load factor of .75, which often are sufficient.

Generics should be used to indicate the classes of the keys and values. They are placed within < and > characters, and the class names are separated by a comma, as in this example:

```
HashMap<String, Long> phonebook = new HashMap<>();
```

This creates a hash map called `phonebook` with keys that are strings and values that are `Long` objects. The second set of < and > characters is empty, which assumes the same classes as those in the previous < and > in the statement.

Objects are stored in a hash map by calling its `put(Object, Object)` method with two arguments, the key and value:

```
phonebook.put("Butterball Turkey Line", 8002888372L);
```

This stores an item in the map with the key "Butterball Turkey Line" and a `Long` object for the value 8002888372—the phone number of that service.

NOTE These statements are putting `Long` objects in the hash map using `long` values. This would have been an error in early versions of Java because a primitive data type such as `long` couldn't be used where an object was required.

But it's no longer an error because of autoboxing and unboxing, a feature of Java that automatically converts between primitive types and their equivalent object classes. When the Java compiler sees a `long` like 8002888372, it converts it to a `Long` object for that value.

An object can be retrieved from the map with its key by calling `get(Object)` with the key as the only argument:

```
long number = phonebook.get("Butterball Turkey Line");
```

The `get()` method returns `null` if there's no value matching that key. This would cause a problem with the preceding example because `null` is not a suitable long value.

Another way to handle that potential problem is to call `getOrDefault(Object, Object)`. If the key specified as the first argument is not found, the second argument is returned by default, as in this statement:

```
long number = phonebook.getOrDefault("Betty Crocker", -1);
```

If a number matching the key "Betty Crocker" is found in the map, that number is returned. Otherwise, −1 is returned.

There are two methods that indicate whether a key or value is present in the map: `containsKey(Object)` and `containsValue(Object)`. These return a boolean of either `true` or `false`.

Hash maps, like array lists, have a `size()` method that indicates the number of items in the data structure.

Looping through a map can be performed by using an entry set, a collection of all the entries in the map. The `entrySet()` method returns these entries as a `Set` object (using the `Set` interface in `java.util`).

Each item in the set is represented by `Map.Entry`, an inner class in the `Map` class of `java.util`. When you have an `Entry` object, you can call its `getKey()` method to retrieve the key and `getValue()` to retrieve the value.

The following `for` loop uses entry sets and entries to access all keys and values in a `phonebook` hash map:

```
for (Map.Entry<String, Long> entry : map.entrySet()) {
    String key = entry.getKey();
    Font value = entry.getValue();
    // ...
}
```

The `FontMapper` project puts all of this together, using a hash map to manage a collection of fonts.

The `Font` class in the `java.awt` package is used to create fonts and use them to display text in a graphical user interface. A font includes the name of the font, the point size, and whether it is plain, bold, or italic in style.

Hash maps can contain any class of objects. In NetBeans, create an empty Java file in the `com.javaminecraft` package and give it the name `FontMapper`. Enter Listing 14.2 into the file, and save it.

LISTING 14.2   The Full Text of `FontMapper.java`

```
 1: package com.javaminecraft;
 2:
 3: import java.awt.*;
 4: import java.util.*;
 5:
 6: public class FontMapper {
 7:     public FontMapper() {
 8:         Font courier = new Font("Courier New", Font.PLAIN, 6);
 9:         Font times = new Font("Times New Roman", Font.BOLD, 12);
10:         Font verdana = new Font("Verdana", Font.ITALIC, 25);
11:         HashMap<String, Font> fonts = new HashMap<>();
12:         fonts.put("smallprint", courier);
13:         fonts.put("body", times);
14:         fonts.put("headline", verdana);
15:         for (Map.Entry<String, Font> entry : fonts.entrySet()) {
16:             String key = entry.getKey();
```

```
17:                    Font value = entry.getValue();
18:                    System.out.println(key + ": " + value.getSize() + "-pt "
19:                        + value.getFontName());
20:                }
21:            }
22:
23:        public static void main(String[] arguments) {
24:            new FontMapper();
25:        }
26: }
```

The `FontMapper` application creates three `Font` objects in Lines 8–10 and then adds them to a hash map called `fonts` in Lines 12–14. They're stored in the map with a string key that describes the font's purpose: "smallprint", "body", and "headline".

A `for` loop in Lines 15–20 loops through the hash map using an entry set and each individual entry in the set.

The output of the application is displayed in Figure 14.2.

FIGURE 14.2

Storing Font *objects in a hash map.*

Why Classes Are Synchronized

Array lists and hash maps are data structures that are new versions of vectors and hash tables. The new versions don't require synchronization, an advanced concept in Java that requires some understanding of how Java programs are run.

Synchronization is how the Java Virtual Machine ensures that an object's instance variables and methods are accessed in a consistent and accurate manner by other users of the object.

This concept will make more sense when you learn about threads in Chapter 16, "Create a Threaded Mod." Java programs can be designed to do more than one task simultaneously. Each task is put in its own thread.

When multiple threads are accessing the same object, it's vital that the object acts the same in each thread. So when the method of a class requires synchronization, as vectors and hash tables do, the Java Virtual Machine has to work harder and can encounter errors that may cause a thread to stop running.

This is why array lists and hash maps replicate the functionality of vectors and hash tables. Data structures were needed that don't require synchronization and run much more efficiently as a consequence.

THE ABSOLUTE MINIMUM

Array lists and hash maps are two of the more useful data structures in the `java.util` package. The array list class expands on the functionality of arrays, making it possible to overcome the fixed-size limitation of that data type. Hash maps enable any kind of object to be used as the key to retrieve a value.

There also are bit sets (the `BitSet` class), which hold 0-and-1 bit values; stacks (`Stack`), which are last-in, first-out collections of data similar to array lists; and properties (`Properties`), a specialized hash map that holds configuration properties for a program in a file or another permanent storage place.

IN THIS CHAPTER

- Respond to exceptions in your Java programs
- Create methods that ignore an exception
- Use methods that cause exceptions
- Create your own exceptions

15

HANDLE ERRORS IN A MOD

Errors—the bugs, blunders, and typos that prevent a program from running correctly—are a natural part of the software development process. "Natural" is probably the kindest word that has ever been used to describe them.

Some errors are flagged by the compiler and prevent you from creating a class. Others are noted by the interpreter in response to a problem that keeps it from running successfully. Java divided errors into two categories:

- **Exceptions**—Events that signal an unusual circumstance has taken place as a program runs

- **Errors**—Events that signal the Java Virtual Machine is having problems that might be unrelated to your program

Errors normally aren't something a Java program can recover from, so they're not the focus of this chapter. You might have encountered an `OutOfMemoryError` as you worked on Java programs. There's nothing that can be done in a Java program to handle that kind of error after it occurs. The program exits with the error.

Exceptions often can be dealt with in a way that keeps a program running properly.

Exceptions

Although you are just learning about them now, you have probably become well-acquainted with exceptions during the previous 14 chapters. These errors turn up when you write a Java program that compiles successfully but encounters a problem as it runs.

For example, a common programming mistake is to refer to an element of an array that doesn't exist, as in the following statements:

```
String[] greek = { "Alpha", "Beta", "Gamma" };
System.out.println(greek[3]);
```

The `String` array `greek` has three elements. Because the first element of an array is numbered 0 rather than 1, the first element is `greek[0]`, the second `greek[1]`, and the third `greek[2]`. So the statement attempting to display `greek[3]` is erroneous. The preceding statements compile successfully, but when you run the program, the Java Virtual Machine (JVM) halts with a message such as the following:

```
Exception in thread "main" java.lang.ArrayIndexOutBoundsException:
    3 at SampleProgram.main(SampleProgram.java:4)
```

This message indicates that the application has generated an exception, which the JVM noted by displaying an error message and stopping the program.

The error message refers to a class called `ArrayIndexOutOfBoundsException` in the `java.lang` package. This class is an exception—an object that represents an exceptional circumstance that has taken place in a Java program.

When a Java class encounters an exception, it alerts users of the class to the error. In this example, the user of the class is the JVM.

NOTE Two terms are used to describe this process: *throw* and *catch*. Objects *throw* exceptions to alert others that they have occurred. These exceptions are *caught* by other objects or the Java Virtual Machine.

All exceptions are subclasses of `Exception` in the `java.lang` package. The `ArrayIndexOutOfBoundsException` does what you would expect—it reports that an array element has been accessed outside the array's boundaries.

There are hundreds of exceptions in Java. Many such as the array exception indicate a problem that can be fixed with a programming change. These are comparable to compiler errors—after you correct the situation, you don't have to concern yourself with the exception any longer.

Other exceptions must be dealt with every time a program runs by using five new keywords: `try`, `catch`, `finally`, `throw`, and `throws`.

Catching Exceptions in a `try-catch` Block

Up to this point, you have dealt with exceptions by fixing the problem that caused them. However, sometimes you can't deal with an exception in that manner and must handle the issue within a Java class.

As an introduction to why this is useful, enter the short Java application in Listing 15.1 in a new empty Java file called `Calculator` in the `com.javaminecraft` package and save the file.

LISTING 15.1 The Full Text of `Calculator.java`

```
 1: package com.javaminecraft;
 2:
 3: public class Calculator {
 4:     public static void main(String[] arguments) {
 5:         float sum = 0;
 6:         for (String argument : arguments) {
 7:             sum = sum + Float.parseFloat(argument);
 8:         }
 9:         System.out.println("Those numbers add up to " + sum);
10:     }
11: }
```

The `Calculator` application takes one or more numbers as command-line arguments, adds them up, and displays the total.

Because all command-line arguments are represented by strings in a Java application, the program must convert them into floating-point numbers before adding them. The `Float.parseFloat()` class method in Line 7 takes care of this, adding the converted number to a variable named `sum`.

Before running the application, give it the following command-line arguments, which can be set in NetBeans with the Run, Set Project Configuration, Customize command: 7 4 8 1 4 1 4. Select Run, Run Project to run the application, and you should see the output in Figure 15.1.

```
Output - Minecraft (run)  ×
    run:
    Those numbers add up to 29.0
    BUILD SUCCESSFUL (total time: 0 seconds)
```

FIGURE 15.1

The output of the `Calculator` *application.*

Run the program several times with different numbers as arguments. It should handle them successfully, which might make you wonder what this has to do with exceptions.

To see the relevance, change the `Calculator` application's command-line arguments to 1 3 5x.

The third argument contains a typo—there shouldn't be an x after the number 5. The `Calculator` application has no way to know this is a mistake, so it tries to add 5x to the other numbers, causing an exception to be displayed.

The message in Figure 15.2 can be informative to a programmer, but it's not something you'd want a user to see. It would be better to hide the error message and deal with the problem in the program.

```
Output - Minecraft2 (run)  ×
    run:
    Exception in thread "main" java.lang.NumberFormatException: For input string: "5x"
            at sun.misc.FloatingDecimal.readJavaFormatString(FloatingDecimal.java:2043)
            at sun.misc.FloatingDecimal.parseFloat(FloatingDecimal.java:122)
            at java.lang.Float.parseFloat(Float.java:451)
            at com.javaminecraft.Calculator.main(Calculator.java:7)
    Java Result: 1
    BUILD SUCCESSFUL (total time: 0 seconds)
```

FIGURE 15.2

An error message displays the Exception class.

Java programs can take care of their own exceptions by using a `try-catch` block statement, which takes the following form:

```
try {
    // statements that might cause the exception
} catch (Exception e) {
    // what to do when the exception occurs
}
```

A `try-catch` block must be used on any exception that you want a method of a class to handle. The `Exception` object that appears in the `catch` statement should be one of three things:

- The class of the exception that might occur
- More than one class of exception, separated by | characters
- A superclass of several different exceptions that might occur

The `try` section of the `try-catch` block contains the statement (or statements) that might throw an exception. In the `Calculator` application, the call to the `Float.parseFloat(String)` method in Line 7 of Listing 15.1 throws a `NumberFormatException` whenever it is used with a string argument that can't be converted to a floating-point value.

To improve the `Calculator` application so that it never stops running with this kind of error, you can use a `try-catch` block.

Create a new empty Java file called `NewCalculator` in the `com.javaminecraft` package, and enter the text of Listing 15.2.

LISTING 15.2 The Full Text of `NewCalculator.java`

```
1: package com.javaminecraft;
2:
3: public class NewCalculator {
4:     public static void main(String[] arguments) {
5:         float sum = 0;
6:         for (String argument : arguments) {
7:             try {
8:                 sum = sum + Float.parseFloat(argument);
9:             } catch (NumberFormatException e) {
```

```
10:                        System.out.println(argument + " is not a
                           ➥number.");
11:                }
12:            }
13:            System.out.println("Those numbers add up to " + sum);
14:        }
15: }
```

After you save the application, customize the project configuration and run `com.javaminecraft.NewCalculator` with the command-line argument `1  3  5x`. You should see the output shown in Figure 15.3.

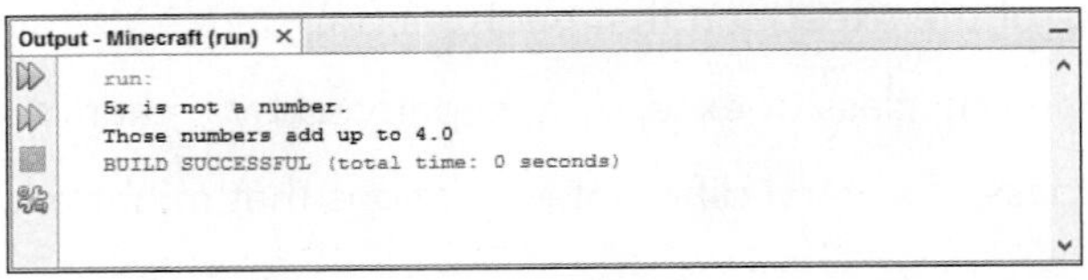

```
Output - Minecraft (run)  ✕
   run:
   5x is not a number.
   Those numbers add up to 4.0
   BUILD SUCCESSFUL (total time: 0 seconds)
```

FIGURE 15.3

The output of the `NewCalculator` *application.*

The `try-catch` block in Lines 7–11 deals with `NumberFormatException` errors thrown by `Float.parseFloat()`. These exceptions are caught within the `NewCalculator` class, which displays an error message for any argument that is not a number. Because the exception is handled within the class, the Java Virtual Machine does not display an error. You can often deal with problems related to user input and other unexpected data by using `try-catch` blocks.

Catching Several Different Exceptions

A `try-catch` block can be used to handle several kinds of exceptions, even if they are thrown by different statements.

One way to handle multiple classes of exceptions is to devote a `catch` block to each one, as in this code:

```
String textValue = "35";
int value;
try {
    value = Integer.parseInt(textValue);
```

```
} catch (NumberFormatException exc) {
    // code to handle exception
} catch (ArithmeticException exc) {
    // code to handle exception
}
```

You also can handle multiple exceptions in the same `catch` block by separating them with pipe (|) characters and ending the list with a name for the exception variable. Here's an example:

```
try {
    value = Integer.parseInt(textValue);
} catch (NumberFormatException | ArithmeticException exc) {
    // code to handle exceptions
}
```

If a `NumberFormatException` or `ArithmeticException` is caught, it will be assigned to the `exc` variable.

Listing 15.3 contains an application called `NumberDivider` that takes two integer arguments from the command line and uses them in a division expression.

This application must be able to deal with two potential problems in user input:

- Non-numeric arguments

- Division by zero

Create a new empty Java file for `NumberDivider` in the `com.javaminecraft` package, and enter the text of Listing 15.3 into the source editor.

LISTING 15.3 The Full Text of `NumberDivider.java`

```
1: package com.javaminecraft;
2:
3: public class NumberDivider {
4:     public static void main(String[] arguments) {
5:         if (arguments.length == 2) {
6:             int result = 0;
7:             try {
8:                 result = Integer.parseInt(arguments[0]) /
9:                     Integer.parseInt(arguments[1]);
```

```
10:                      System.out.println(arguments[0] + " divided by
                 ➡" +
11:                         arguments[1] + " equals " + result);
12:                  } catch (NumberFormatException e) {
13:                      System.out.println("Both arguments must be
                 ➡integers.");
14:                  } catch (ArithmeticException e) {
15:                      System.out.println("You cannot divide by
                 ➡zero.");
16:                  }
17:              }
18:          }
19: }
```

Using command-line arguments to specify two arguments, you can run it with integers, floating-point numbers, and nonnumeric arguments.

The if statement in Line 5 checks to make sure that two arguments are sent to the application. If not, the program exits without displaying anything.

The NumberDivider application performs integer division, so the result is an integer. In integer division, 5 divided by 2 equals 2, not 2.5.

If you use a floating-point or nonnumeric argument, a NumberFormatException is thrown by Lines 8–9 and caught by Lines 15–16.

If you use an integer as the first argument and a zero as the second argument, an ArithmeticExpression is thrown in Lines 8–9 and caught by Lines 14–15.

Some sample output from a successful run of the program is shown in Figure 15.4.

FIGURE 15.4

The output of the NumberDivider application.

Handling Something After an Exception

When you are dealing with multiple exceptions by using `try` and `catch`, there are times when you want the program to do something at the end of the block whether an exception occurred or not.

You can handle this by using a `try-catch-finally` block, which takes the following form:

```
try {
    // statements that might cause the exception
} catch (Exception e) {
    // what to do when the exception occurs
} finally {
    // statements to execute no matter what
}
```

The statement(s) within the `finally` section of the block is executed after everything else in the block, even if an exception occurs.

One place this is useful is in a program that reads data from a file on disk, which you do in Chapter 17, "Read and Write Files." There are several ways an exception can occur when you are accessing data—the file might not exist, a disk error could occur, and so on. If the statements to read the disk are in a `try` section and errors are handled in a `catch` section, you can close the file in the `finally` section. This ensures that the file is closed whether or not an exception is thrown as it is read.

Throwing Exceptions

When you call a method of another class, that class can control how the method is used by throwing exceptions.

As you make use of the classes in the Java Class Library, the compiler often displays a message such as the following:

```
NetReader.java:14: unreported exception java.net.
MalformedURLException; must be caught or declared to be thrown
```

Whenever you see an error stating that an exception "must be caught or declared to be thrown," it indicates the method you are trying to use throws an exception.

Any class that calls these methods, such as an application that you write, must do one of the following things:

- Handle the exception with a `try-catch` block
- Throw the exception
- Handle the exception with a `try-catch` block and then throw it

Up to this point in the chapter, you have seen how to handle exceptions. If you would like to throw an exception after handling it, you can use a `throw` statement followed by the exception object to throw.

The following statements handle a `NumberFormatException` error in a `catch` block and then throw the exception:

```
float principal;
try {
    principal = Float.parseFloat(arguments[0]) * 1.1F;
} catch (NumberFormatException e) {
    System.out.println(arguments[0] + " is not a number.");
    throw e;
}
```

This rewritten code handles all exceptions that could be generated in the `try` block and throws them:

```
float principal;
try {
    principal = Float.parseFloat(arguments[0]) * 1.1F;
} catch (Exception e) {
    System.out.println("Error " + e.getMessage());
    throw e;
}
```

`Exception` is the parent of all exception subclasses. A `catch` statement will catch the class and any subclass below it in the class hierarchy.

When you throw an exception with `throw`, it generally means you have not done everything that needs to be done to take care of the exception.

An example of where this might be useful: Consider a hypothetical program called `CreditCardChecker`, an application that verifies credit card purchases. This application uses a class called `CheckDatabase`, which has the following job:

1. Make a connection to the credit card lender's computer.

2. Ask that computer whether the customer's credit card number is valid.

3. Ask the computer whether the customer has enough credit to make the purchase.

As the `CheckDatabase` class is doing its job, what happens if the credit card lender's computer doesn't respond to any attempts to connect? This kind of error is exactly the kind of thing that the `try-catch` block was designed for, and it is used within `CheckDatabase` to handle connection errors.

If the `CheckDatabase` class handles this error by itself, the `CreditCardChecker` application doesn't know that the exception took place at all. This isn't a good idea—the application should know when a connection cannot be made so it can report this to the person using the application.

One way to notify the `CreditCardChecker` application is for `CheckDatabase` to catch the exception in a `catch` block and then throw it again with a `throw` statement. The exception is thrown in `CheckDatabase`, which must then deal with it like any other exception.

Exception handling is a way that classes can communicate with each other in the event of an error or other unusual circumstance.

When using `throw` in a `catch` block that catches a parent class, such as `Exception`, throwing the exception throws that class. This loses some detail of what kind of error occurred because a subclass such as `NumberFormatException` tells you a lot more about the problem than simply the `Exception` class.

Java offers a way to keep this detail—the `final` keyword in a `catch` statement:

```
try {
    principal = Float.parseFloat(loanText) * 1.1F;
} catch (final Exception e) {
    System.out.println("Error " + e.getMessage());
    throw e;
}
```

That `final` keyword in `catch` causes `throw` to behave differently. The specific class that was caught is thrown.

NOTE You can create your own exceptions by making a new class that is a subclass of an existing exception, such as `Exception`, the superclass of all exceptions. In a subclass of `Exception`, there are only two things you might want to override: the constructor `Exception()` with no arguments and the constructor with a `String` as an argument. The string should be a message describing the error that has occurred.

Ignoring Exceptions

The next technique covered in this chapter is how to ignore an exception completely. A method in a class can ignore exceptions by using a `throws` clause as part of the method definition.

The following method throws a `MalformedURLException`, an error that can occur when you are working with web addresses in a Java program:

```java
public void loadURL(String address) throws MalformedURLException {
    URL page = new URL(address);
    // code to load web page
}
```

The second statement in this example creates a `URL` object, which represents an address on the Web. The constructor method of the `URL` class throws a `MalformedURLException` to indicate that an invalid address is used, so no object can be constructed. The following statement causes one of these exceptions to be thrown when you attempt to open a connection to that URL:

```java
URL source = new URL("http:www.javaminecraft.com");
```

The string `http:www.javaminecraft.com` is not a valid URL. It's missing some punctuation—two slash characters (`//`) after the colon.

Because the `loadURL()` method has been declared to throw `MalformedURLException` errors, it does not have to deal with them inside the method. The responsibility for catching this exception falls to any method that calls the `loadURL()` method.

Exceptions That Don't Need Catch

Although this chapter has shown that exceptions need to be caught with `try-catch` or declared to be thrown with a `throws` clause, there's an exception.

Some exceptions that might occur as a Java program runs don't have to be handled in any way. The compiler won't come to a screeching halt when it detects that the exception is being ignored.

These exceptions are called *unchecked* exceptions, while the others are *checked* exceptions.

Unchecked exceptions are all subclasses of `RuntimeException` in the `java.lang` package. A common example of an unchecked exception is `IndexOutOfBoundsException`, which indicates that the index used to access an array, a string, or an array list is not within its boundaries. If an array has five elements and you attempt to read element number 10, this exception occurs.

Another is `NullPointerException`, which occurs when an object is used that has no value. Object variables have the value `null` before they are assigned an object. Some methods also return `null` when an object can't be returned. If a statement incorrectly assumes an object has a value, a `NullPointerException` occurs.

Both of these errors are things a programmer could (and should) prevent in the code, not things that require exception handling. If you write a program that accesses an out-of-bounds array element, fix the code that does this and recompile it. If you expect an object in a variable and it equals `null`, check for that with an `if` conditional before using the object.

The rationale for unchecked exceptions in Java is that they either can be prevented by well-written code or they could occur so often that catching them all the time would make programs unnecessarily complex. A `NullPointerException` could occur in every statement in a program where an object's methods are called.

Of course, just because an exception can be ignored doesn't mean it should be. You still have the option of using `try`, `catch`, and `throws` with unchecked exceptions.

Throwing and Catching Exceptions

For the chapter's final project, you create a class that uses exceptions to tell another class about an error that has taken place.

The classes in this project are `HomePage`, a class that represents a personal home page on the Web, and `PageCatalog`, an application that catalogs these pages.

Enter the text of Listing 15.4 in a new empty Java file called `HomePage` in the `com.javaminecraft` package.

LISTING 15.4   The Full Text of `HomePage.java`

```
 1: package com.javaminecraft;
 2:
 3: import java.net.*;
 4:
 5: public class HomePage {
 6:     String owner;
 7:     URL address;
 8:     String category = "none";
 9:
10:     public HomePage(String inOwner, String inAddress)
11:         throws MalformedURLException {
12:
13:         owner = inOwner;
14:         address = new URL(inAddress);
15:     }
16:
17:     public HomePage(String inOwner, String inAddress, String
        ➥inCategory)
18:         throws MalformedURLException {
19:
20:         this(inOwner, inAddress);
21:         category = inCategory;
22:     }
23: }
```

You can use the compiled `HomePage` class in other programs. This class represents personal web pages. It has three instance variables: `address`, a `URL` object representing the address of the page; `owner`, the person who owns the page; and `category`, a short comment describing the page's primary subject matter.

Like any class that creates `URL` objects, `HomePage` must either deal with `MalformedURLException` errors in a `try-catch` block or declare that it is ignoring these errors.

The class takes the latter course, as shown in Lines 10–11 and Lines 17–18. By using `throws` in the two constructor methods, `HomePage` removes the need to deal with `MalformedURLException` errors in any way.

To create an application that uses the `HomePage` class, return to NetBeans and create an empty Java file called `PageCatalog` that contains the text of Listing 15.5.

LISTING 15.5 The Full Text of `PageCatalog.java`

```
 1: package com.javaminecraft;
 2:
 3: import java.net.*;
 4:
 5: public class PageCatalog {
 6:     public static void main(String[] arguments) {
 7:         HomePage[] catalog = new HomePage[5];
 8:         try {
 9:             catalog[0] = new HomePage("Minecraft",
10:                 "http://www.minecraft.net", "software");
11:             catalog[1] = new HomePage("Wiki",
12:                 "http://minecraft.gamepedia.com", "reference");
13:             catalog[2] = new HomePage("Facebook",
14:                 "https://www.facebook.com/minecraft",
                    ➥"social");
15:             catalog[3] = new HomePage("Programming",
16:                 "http://www.javaminecraft.com", "reference");
17:             catalog[4] = new HomePage("Company",
18:                 "mojang.com");
19:             for (int i = 0; i < catalog.length; i++) {
20:                 System.out.println(catalog[i].owner + ": " +
21:                     catalog[i].address + " -- " +
22:                     catalog[i].category);
23:             }
24:         } catch (MalformedURLException e) {
25:             System.out.println("Error: " + e.getMessage());
26:         }
27:     }
28: }
```

When you run the compiled application, the output shown in Figure 15.5 is displayed.

FIGURE 15.5

The erroneous output of the PageCatalog *application.*

The PageCatalog application creates an array of HomePage objects and then displays the contents of the array. Each HomePage object is created using up to three arguments:

- A short description of the page
- The address of the page (as a String, not a URL)
- The category of the page

The third argument is optional, and it is not used in Lines 17–18.

The constructor methods of the HomePage class throw MalformedURLException errors when they receive a string that cannot be converted into a valid URL object. These exceptions are handled in the PageCatalog application by using a try-catch block.

To correct the problem causing the "no protocol" error, edit Line 18 so the string begins with the text http:// like the other web addresses in Lines 9–16. When you run the program again, you see the output shown in Figure 15.6.

FIGURE 15.6

The corrected output of the PageCatalog *application.*

THE ABSOLUTE MINIMUM

Now that you have put Java's exception handling techniques to use, the subject of errors ought to be a bit more popular than it was at the beginning of the chapter.

You can do a lot with these techniques:

- Catch an exception and deal with it.

- Ignore an exception, leaving it for another class or the Java Virtual Machine to take care of.

- Catch several exceptions in the same `try-catch` block.

- Throw your own exception.

Managing exceptions in your Java programs makes them more reliable, more versatile, and easier to use because you don't display any cryptic error messages to people who are running your software.

IN THIS CHAPTER

- Use an interface with a program
- Create threads
- Start, stop, and pause threads
- Catch errors

16

CREATE A THREADED MOD

A computer term used often to describe the hectic pace of daily life is *multitasking*, which means to do more than one thing at once—such as browsing the Web while posting a message on Twitter and branch mining for diamonds at level 12 in Minecraft. A multitasking computer is one that can run more than one program at a time.

One sophisticated feature of the Java language is the ability to write programs that can multitask, which is made possible through a class of objects called *threads*.

Threads

In a Java program, each of the simultaneous tasks the computer handles is called a thread and the overall process is called multithreading. Threading is useful in animation and many other programs.

Threads are a way to organize a program so it does more than one thing at a time. Each task that must occur simultaneously is placed in its own thread, and this often is accomplished by implementing each task as a separate class.

Threads are represented by the `Thread` class and the `Runnable` interface, which are both part of the `java.lang` package of classes. Because they belong to this package, you don't have to use an `import` statement to make them available in your programs.

One of the simplest uses of the `Thread` class is to slow down how fast a program does something.

Slowing Down a Program

The `Thread` class has a `sleep()` method that you can call in any program that should stop running for a short period of time. You often see this technique used in a program that features animation because it prevents images from being displayed faster than the Java Virtual Machine (JVM) can handle them.

To use the `sleep()` method, call `Thread.sleep()` with the number of milliseconds to pause, as in the following statement:

```
Thread.sleep(5000);
```

The preceding statement causes the JVM to pause for five seconds before doing anything else. If for some reason the JVM can't pause that long, an `InterruptedException` is thrown by the `sleep()` method.

Because this exception might be thrown, you must deal with it in some manner when using the `sleep()` method. One way to do this is to place the `Thread.sleep()` statement inside a `try-catch` block:

```
try {
    Thread.sleep(5000);
} catch (InterruptedException e) {
    // wake up early
}
```

When you want a Java program to handle more than one thing at a time, you must organize the program into threads. Your program can have as many threads as needed, and they all can run simultaneously without affecting each other.

Creating a Thread

A Java class that can be run as a thread is referred to as a *runnable* (or threaded) class. Although you can use threads to pause a program's execution for a few seconds, programmers often use them for the opposite reason—to speed up a program. If you put time-consuming tasks in their own threads, the rest of the program runs more quickly. This often is used to prevent a task from slowing down the responsiveness of a program's graphical user interface (GUI).

For example, if you have written an application that loads stock market price data from disk and compiles statistics, the most time-consuming task is to load the data. If threads are not used in the application, the program's interface might respond sluggishly as the data is being loaded. This can be extremely frustrating to a user.

Two ways to place a task in its own thread are the following:

- Putting the task in a class that implements the Runnable interface
- Putting the task in a class that is a subclass of Thread

To support the Runnable interface, the implements keyword is used when the class is created, as in this example:

```
public class LoadStocks implements Runnable {
    // body of the class
}
```

When a class implements an interface, it indicates that the class contains some extra behavior in addition to its own methods.

Classes that implement the Runnable interface must include the run() method, which has the following structure:

```
public void run() {
    // body of the method
}
```

The run() method should take care of the task that the thread was created to accomplish. In the stock-analysis example, the run() method could contain statements to load data from disk and compile statistics based on that data.

When a threaded application is run, the statements in its run() method are not executed automatically. Threads can be started and stopped in Java, and a thread doesn't begin running until you do two things:

- Create an object of the threaded class by calling the Thread constructor.

- Start the thread by calling its start() method.

The Thread constructor takes a single argument—the object that contains the thread's run() method. Often, you use the this keyword as the argument, which indicates the current class includes the run() method.

Listing 16.1 contains a Java application that stores a sequence of 10,000 prime numbers in a StringBuilder object that is not displayed until all 10,000 have been found. The prime numbers are discovered in their own thread while the application's main thread runs.

In NetBeans, create a new empty Java file named PrimeFinder, put it in the com.javaminecraft package, enter the text from the listing in the file, and remember to save it.

LISTING 16.1 The Full Text of PrimeFinder.java

```
 1: package com.javaminecraft;
 2:
 3: public class PrimeFinder implements Runnable {
 4:     Thread go;
 5:     StringBuilder primes;
 6:     boolean done = false;
 7:
 8:     public PrimeFinder() {
 9:         primes = new StringBuilder();
10:     }
11:
12:     public void start() {
13:         if (go == null) {
14:             go = new Thread(this);
15:             go.start();
16:         }
17:     }
18:
```

```
19:     @Override
20:     public void run() {
21:         int quantity = 500000;
22:         int numPrimes = 0;
23:         // candidate: the number that might be prime
24:         int candidate = 2;
25:         primes.append("\nFirst ");
26:         primes.append(quantity);
27:         primes.append(" primes: ");
28:         while (numPrimes < quantity) {
29:             if (isPrime(candidate)) {
30:                 primes.append(candidate);
31:                 primes.append(" ");
32:                 numPrimes++;
33:             }
34:             candidate++;
35:         }
36:         done = true;
37:     }
38:
39:     public static boolean isPrime(int checkNumber) {
40:         double root = Math.sqrt(checkNumber);
41:         for (int i = 2; i <= root; i++) {
42:             if (checkNumber % i == 0) {
43:                 return false;
44:             }
45:         }
46:         return true;
47:     }
48:
49:     public static void main(String[] arguments) {
50:         PrimeFinder app = new PrimeFinder();
51:         app.start();
52:         int count = 1;
53:         while (!app.done) {
54:             System.out.print(count + " ");
```

```
55:                    count++;
56:                    try {
57:                        Thread.sleep(1000);
58:                    } catch (InterruptedException ex) {
59:                        // do nothing
60:                    }
61:                }
62:                System.out.println(app.primes.toString());
63:        }
64: }
```

The `PrimeFinder` application displays a count of seconds while the prime numbers are being calculated and then displays them all by converting the `StringBuilder` object to a string. A portion of the output is shown in Figure 16.1 (displaying the whole thing would take up too much space).

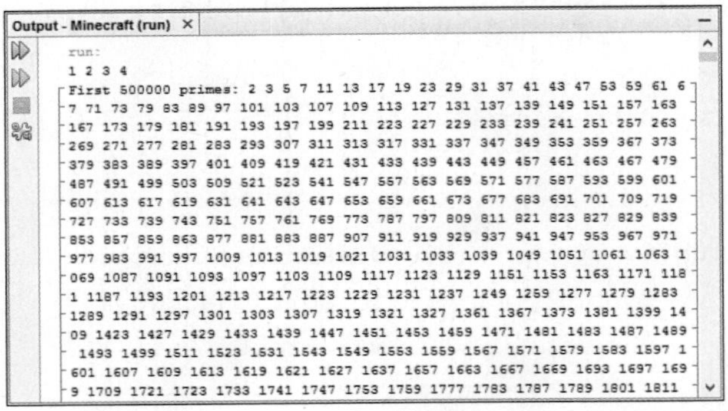

FIGURE 16.1

Running the PrimeFinder *application.*

Most statements in the application are used to find the prime numbers. The following statements are used to implement threads in this program:

- In Line 3, the `Runnable` interface is applied to the `PrimeFinder` class.

- In Line 4, a `Thread` object variable is created with the name go but isn't assigned a value.

- In Lines 13–16, if the go object variable has a value of `null`, which indicates the thread hasn't been created yet, a new `Thread` object is created and stored in the variable. The thread is started by calling the thread's `start()` method, which causes the `run()` method of the `PrimeFinder` class to be called.

- In Lines 19–37, the `run()` method looks for a sequence of prime numbers beginning with 2, storing each one in the `primes StringBuilder` object component by calling its `append()` method. When it has found all 10,000, the `done` instance variable is set to `true`.

The `main()` method of this application does more work than other projects in this book. First, an object of the program's class is created and its `start()` method is called in Line 51. This method gets the `Thread` that finds prime numbers started.

A `while` loop in Lines 53–61 keeps looping until the program's `done` variable is `true`. Each trip through the loop displays the value of the `count` variable and increments it by 1.

The call to `Thread.sleep(1000)` causes the loop to pause for 1 second (1,000 milliseconds).

When `app` equals `true`, the loop ends and contents of the `primes` variable are displayed in Line 62.

Working with Threads

You can start a thread by calling its `start()` method, which might lead you to believe there's also a `stop()` method to bring it to a halt.

Although Java includes a `stop()` method in the `Thread` class, it has been deprecated. In Java, a *deprecated* element is a class, interface, method, or variable that has been replaced with something that works better.

 CAUTION   It's a good idea to heed this deprecation warning. Oracle has deprecated the `stop()` method because it can cause problems for other threads running in the Java Virtual Machine. The `resume()` and `suspend()` methods of the class also are deprecated.

The next project you undertake shows how you can stop a thread. The program you are undertaking rotates through a list of website titles and the addresses used to visit them.

The title of each page and the web address are displayed in a continuous cycle. Users are able to visit the currently displayed site by clicking a button on the application's graphical user interface. This program operates over a period of time, displaying information about each website in sequence. Because of this time element, threads are the best way to control the program.

This project requires a graphical user interface, a type of Java programming that's not covered in this book because it isn't necessary for creating Minecraft mods. A single window is displayed with a button to click.

Instead of entering this program into the NetBeans source editor first and learning about it afterward, you get a chance to enter the full text of the LinkRotator application at the end of the chapter. Before then, each section of the program is described.

The `class` Declaration

The first thing you need to do in this program is to use import for classes in the packages java.awt, java.io, java.net, java.awt.event, and javax.swing.

After you have used import to make some classes available, you're ready to begin the application with the following statement:

```
public class LinkRotator extends JFrame
    implements Runnable, ActionListener {
```

This statement creates the LinkRotator class as a subclass of the JFrame class, which represents a graphical user interface in Java. The statement also indicates that two interfaces are supported by this class—Runnable and ActionListener. By implementing the Runnable class, you are able to use a run() method in this program to make a thread begin running. The ActionListener interface enables the program to respond to mouse clicks.

Setting Up Variables

The first thing to do in LinkRotator is create the variables and objects of the class. Create a six-element array of String objects called pageTitle and a six-element array of URI objects called pageLink:

```
String[] pageTitle = new String[6];
URI[] pageLink = new URI[6];
```

The pageTitle array holds the titles of the six websites that are displayed. The URI class of objects stores the value of a website address. URI has all the behavior and attributes needed to keep track of a web address.

The last three things to create are an integer variable, a Thread object, and a user interface label:

```
int current = 0;
Thread runner;
JLabel siteLabel = new JLabel();
```

The current variable keeps track of which site is being displayed so you can cycle through the sites. The Thread object runner represents the thread this program runs. You call methods of the runner object when you start, stop, and pause the operation of the program.

The Constructor

The program's constructor automatically is executed when the program is run. This method is used to assign values to the arrays pageTitle and pageLink. It also is used to create a clickable button that appears on the user interface. The method includes the following statements:

```
pageTitle = new String[] {
    "Oracle's Java site",
    "Cafe au Lait",
    "JavaWorld",
    "JavaMinecraft.Com",
    "Sams Publishing",
    "Workbench"
};
pageLink[0] = getURI("http://www.oracle.com/technetwork/java");
pageLink[1] = getURI("http://www.ibiblio.org/javafaq");
pageLink[2] = getURI("http://www.javaworld.com");
pageLink[3] = getURI("http://www.javaminecraft.com");
pageLink[4] = getURI("http://www.samspublishing.com");
pageLink[5] = getURI("http://workbench.cadenhead.org");
Button visitButton = new Button("Visit Site");
goButton.addActionListener(this);
add(visitButton);
```

The title of each page is stored in the six elements of the pageTitle array, which is initialized using six strings. The elements of the pageLink array are assigned a value returned by the getURI() method, yet to be created.

The last three statements of the init() method create a button labeled "Visit Site" and add it to the application's frame.

Catching Errors as You Set Up URLs

When you set up a URI object, you must make sure the text used to set up the address is in a valid format. http://workbench.cadenhead.org and http://www.quepublishing.com are valid, but http:www.javaworld.com would not be because of missing "/" marks.

The getURI(*String*) method takes a web address as an argument, returning a URI object representing that address. If the string is not a valid address, the method returns null instead:

```
URI getURI(String urlText) {
    URI pageURI = null;
    try {
        pageURI = new URI(urlText);
    } catch (URISyntaxException m) {
        // do nothing
    }
    return pageURI;
}
```

The try-catch block deals with any URISyntaxLException errors that occur when URI objects are created. Because nothing needs to happen if this exception is thrown, the catch block contains only a comment.

Starting the Thread

In this program, the runner thread starts when its start() method is called.

The start() method is called as the last statement of the constructor. Here's the method:

```
public void start() {
    if (runner == null) {
        runner = new Thread(this);
        runner.start();
    }
}
```

This method starts the runner thread if it is not already started.

The statement `runner = new Thread(this)` creates a new `Thread` object with one argument—the `this` keyword. The `this` keyword refers to the program itself, designating it as the class that runs within the thread.

The call to `runner.start()` causes the thread to begin running. When a thread begins, the `run()` method of that thread is called. Because the `runner` thread is the `LinkRotator` application itself, the `run()` method of the application is called.

Running the Thread

The `run()` method is where the main work of a thread takes place. In the `LinkRotator` program, the following represents the `run()` method:

```
public void run() {
    Thread thisThread = Thread.currentThread();
    while (runner == thisThread) {
        current++;
        if (current > 5) {
            current = 0;
        }
        siteLabel.setText(pageTitle[current]);
        repaint();
        try {
            Thread.sleep(1000);
        } catch (InterruptedException e) {
            // do nothing
        }
    }
}
```

The first thing that takes place in the `run()` method is the creation of a `Thread` object called `thisThread`. A class method of the `Thread` class, `currentThread()`, sets up the value for the `thisThread` object. The `currentThread()` method keeps track of the thread that's currently running.

All statements in this method are part of a `while` loop that compares the `runner` object to the `thisThread` object. Both objects are threads, and as long as they refer to the same object, the `while` loop continues looping. There's no statement inside this loop that causes the `runner` and `thisThread` objects to have different values, so it loops indefinitely unless something outside of the loop changes one of the `Thread` objects.

The run() method calls repaint(). Next, the value of the current variable increases by 1, and if current exceeds 5, it is set to 0 again. The current variable is used to determine which website's information to display. It is used as the index to the pageTitle array of strings, and the title is set as the text of the siteLabel user interface component.

The run() method includes another try-catch block that handles errors. The Thread.sleep(1000) statement causes a thread to pause 1 second—long enough for users to read the name of the website and its address. The catch statement takes care of any InterruptedException errors that might occur while the Thread.sleep() statement is being handled. These errors would occur if something interrupted the thread as it slept.

Handling Mouse Clicks

The last thing to take care of in the LinkRotator program is event handling. Whenever a user clicks the Visit Site button, the application should open the displayed website with a web browser. This is done with a method called actionPerformed(), which is called whenever the button is clicked.

The following is the actionPerformed() method of LinkRotator:

```
public void actionPerformed(ActionEvent event) {
    Desktop desktop = Desktop.getDesktop();
    if (pageLink[current] != null) {
        try {
            desktop.browse(pageLink[current]);
            runner = null;
            System.exit(0);
        } catch (IOException exc) {
            // do nothing
        }
    }
}
```

The first thing that happens in this method is that a Desktop object is created. The Desktop class in the java.awt package represents the desktop environment of the computer running the application. After you have this object, you can use it to launch an email client using a "mailto:" link, open a file for editing with another program, print a file, and make other programs outside of Java perform tasks.

Here, the Desktop object is used to open a web page with the computer's default web browser.

The browse(URI) method loads the specified web address in a browser. If pageLink[current] is a valid address, browse() requests that the browser load the page.

Displaying Revolving Links

You're now ready to create the program and test it. Create a new empty Java file named LinkRotator, and type in the text from Listing 16.2.

LISTING 16.2 The Full Text of LinkRotator.java

```
 1: package com.javaminecraft;
 2:
 3: import java.awt.*;
 4: import java.awt.event.*;
 5: import java.io.*;
 6: import javax.swing.*;
 7: import java.net.*;
 8:
 9: public class LinkRotator extends JFrame
10:     implements Runnable, ActionListener {
11:
12:     String[] pageTitle = new String[6];
13:     URI[] pageLink = new URI[6];
14:     int current = 0;
15:     Thread runner;
16:     JLabel siteLabel = new JLabel();
17:
18:     public LinkRotator() {
19:         setDefaultCloseOperation(JFrame.EXIT_ON_CLOSE);
20:         setSize(300, 100);
21:         FlowLayout flo = new FlowLayout();
22:         setLayout(flo);
23:         add(siteLabel);
24:         pageTitle = new String[] {
```

```
25:                    "Oracle's Java site",
26:                    "Cafe au Lait",
27:                    "JavaWorld",
28:                    "JavaMinecraft.Com",
29:                    "Que Publishing",
30:                    "Workbench"
31:            };
32:            pageLink[0] = getURI("http://www.oracle.com/
            ➥technetwork/java");
33:            pageLink[1] = getURI("http://www.ibiblio.org/javafaq");
34:            pageLink[2] = getURI("http://www.javaworld.com");
35:            pageLink[3] = getURI("http://www.javaminecraft.com");
36:            pageLink[4] = getURI("http://www.quepublishing.com");
37:            pageLink[5] = getURI("http://workbench.cadenhead.org");
38:            Button visitButton = new Button("Visit Site");
39:            visitButton.addActionListener(this);
40:            add(visitButton);
41:            setVisible(true);
42:            start();
43:        }
44:
45:        private URI getURI(String urlText) {
46:            URI pageURI = null;
47:            try {
48:                pageURI = new URI(urlText);
49:            } catch (URISyntaxException ex) {
50:                // do nothing
51:            }
52:            return pageURI;
53:        }
54:
55:        public void start() {
56:            if (runner == null) {
57:                runner = new Thread(this);
58:                runner.start();
59:            }
```

```
60:     }
61:
62:     public void run() {
63:         Thread thisThread = Thread.currentThread();
64:         while (runner == thisThread) {
65:             current++;
66:             if (current > 5) {
67:                 current = 0;
68:             }
69:             siteLabel.setText(pageTitle[current]);
70:             repaint();
71:             try {
72:                 Thread.sleep(1000);
73:             } catch (InterruptedException exc) {
74:                 // do nothing
75:             }
76:         }
77:     }
78:
79:     public void actionPerformed(ActionEvent event) {
80:         Desktop desktop = Desktop.getDesktop();
81:         if (pageLink[current] != null) {
82:             try {
83:                 desktop.browse(pageLink[current]);
84:                 runner = null;
85:                 System.exit(0);
86:             } catch (IOException exc) {
87:                 // do nothing
88:             }
89:         }
90:     }
91:
92:     public static void main(String[] arguments) {
93:         new LinkRotator();
94:     }
95: }
```

Figure 16.2 shows two windows open on a computer desktop. The smaller window, which is circled, is the `LinkRotator` application running. The larger one behind is one of the links that can be opened with the program: the web page for Que Publishing.

FIGURE 16.2

Displaying revolving links in an application.

Stopping a Thread

The `LinkRotator` application does not have a way to stop the thread, but it has been designed in a way that would make it simple to do so. Here's one method that could be called to end execution of the thread:

```
public void stop() {
    if (runner != null) {
        runner = null;
    }
}
```

The `if` statement tests whether the `runner` object is equal to `null`. If it is, there isn't an active thread that needs to be stopped. Otherwise, the statement sets `runner` equal to `null`.

Setting the `runner` object to a `null` value causes it to have a different value than the `thisThread` object. When this happens, the `while` loop inside the `run()` method stops running.

CAUTION   The `LinkRotator` application has a `try-catch` block in Lines 47–51 that does nothing in the `catch` block in response to an exception. This might seem like bad programming practice because it ignores the error, but it can be okay when you know that doing nothing is appropriate.

Here, the only cause of a `URISyntaxException` is when the URI sent to the method is invalid. This situation already is handled by setting the value returned by the method to `null` in Line 46, so nothing more needs to be done inside the `catch` block.

THE ABSOLUTE MINIMUM

Threads are a powerful concept implemented with a small number of classes and interfaces in Java. By supporting multithreading in your programs, you make them more responsive and can speed up how quickly they perform tasks.

Every Minecraft mod has to be careful not to cause the server to lag, which players hate more than creepers dropping by and blowing up their house. One way to reduce this possibility is to put time-intensive tasks in their own threads.

READ AND WRITE FILES

There are numerous ways to represent data on a computer. You already have worked with one by creating objects. An object includes data in the form of variables and references to objects. It also includes methods that use the data to accomplish tasks.

To work with other kinds of data, such as files on your hard drive and documents on a web server, you can use the classes of the `java.io` package. The `io` part of its name stands for *input/output*, and the classes are used to access a source of data, such as a hard drive, a DVD, or the computer's memory.

You can bring data into a program and send data out by using either a communications system called *streams*, which are objects that take information from one place to another.

Streams

To save data permanently within a Java program or to retrieve that data later, you must use at least one stream.

A stream is an object that takes information from one source and sends it somewhere else, taking its name from water streams that take squids, boats, chickens, sheep, and industrial pollutants from one place to another.

Streams connect a diverse variety of sources, including computer programs, hard drives, Internet servers, computer memory, and thumb drives. After you learn how to work with one kind of data using streams, you are able to work with others in the same manner.

During this chapter, you use streams to read and write data stored in files on your computer.

There are two kinds of streams:

- Input streams, which read data from a source

- Output streams, which write data to a source

All input and output streams are made up of bytes, individual integers with values ranging from 0 to 255. You can use this format to represent data, such as executable programs, word-processing documents, and MP3 music files, but those are only a small sampling of what bytes can represent. A byte stream is used to read and write this kind of data.

NOTE   Java class files are stored as bytes in a form called bytecode. The Java Virtual Machine (JVM) runs bytecode, which doesn't actually have to be produced by the Java language. It can run compiled bytecode produced by other languages, including NetRexx and Jython. You also hear the JVM referred to as the *bytecode interpreter*.

A more specialized way to work with data is in the form of characters—individual letters, numbers, punctuation, and the like. You can use a character stream when you are reading and writing a text source.

Whether you work with a stream of bytes, characters, or other kinds of information, the overall process is the same:

- Create a stream object associated with the data.

- Call methods of the stream to either put information in the stream or take information out of it.

- Close the stream by calling the object's `close()` method.

Files

In Java, files are represented by the `File` class, which also is part of the `java.io` package. Files can be read from hard drives, floppy drives, CD-ROMs, and other storage devices.

A `File` object can represent files that already exist or files you want to create. To create a `File` object, use the name of the file as the constructor, as in this example:

```
File bookName = new File("address.dat");
```

This creates an object for a file named `address.dat` in the current folder. You also can include a path in the filename:

```
`File bookName = new File("data\\address.dat");
```

 NOTE   This example works on a Windows system, which uses the backslash (\ \) character as a separator in pathnames and file-names. Linux and other Unix-based systems use a forward slash (/) character instead. To write a Java program that refers to files in a way that works regardless of the operating system, use the class variable `File.pathSeparator` instead of a forward or backslash, as in this statement:

```
File bookName = new File("data" + File.pathSeparator
    + "address.dat");
```

When you have a `File` object, you can call several useful methods on that object:

- `exists()`—`true` if the file exists; `false` otherwise

- `getName()`—The name of the file, as a `String`

- `length()`—The size of the file, as a `long` value

- `createNewFile()`—Creates a file of the same name, if one does not exist already

- `delete()`—Delete the file, if it exists

- `renameTo(File)`—Renames the file, using the name of the `File` object specified as an argument

You also can use a `File` object to represent a folder on your system rather than a file. Specify the folder name in the `File` constructor, which can be absolute (such as `C:\\MyDocuments\\`) or relative (such as `java\\database`).

After you have an object representing a folder, you can call its `listFiles()` method to see what's inside the folder. This method returns an array of `File` objects representing every file and subfolder it contains.

Reading Data from a Stream

The first project of the chapter is to read data from a file using an input stream. You can do this using the `FileInputStream` class, which represents input streams that are read as bytes from a file.

You can create a file input stream by specifying a filename or a `File` object as the argument to the `FileInputStream()` constructor method.

Methods that read or write files can fail with an `IOException` if there's an error accessing the file. Many of the methods associated with reading and writing files generate this exception, so a `try-catch` block is often used.

Streams are one of the resources in Java that must be closed when they're no longer being used. Leaving a stream open is a significant drain on resources in the JVM as a program runs.

A special `try` statement called `try`-with-resources makes it easy to ensure that a resource such as a file input stream will be closed when it's no longer needed.

The `try` statement is followed by parentheses. Inside the parentheses are one or more Java statements that declare variables that read or write data through a resource.

Here's an example that reads a text file called "cookie.web" using a file input stream named `stream`:

```
File cookie = new File("cookie.web");
try (FileInputStream stream = new FileInputStream(cookie)) {
    System.out.println("Length of file: " + cookie.length());
} catch (IOException ioe) {
    System.out.println("Could not read file");
}
```

Because the stream is in the `try` statement, the stream is closed automatically when the `try-catch` block completes (if it hasn't been closed).

File input streams read data in bytes. You can read a single byte by calling the stream's `read()` method without an argument. If no more bytes are available in the stream because you have reached the end of the file, a byte value of –1 is returned.

When you read an input stream, it begins with the first byte in the stream, such as the first byte in a file. You can skip some bytes in a stream by calling its `skip()` method with one argument: an `int` representing the number of bytes to skip. The following statement skips the next 1,024 bytes in a stream named `scanData`:

```
scanData.skip(1024);
```

If you want to read more than one byte at a time, do the following:

- Create a byte array that is exactly the size of the number of bytes you want to read.

- Call the stream's `read()` method with that array as an argument. The array is filled with bytes read from the stream.

For the next project, you create an application that reads ID3 data from an MP3 audio file. Because MP3 is such a popular format for music files, 128 bytes are often added to the end of an ID3 file to hold information about the song, such as the title, artist, and album.

The `ID3Reader` application reads an MP3 file using a file input stream, skipping everything but the last 128 bytes. The remaining bytes are examined to see if they contain ID3 data. If they do, the first three bytes are the numbers 84, 65, and 71.

 NOTE On the ASCII character set, which is included in the Unicode Standard character set supported by Java, those three numbers represent the capital letters *T*, *A*, and *G*, respectively.

Create a new empty Java file called `ID3Reader`, and fill it with the text from Listing 17.1.

LISTING 17.1 The Full Text of `ID3Reader.java`

```
1: package com.javaminecraft;
2:
3: import java.io.*;
4:
```

```
 5: public class ID3Reader {
 6:     public static void main(String[] arguments) {
 7:         File song = new File(arguments[0]);
 8:         try (FileInputStream file = new FileInputStream(song))
            ➡ {
 9:             int size = (int) song.length();
10:             file.skip(size - 128);
11:             byte[] last128 = new byte[128];
12:             file.read(last128);
13:             String id3 = new String(last128);
14:             String tag = id3.substring(0, 3);
15:             if (tag.equals("TAG")) {
16:                 System.out.println("Title: " + id3.substring(3,
                    ➡ 32));
17:                 System.out.println("Artist: " +
                    ➡ id3.substring(33, 62));
18:                 System.out.println("Album: " +
                    ➡ id3.substring(63, 91));
19:                 System.out.println("Year: " + id3.substring(93,
                    ➡ 97));
20:             } else {
21:                 System.out.println(arguments[0] + " does not
                    ➡ contain"
22:                     + " ID3 info.");
23:             }
24:             file.close();
25:         } catch (IOException ioe) {
26:             System.out.println("Error -- " + ioe.toString());
27:         }
28:     }
29: }
```

Before running this class as an application, you must specify an MP3 file as a command-line argument (using Run, Set Project Configuration, Configure in NetBeans). The program can be run with any MP3. Figure 17.1 shows what the ID3Reader application displays when the song specified is Minecraft by C418.

```
Output - Minecraft (run)  ×
    run:
    Title: Minecraft
    Artist: C418
    Album: Minecraft - Volume Alpha
    Year: 2011
    BUILD SUCCESSFUL (total time: 0 seconds)
```

FIGURE 17.1

Running the ID3Reader *application.*

TIP   If you don't have any MP3s, you can look for songs to examine using the Creative Commons license at http://search.creativecommons.org.

Creative Commons is a set of copyright licenses that stipulate how a work such as a song or book can be distributed, edited, or republished. The website Rock Proper at www.rockproper. com also offers a collection of MP3 albums that are licensed for sharing under Creative Commons.

The application reads the last 128 bytes from the MP3 in Lines 11–12 of Listing 17.1, storing them in a byte array. This array is used in Line 13 to create a String object that contains the characters represented by those bytes.

If the first three characters in the string are "TAG," the MP3 file being examined contains ID3 information in a format the application understands.

In Lines 16–19, the string's substring() method is called to display portions of the string. The characters to display are from the ID3 format, which always puts the artist, song, title, and year information in the same positions in the last 128 bytes of an MP3 file.

Some MP3 files either don't contain ID3 information at all or contain ID3 information in a different format from what the application can read.

The file Minecraft.mp3 from C418 contains readable ID3 information if you created it from a copy of the *Volume Alpha* album purchased from Amazon, Apple iTunes, or another retailer. Programs that create MP3 files from commercial albums read song information from a music industry database called CDDB.

After everything related to the ID3 information has been read from the MP3's file input stream, the stream is closed in Line 24. You should always close streams when you are finished with them to conserve JVM resources.

NOTE C418 is another name for Daniel Rosenfeld, the music producer for Minecraft. He created the music for the world and the CDs found in the game that can be played on a jukebox. He has released the albums *Volume Alpha* and *Volume Beta* to collect his music for the game.

Buffered Input Streams

One of the ways to improve the performance of a program that reads input streams is to buffer the input. Buffering is the process of saving data in memory for use later when a program needs it. When a Java program needs data from a buffered input stream, it looks in the buffer first, which is faster than reading from a source such as a file.

To use a buffered input stream, you create an input stream such as a `FileInputStream` object and then use that object to create a buffered stream. Call the `BufferedInputStream(InputStream)` constructor with the input stream as the only argument. Data is buffered as it is read from the input stream.

To read from a buffered stream, call its `read()` method with no arguments. An integer from 0 to 255 is returned and represents the next byte of data in the stream. If no more bytes are available, –1 is returned instead.

As a demonstration of buffered streams, the next program you create adds a feature to Java that many programmers miss from other languages they have used: console input.

Console input is the ability to read characters from the console (also known as the command line) while running an application.

The `System` class, which contains the `out` variable used in the `System.out.print()` and `System.out.println()` statements, has a class variable called `in` that represents an `InputStream` object. This object receives input from the keyboard and makes it available as a stream.

You can work with this input stream like any other. The following statement creates a buffered input stream associated with the `System.in` input stream:

```
BufferedInputStream bin = new BufferedInputStream(System.in);
```

The next project, the `Console` class, contains a class method you can use to receive console input in any of your Java applications. Enter the text from Listing 17.2 in a new empty Java file named `Console`.

LISTING 17.2 The Full Text of `Console.java`

```
1: package com.javaminecraft;
2:
3: import java.io.*;
4:
5: public class Console {
6:     public static String readLine() {
7:         StringBuilder response = new StringBuilder();
8:         try {
9:             BufferedInputStream bin = new
10:                 BufferedInputStream(System.in);
11:             int in = 0;
12:             char inChar;
13:             do {
14:                 in = bin.read();
15:                 inChar = (char) in;
16:                 if (in != -1) {
17:                     response.append(inChar);
18:                 }
19:             } while ((in != -1) & (inChar != '\n'));
20:             bin.close();
21:             return response.toString();
22:         } catch (IOException e) {
23:             System.out.println("Exception: " + e.getMessage());
24:             return null;
25:         }
26:     }
27:
28:     public static void main(String[] arguments) {
29:         System.out.print("You are standing at the end of the
            ➥road ");
30:         System.out.print("before a small brick building. Around
            ➥you ");
31:         System.out.print("is a forest. A small stream flows out
            ➥of ");
32:         System.out.println("the building and down a gully.\n");
```

```
33:             System.out.print("> ");
34:             String input = Console.readLine();
35:             System.out.println("That's not a verb I recognize.");
36:        }
37: }
```

The `Console` class includes a `main()` method that demonstrates how it can be used. When you run the application, the output should resemble Figure 17.2.

```
Output - Minecraft (run)  ×
run:
You are standing at the end of the road before a small brick building. Around you is a forest. A small s
tream flows out of the building and down a gully.

> go north
That's not a verb I recognize.
BUILD SUCCESSFUL (total time: 11 seconds)
```

FIGURE 17.2

Running the `Console` *application.*

The `Console` class contains one class method, `readLine()`, which receives characters from the console. When the Enter key is pressed, `readLine()` returns a `String` object that contains all the characters that are received.

NOTE The `Console` class is also the world's least satisfying text adventure game. You can't enter the building, wade in the stream, or even wander off. For a real version of the game referenced in this program's output, which is called Adventure, visit Web-Adventures at www.web-adventures.org.

Writing Data to a Stream

In the `java.io` package, the classes for working with streams come in matched sets. There are `FileInputStream` and `FileOutputStream` classes for working with byte streams, `FileReader` and `FileWriter` classes for working with character streams, and many other sets for working with other kinds of stream data.

To begin writing data, you first create a `File` object that is associated with an output stream. This file doesn't have to exist on your system.

You can create a `FileOutputStream` in two ways. If you want to append bytes onto an existing file, call the `FileOutputStream()` constructor method with two arguments: a `File` object representing the file and the `boolean` of `true`. The bytes you write to the stream are tacked onto the end of the file.

If you want to write bytes into a new file, call the `FileOutputStream()` constructor method with a `File` object as its only object.

After you have an output stream, you can call different `write()` methods to write bytes to it:

- Call `write()` with a byte as its only argument to write that byte to the stream.

- Call `write()` with a byte array as its only argument to write all the array's bytes to the stream.

- Specify three arguments to the `write(byte[], int, int)` method: a byte array, an integer representing the first element of the array to write to the stream, and the number of bytes to write.

The following statement creates a byte array with 10 bytes and writes the last 5 to an output stream:

```
File dat = new File("data.dat");
FileOutputStream datStream = new FileOutputStream(dat);
byte[] data = new byte[] { 5, 12, 4, 13, 3, 15, 2, 17, 1, 18 };
datStream.write(data, 5, 5);
```

When writing bytes to a stream, you can convert text to an array of bytes by calling the `String` object's `getBytes()` method, as in this example:

```
String name = "Puddin N. Tane";
byte[] nameBytes = name.getBytes();
```

After you have finished writing bytes to a stream, you close it by calling the stream's `close()` method.

The next project you write is a simple application, `ConfigWriter`, that saves several lines of text to a file by writing bytes to a file output stream. Create an empty Java file of that name, and enter the text from Listing 17.3 into the source editor.

LISTING 17.3   The Full Text of `ConfigWriter.java`.

```
1: package com.javaminecraft;
2:
3: import java.io.*;
4:
5: public class ConfigWriter {
6:     String newline = System.getProperty("line.separator");
```

```
 7:
 8:      public ConfigWriter() {
 9:          try {
10:              File file = new File("program.properties");
11:              FileOutputStream fileStream = new
              ➥FileOutputStream(file);
12:              write(fileStream, "username=max");
13:              write(fileStream, "score=12550");
14:              write(fileStream, "level=5");
15:              fileStream.close();
16:          } catch (IOException ioe) {
17:              System.out.println("Could not write file");
18:          }
19:      }
20:
21:      void write(FileOutputStream stream, String output)
22:          throws IOException {
23:
24:          output = output + newline;
25:          byte[] data = output.getBytes();
26:          stream.write(data, 0, data.length);
27:      }
28:
29:      public static void main(String[] arguments) {
30:          ConfigWriter cw = new ConfigWriter();
31:      }
32: }
```

When this application is run, it creates a file called program.properties that
contains the following three lines of text:

```
username=max
score=12550
level=5
```

The file is created in Line 10 and associated with a file output stream in Line 11.
The three properties are written to the stream in Lines 12–14.

An application run in NetBeans will save the file(s) it creates in the project's main folder if no other folder is specified. To see the `program.properties` file in NetBeans, in the Projects pane, click the Files tab to bring it to the front. The file is in the top `Minecraft` folder, as shown in Figure 17.3.

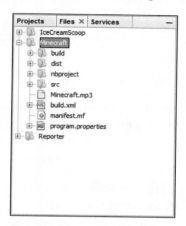

FIGURE 17.3

Finding the `program.properties` *file.*

Double-click the filename to open it in the NetBeans source code editor.

Reading and Writing Configuration Properties

Java programs are more versatile when they can be configured using command-line arguments, as you have demonstrated in several applications created in preceding chapters. The `java.util` package includes a class, `Properties`, that enables configuration settings to be loaded from another source: a text file.

The file can be read like other file sources in Java:

- Create a `File` object that represents the file.

- Create a `FileInputStream` object from that `File` object.

- Call `load()` to retrieve the properties from that input stream.

A properties file has a set of property names followed by an equal sign (=) and their values. Here's an example:

```
username=lepton
lastCommand=open database
windowSize=32
```

Each property has its own line, so this sets up properties named `username`, `lastCommand`, and `windowSize` with the values `lepton`, `open database`, and `32`, respectively. (The same format was used by the `ConfigWriter` application.)

The following code loads a properties file called `config.dat`:

```
File configFile = new File("config.dat");
FileInputStream inStream = new FileInputStream(configFile);
Properties config = new Properties();
config.load(inStream);
```

Configuration settings, which are called properties, are stored as strings in the `Properties` object. Each property is identified by a key. The `getProperty()` method retrieves a property using its key, as in this statement:

```
String username = config.getProperty("username");
```

Because properties are stored as strings, you must convert them in some manner to use a numerical value, as in this code:

```
String windowProp = config.getProperty("windowSize");
int windowSize = 24;
try {
    windowSize = Integer.parseInt(windowProp);
} catch (NumberFormatException exception) {
    // do nothing
}
```

Properties can be stored by calling the `setProperty()` method with two arguments—the key and value:

```
config.setProperty("username", "max");
```

You can display all properties by calling the `list(PrintStream)` method of the `Properties` object. `PrintStream` is the class of the `out` variable of the `System` class, which you've been using throughout the book to display output in `System.out.println()` statements. The following code calls `list()` to display all properties:

```
config.list(System.out);
```

After you have made changes to the properties, you can store them back to the file:

- Create a `File` object that represents the file.
- Create a `FileOutputStream` object from that `File` object.

- Call store(*OutputStream, String*) to save the properties to the designated output stream with a description of the properties file as the string.

For the next project, you build on the ConfigWriter application, which wrote several program settings to a file. The Configurator application reads those settings into a Java properties file, adds a new property named runtime with the current date and time, and saves the altered file.

Create a new empty Java file to hold the Configurator class, and enter the text from Listing 17.4.

LISTING 17.4 The Full Text of Configurator.java

```
 1: package com.javaminecraft;
 2:
 3: import java.io.*;
 4: import java.util.*;
 5:
 6: public class Configurator {
 7:
 8:     public Configurator() {
 9:         try {
10:             // load the properties file
11:             File configFile = new File("program.properties");
12:             FileInputStream inStream = new
                    ➥FileInputStream(configFile);
13:             Properties config = new Properties();
14:             config.load(inStream);
15:             // create a new property
16:             Date current = new Date();
17:             config.setProperty("runtime", current.toString());
18:             // save the properties file
19:             FileOutputStream outStream = new
                    ➥FileOutputStream(configFile);
20:             config.store(outStream, "Properties settings");
21:             inStream.close();
22:             config.list(System.out);
23:         } catch (IOException ioe) {
24:             System.out.println("IO error " + ioe.getMessage());
```

```
25:                 }
26:         }
27:
28:         public static void main(String[] arguments) {
29:             Configurator con = new Configurator();
30:         }
31: }
```

In this application, the `File` object for `program.properties` is created and associated with a file input stream in Lines 11–12. The contents of this file are loaded into a `Properties` object from the stream in Lines 13–14.

A new property for the current date and time is created in Lines 16–17. The file is then associated with an output stream in Line 19, and the entire properties file is written to that stream in Line 20.

The output of the `Configurator` application is shown in Figure 17.4.

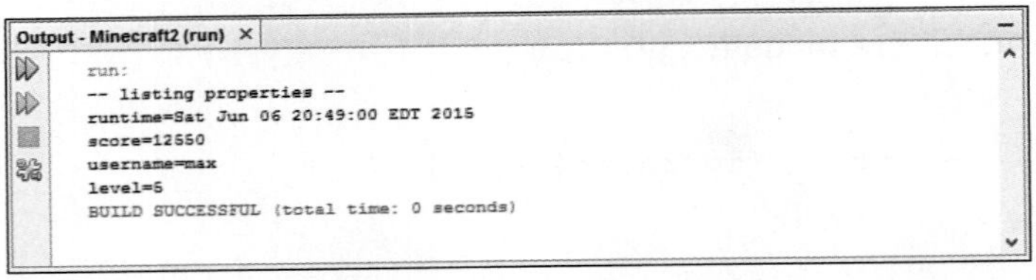

FIGURE 17.4

Running the Configurator *application.*

The `program.properties` file now contains the following text:

```
#Properties settings
#Sat Jun 06 20:49:00 EDT 2015
runtime=Sat Jun 06 20\:49\:00 EDT 2015
score=12550
level=5
username=max
```

The backslash character's (\\) formatting, which differs from the output of the application, ensures the properties file is stored properly.

THE ABSOLUTE MINIMUM

During this chapter, you worked with input streams and output streams that wrote bytes, the simplest way to represent data over a stream.

There are many more classes in the `java.io` package to work with streams in other ways. There's also a package of classes called `java.net` that enables you to read and write streams over an Internet connection.

Byte streams can be adapted to many uses because you can easily convert bytes into other data types, such as integers, characters, and strings.

18

IN THIS CHAPTER

- Use Spigot to create a mod
- Design a mod framework
- Respond to a player command
- Generate random numbers
- Work with (x,y,z) locations in the game world
- Spawn a mob at a specified location
- Find the block at a location
- Determine the material of a block
- Customize a chicken

SPAWN A MOB

Armed with the Java knowledge that is filling your brain, assuming you didn't skip past the last 14 chapters, you are ready to put it to use writing Minecraft mods.

One of the strengths of Java is that it employs object-oriented programming, which makes it possible to acquire the capabilities of an existing Java class through inheritance. You inherit the code through the `extends` keyword, and everything the existing class does your new class also can do. You inherit the attributes (variables) and behavior (methods) from this superclass.

Because of inheritance, the code you write in your new class can focus on the new things it does and the things it does differently than its superclass.

All Minecraft mods are subclasses of `JavaPlugin` in the `org.bukkit.plugin.java` package. You inherit all the code necessary for your program and the Minecraft server to communicate with each other. This code, plus a configuration file in YAML format called `plugin.yml`, tell the server what should happen when the mod's command is entered by a player in the game.

This chapter's mod spawns 1–30 chickens in the skies around the player, demonstrating how to spawn mobs in Minecraft and work with (x,y,z) locations in the game world. It also shows how to generate random numbers in Java.

So let's get clucking.

The Mod Framework

All Minecraft mods can be built from the same basic framework of Java code. Here's a look at it:

```java
public class ChickenStorm extends JavaPlugin {
    public static final Logger LOG = Logger.getLogger("Minecraft");


    @Override
    public boolean onCommand(CommandSender sender,
        Command command, String label, String[] arguments) {

        if (label.equalsIgnoreCase("chickenstorm")) {
            if (sender instanceof Player) {
                executeCommand(sender);
                return true;
            }
        }
        return false;
    }


    // handle the command
    public void executeCommand(CommandSender sender) {
        Player me = (Player) sender;
        Location spot = me.getLocation();
        World world = me.getWorld();

        // do something cool here
```

```
    // tell the server log what the mod did
    LOG.info("[ChickenStorm] The mod did something!");
  }
}
```

Only three things in this code will need to be changed with each mod you develop in the coming chapters: the name of the Java class (`ChickenStorm`), the command a player enters to run the mod (`chickenstorm`), and the message displayed to the server log (which begins with `[ChickenStorm]`).

When a player types a command, the Spigot server looks for an `onCommand()` method in that mod that can do something in response to that command. The command has four arguments:

- A `CommandSender` object that represents the player who issued the command (which in this framework is stored in a variable named `sender`)
- A `Command` object that represents the command (which is stored in `command`)
- A `String` that holds the text of the command (stored in `label`)
- A `String[]` array that contains the arguments entered by the player after the command, if any (stored in `arguments`)

The `onCommand()` method is inherited from `JavaPlugin`. The method must return a Boolean value to indicate whether it handled the command successfully. The mod returns `false` if it didn't and `true` if it did. The Spigot server needs to know this as it processes player commands in all the mods on that server.

A mod must ensure that the player's command is one that it handles. This is accomplished by calling the `equalsIgnoreCase(String)` method of the `label` variable, which ignores the capitalization of the text when comparing it to the string specified as the argument.

The mod also must make sure that the `CommandSender` object that issued the command belongs to the `Player` class, which can be checked with the `instanceof` keyword.

Here are two `if` conditionals that verify these things:

```
if (label.equalsIgnoreCase("chickenstorm")) {
    if (sender instanceof Player) {
        // player issued that command
    }
}
```

The framework puts the code that handles the mod in its own method, `executeCommand()`. This command has the `CommandSender` object as its only argument because it makes use of that object. Other mods also might make use of the other three arguments sent to the `onCommand()` method.

All the code that implements the mod will be put at the line denoted by the comment `// do something cool here`.

The `executeCommand()` method begins with the following three statements:

```
Player me = (Player) sender;
Location spot = me.getLocation();
World world = me.getWorld();
```

These statements do three things you're likely to need in every mod you create:

- Create a `Player` object that represents the player who entered the command. `Player` is in the `org.bukkit.entity` package.
- Call the player's `getLocation()` method to determine the (x,y,z) location of the player, which is stored as a `Location` object from the `org.bukkit` package.
- Call the player's `getWorld()` method to access the `World` object that holds the entire game world. This also is part of the `org.bukkit` package.

The `Player` is stored in `me`, `Location` in `spot`, and `World` in `world`.

After the mod has completed its work, a message should be written to the server window that reveals what it did. The server window is accessed through a static class variable of the mod named `LOG`:

```
public static final Logger LOG = Logger.getLogger("Minecraft");
```

`LOG` is a variable of the `Logger` class in the `java.util.logging` package, which enables Java programs to store information to log files. As the Spigot server runs, log messages from the server and its mods are displayed in the server window.

The variable's name `LOG` is capitalized, which is a style convention adopted by Java programmers that indicates the variable is `static` so its value cannot be changed.

The `LOG` object has an `info(String)` method for writing an informational message to the log. The framework does this after the mod's work is done in this statement:

```
LOG.info("[ChickenStorm] The mod did something!");
```

The first part of the message provides the name of the mod's class surrounded by brackets ([ChickenStorm]). This is important to include—without it, the server log won't contain anything that identifies which mod sent the message.

When customizing the framework, you should come up with something better to tell the server than "The mod did something!"

Here's what this chapter's mod tells the server:

```
LOG.info(quantity + " chickens summoned");
```

 NOTE   The mod framework includes something unusual in the line immediately preceding the start of the onCommand() method: the text @Override. This is a special message about the code called an *annotation*. Annotations provide extra information about a program that can be helpful for the Java compiler and Java Virtual Machine. They're like comments that are readable by both humans and computers, although they do not in any way change the code itself.

All annotations begin with the at sign (@). The purpose of the annotation @Override is to indicate that a method overrides a method in the superclass of this class. This enables the Java compiler (and NetBeans) to check whether the method actually is overriding a superclass method.

If you put in @Override and spelled the method name as onComand() instead of onCommand(), the compiler would alert you to this error because of the annotation.

Now that the framework has been covered, it's time to do something cool.

Starting a Mod Project

As you probably have guessed, this chapter's mod is called ChickenStorm. Its job is to fill the sky around a Minecraft player with from 1 to 30 chickens, 40 percent of which will be baby chicks.

Every mod is its own project in NetBeans, which is necessary because the mod's files must be packaged as a single Java archive (JAR) file.

Create the new project by following these steps in NetBeans:

1. Select the menu command File, New Project. The New Project dialog opens.

2. Select the project category Java and the project type Java Application, and then click Next.

3. Enter **ChickenStorm** as the project's name.

4. Deselect the Create Main Class check box.

5. Click Finish.

Mods require the Spigot class library, so you must add it to this project and every other mod project so that the Java classes in the library can be used in your program.

Here's how to do this:

1. In the Projects pane, right-click the Libraries folder and select the menu command Add Library. The Add Library dialog opens.

2. The Available Libraries pane lists all the class libraries that NetBeans knows about. You should have Spigot in this list because you added it to NetBeans during Chapter 3, "Create a Minecraft Mod." Select Spigot.

3. Click Add Library.

The Projects pane in NetBeans will be updated. The Libraries folder now will contain the item Spigot that includes its name and the filename of the JAR file, as shown in Figure 18.1.

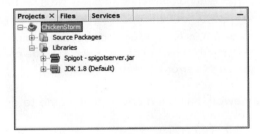

FIGURE 18.1

Adding the Spigot library to a Minecraft mod project.

The new project is created with no files in it. The first file to create is a configuration file for the mod that's required by the Spigot server. The file is a simple properties file in a format called YAML (Yet Another Markup Language). It must have the filename `plugin.yml` and be stored in a special subfolder of the project.

NetBeans makes this easy. Undertake these steps:

1. Select File, New File. The New File wizard opens.

2. In the Categories pane, scroll down and then select Other.

3. In the File Types pane, select YAML File and click Next.

4. In the File Name field, enter `plugin`. (Don't put `.yml` on the end; this is done for you by NetBeans.)

5. In the Folder field, enter `src`.

6. Click Finish.

The source code editor opens with the new file `plugin.yml` ready for editing. Delete the text that NetBeans puts in the editor, enter the text of Listing 18.1 into that file, and save it when you're done.

LISTING 18.1 The Full Text of `plugin.yml`

```
 1: name: ChickenStorm
 2:
 3: author: Your Name Here
 4:
 5: main: com.javaminecraft.ChickenStorm
 6:
 7: commands:
 8:     chickenstorm:
 9:         description: Spawn 1-30 chickens.
10:
11: version: 1.0
```

The Spigot server is persnickety about the spacing and formatting of this file. Make sure you use spaces in front of Lines 8 and 9, and put the right number of spaces (which is four before the text `chickenstorm` on Line 8 and eight before `description` on Line 9). Do not use the Tab key; only spaces.

In a YAML file, property names are followed by a colon and the value of that property.

The `name` property is the name of the mod.

The `author` property is the programmer who wrote it, which you should change from `Your Name Here` to your actual name—give yourself some props.

The `main` property is the full class name of the mod, which is the package name followed by the class name. It is `com.javaminecraft.ChickenStorm` for this project.

The `commands` property is defined in Lines 7–9 and lists all commands the mod handles, which can be more than one, although `ChickenStorm` has only one.

Line 8 matches the mod command, capitalized properly, and is followed by a colon.

Line 9 is that command's `description` property, which is a short description of what the mod does.

The `version` property is the version number of the mod.

The `plugin.yml` file must be stored in the correct subfolder for the `ChickenStorm` mod to work when it is added to a Spigot server.

You can check the Projects pane in NetBeans to ensure the file is in the proper place, which is shown in Figure 18.2.

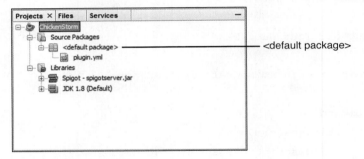

FIGURE 18.2

Checking the location of the `plugin.yml` *file.*

The `plugin.yml` file must be in the Source Packages item in the `<default package>` sub-item. If it is someplace else such as the `com.javaminecraft` sub-item, drag `plugin.yml` to the `Source Packages` item and drop it there. NetBeans will make the changes necessary and update the Projects pane accordingly.

Writing the Mod's Code

The project has been created, the framework is established, and a `plugin.yml` file has been authored that describes what the mod does.

All that remains is to write the `ChickenStorm` mod by extending the framework.

The mod stores the maximum number of chickens to spawn in a static class variable called `CHIX`:

```
private static final int CHIX = 30;
```

This could be changed to something higher or lower, although you have indicated in `plugin.yml` that from 1 to 30 chickens will be brought into the world.

CAUTION   Before you go crazy, keep in mind that spawning 1,000 chickens is a good way to send many Minecraft servers deep into lag—chicken-clucking, server-throttling, maybe-this-wasn't-the-best-idea lag. In a later mod, you'll be shown how to use lightning bolts to bring some sanity to a game world that has become overpopulated with mobs, but for now take care not to overcount your chickens.

This mod creates a random number of chickens, so you need a way in Java to generate a random value.

The `Math` class in the `java.lang` package has a `Random()` class method that returns a random double value that is from 0.0 to 1.0, including 0.0 as a potential value but not 1.0. You can multiply this value by an integer to get a random number from 0 to one less than that integer.

`ChickenStorm` multiplies `Math.random()` times `CHIX` and adds 1, which produces a random number from 1 to the maximum number of chickens. This is used in the conditional of a `for` loop that spawns the chickens:

```
for (int i = 0; i < Math.random() * CHIX + 1; i++) {
    // code to spawn a chicken here
}
```

When a chicken is spawned, it requires the location where that mob should be placed. Locations are created with the constructor `Location(World, double, double, double)`. The four arguments to the constructor are the game world and the (x,y,z) coordinates of that location.

Mobs often are spawned near the player who issued the command to create them. You can find a player's (x,y,z) coordinates by calling the `Location` object of the player's `getX()`, `getY()`, and `getZ()` methods.

Putting a chicken at the same location as the player would be accomplished with this statement:

```
Location cSpot = new Location(world, spot.getX(),
    spot.getY(), spot.getZ());
```

This mod does something more complicated. It puts each chicken from 10 to 109 blocks above the player and up to 14 or 15 blocks away from the player in the

X and Z planes. Here's the statement to do that, which makes use of `Math.random()` again:

```
Location cSpot = new Location(world,
    spot.getX() - 15 + Math.random() * 30,
    spot.getY() + 10 + Math.random() * 100,
    spot.getZ() - 15 + Math.random() * 30);
```

In Minecraft, the Y plane goes up and down, starting with 0 at the bottom of the game world and counting up as it ascends. Because `spot` holds the player's location, the code `spot.getY() + 10 + Math.random() * 100` is a value from 10 to 109 blocks above the player's Y location.

The X and Z locations are from −15 to 14 away from the player's X and Z location.

The result of this is to pick a spot for the chicken that's above the player—potentially way above—but pretty close in the other two dimensions.

When you generate a location at random in a Minecraft mod, keep in mind that each block in the game can be air or some other material. If you put a chicken in a stone block, that would be a fate most fowl, and it would be instantly killed.

You can prevent this by figuring out what kind of material is at a specific location. This mod accomplishes that with the following code:

```
if (cSpot.getBlock().getType() != Material.AIR) {
    // don't put the chicken in a solid block
}
```

The `if` conditional uses a pretty complex Java statement in which a method returns an object and that object's method is called. (You did something similar earlier in the book any time you called `System.out.println()` to display text.)

A `Location` object has a `getBlock()` method that returns the block at that location as a `Block` object from the `org.bukkit.block` package.

A `Block` object has a `getType()` method that returns the block's material type, which is a value represented by a `Material` variable. The `AIR` variable represents a block of air (naturally).

So calling `cSpot.getBlock().getType()` returns the type of material in the block at that location. Comparing this to `Material.AIR` checks whether it is air.

The chicken is spawned by calling a factory method of the `World` object holding the game world:

```
Chicken clucky = world.spawn(cSpot, Chicken.class);
```

The `spawn(Location, Class)` method spawns a mob of the specified class at the specified location. It also returns this mob as an object you can store in a variable.

The `Chicken.class` argument represents the class of the mob you want to spawn. In Java, following a class name with `.class` accomplishes this purpose.

The chicken created by this statement is stored in the variable `clucky`. It is a `Chicken` object in the `org.bukkit.entity` package.

A chicken mob has `setBaby()` and `setAdult()` methods that do what you'd expect them to do. These are used with `Math.random()` to make 40 percent of the chickens into chicks:

```
if (Math.random() < .4) {
    // make 40% of them babies
    clucky.setBaby();
} else {
    // make the rest adults
    clucky.setAdult();
}
```

You now can put all of this together into a Java class that spawns chickens.

Create the `ChickenStorm` program by undertaking these steps:

1. Click File, New File. The New File dialog appears.
2. In the Categories pane, select Java.
3. In the File Types pane, select Empty Java File; then click Next.
4. In the Class Name field, enter **ChickenStorm**.
5. In the Package field, enter **com.javaminecraft**.
6. Click Finish.

The empty file `ChickenStorm.java` opens for editing in the NetBeans source code editor. Enter the text of Listing 18.2, and save the file when this is complete.

LISTING 18.2   The Full Text of `ChickenStorm.java`

```
1: package com.javaminecraft;
2:
3: import java.util.logging.Logger;
4: import org.bukkit.Location;
```

```
 5: import org.bukkit.Material;
 6: import org.bukkit.World;
 7: import org.bukkit.command.Command;
 8: import org.bukkit.command.CommandSender;
 9: import org.bukkit.entity.Chicken;
10: import org.bukkit.entity.Player;
11: import org.bukkit.plugin.java.JavaPlugin;
12:
13: public class ChickenStorm extends JavaPlugin {
14:     public static final Logger LOG = Logger.getLogger(
15:         "Minecraft");
16:     // the maximum number of chickens
17:     private static final int CHIX = 30;
18:
19:     @Override
20:     public boolean onCommand(CommandSender sender,
21:         Command command, String label, String[] arguments) {
22:
23:         if (label.equalsIgnoreCase("chickenstorm")) {
24:             if (sender instanceof Player) {
25:                 executeCommand(sender);
26:                 return true;
27:             }
28:         }
29:         return false;
30:     }
31:
32:     // handle the chickenstorm command
33:     public void executeCommand(CommandSender sender) {
34:         Player me = (Player) sender;
35:         Location spot = me.getLocation();
36:         World world = me.getWorld();
37:
38:         int quantity = 0;
39:         // loop from 1 to CHIX times
40:         for (int i = 0; i < Math.random() * CHIX + 1; i++) {
```

```
41:            // pick a spot for the chicken above the player
42:            Location cSpot = new Location(world,
43:                spot.getX() - 15 + Math.random() * 30,
44:                spot.getY() + 10 + Math.random() * 100,
45:                spot.getZ() - 15 + Math.random() * 30);
46:            if (cSpot.getBlock().getType() != Material.AIR) {
47:                // don't put the chicken in a solid block
48:                continue;
49:            }
50:            // create the chicken
51:            Chicken clucky = world.spawn(cSpot, Chicken.class);
52:            if (Math.random() < .4) {
53:                // make 40% of them babies
54:                clucky.setBaby();
55:            } else {
56:                // make the rest adults
57:                clucky.setAdult();
58:            }
59:            quantity++;
60:        }
61:        // tell the server log how many were created
62:        LOG.info(quantity + " chickens summoned");
63:    }
64: }
```

Because this program is a Minecraft mod, it cannot be run directly in NetBeans like the programs you have written in Chapters 4–17.

Instead, you must build the project.

Select the menu command Run, Clean and Build Project. If this is a success, the message Finished Building ChickenStorm (clean, jar) appears in the lower-left corner of the NetBeans user interface.

The mod is packaged as a file called ChickenStorm.jar in a subfolder of the project. To find it, click the Files tab in the Projects pane to bring it to the front. Then click the + sign to expand the ChickenStorm folder (if necessary), and expand the dist subfolder. The Files tab lists all the files that make up the project, as shown in Figure 18.3.

JAR File

FIGURE 18.3

Finding the ChickenStorm *mod's JAR file.*

The presence of the ChickenStorm.jar file indicates that you have built the mod and are ready to deploy it on the server.

Deploying a Mod

The ChickenStorm mod is packaged into a JAR file named ChickenStorm.jar. This file must be copied from the project folder to the Spigot server while that server is not running.

To deploy the mod, follow these steps:

1. If the Minecraft server is running, stop it by going to the server window and typing the command **stop**. You will see messages related to the shutdown until it is finished.

2. Hit the spacebar or any other key to close the server window.

3. Outside of NetBeans in your computer's file system, open the folder where you installed the Minecraft server.

4. Open the ChickenStorm subfolder.

5. Open that folder's dist subfolder.

6. Select the ChickenStorm file (a JAR file), and press Ctrl+C to copy it.

7. Go back to the Minecraft server folder.

8. Open the plugins subfolder.

9. Press Ctrl+V to copy ChickenStorm into it.

You have deployed this mod on the Minecraft server. Start the server the same way you have done before: Click the `start-server` command. As the server starts, you will see two new messages in the window:

```
[ChickenStorm] Loading ChickenStorm v1.0
[ChickenStorm] Enabling ChickenStorm v1.0
```

If you don't see these messages, but instead see some long error messages, double-check everything in `ChickenStorm.java` against Listing 18.2 and `plugin.yml` against Listing 18.1 and ensure all the lines were entered correctly. When you're sure, rebuild and redeploy the mod.

You can test the mod by playing Minecraft on your server.

In the game, enter the command `/chickenstorm`. From 1 to 30 chickens will begin drifting slowly down all around you, landing safely because they are one of the mobs that is immune to falling damage.

(Try the same thing with zombies, and the living dead will splat all around, ending their newly spawned existence quite gruesomely.)

Figure 18.4 shows an island full of chickens with more falling from the skies.

FIGURE 18.4

Cluck cluck cluck cluck cluck!

THE ABSOLUTE MINIMUM

There's a lot of ground to cover when you begin creating Minecraft mods.

You must learn a framework for mods that inherits from the `JavaPlugin` class in the `org.bukkit.plugin.java` package. Your subclass overrides the `onCommand()` method of that superclass and responds to a command typed by a player in the game.

The command that is the mod's responsibility is indicated by the `plugin.yml` file, a short and simple properties file in the YAML format.

The `ChickenStorm` mod was packaged into a single JAR file and stored in the Spigot server's `plugins` subfolder. When the server was run again, it discovered this file and tried to load it as a mod, reporting back whether it was successful or not in the server log window.

This first full-fledged mod went over a lot of stuff that won't have to be covered again. You now know all the fundamentals necessary to create and deploy a mod.

On the mods you code in upcoming chapters, you learn about the Spigot class library and all the different things mods can do.

19

MAKE ONE MOB RIDE ANOTHER

The first Minecraft mods you create in this book all involve mobs—the animals and foes who make the game world a more lively place. Spawning a mob and making changes to a mob you encounter in the game are a good starting place for this kind of programming.

Each mob you can encounter in Minecraft can be created and manipulated as an object in Java.

The class names are in the `org.bukkit.entity` package and are largely what you'd expect them to be, such as `Zombie`, `Villager`, `Creeper`, `MushroomCow`, and `CaveSpider`.

Mobs can interact with other mobs. In your Java code, one mob will have methods to call that establish the relationship to the other mob.

The mod you code in this chapter covers a common interaction: making one mob ride another. You create a `ZombieChicken` mod that spawns zombies who are mounted on chickens.

Starting the Project

The `ZombieChicken` mod spawns from 1–10 chicken-riding zombies. The zombies are turned into baby zombies because a full-grown member of the living dead would be too big to ride a chicken.

(This book has some weird sentences in it—and the last one might be the weirdest.)

Before you can begin writing any Java code, you must take care of the standard tasks every mod requires.

Because every Minecraft mod must be its own project, you create one in NetBeans by following these steps:

1. Select File, New Project. The New Project dialog opens.

2. Select the project category `Java` and the project type `Java Application`, and click Next.

3. Enter the project name **ZombieChicken**.

4. Deselect the Create Main Class check box (if necessary).

5. Click Finish.

Remember to add the Spigot class library to the new project to make its classes available in your program. Follow these steps:

1. In the Projects pane, right-click the Libraries folder and select the pop-up menu command Add Library. That dialog opens.

2. In the Available Libraries pane, select Spigot.

3. Click Add Library.

The Projects pane in NetBeans will now reflect that Spigot is one of the libraries in this project.

Next, you must create the mod's plug-in configuration file `plugin.yml` and make sure it is stored in the proper folder. Do this:

1. Select File, New File. The New File dialog opens.

2. In the Categories pane, select Other.

3. In the File Types pane, select YAML File; then click Next.

4. In the File Name field, enter **plugin** (without the `.yml`).

5. In the Folder field, enter `src`.

6. Click Finish.

The source code editor opens with the new file `plugin.yml` ready to be written. Enter the text of Listing 19.1 into the editor, and save it by selecting the menu command File, Save or clicking Save All on the NetBeans toolbar.

LISTING 19.1   The Full Text of `plugin.yml`

```
 1: name: ZombieChicken
 2:
 3: author: Your Name Here
 4:
 5: main: com.javaminecraft.ZombieChicken
 6:
 7: commands:
 8:     zombiechicken:
 9:         description: Spawn 1-10 chicken-riding zombies.
10:
11: version: 1.0
```

There should be no surprises in this file, which establishes that a mod named ZombieChicken is in a class called com.javaminecraft.ZombieChicken, has version number 1.0, and takes the player command zombiechicken. The mod's purpose is to "Spawn 1–10 chicken-riding zombies."

As long as you remembered to use spaces instead of tabs to indent Lines 8 and 9 and have the proper number of spaces, this file is likely set up correctly.

Now let's make some zombies and teach them to ride chickens.

Writing the Mod

Before you begin entering the source code of the mod, there's a NetBeans feature you should learn that saves you some typing time.

NetBeans is a powerful integrated development environment (IDE) that analyzes the code of the program you're writing as you enter each line.

If you make an error and NetBeans knows how to fix it, it will offer to do that for you.

One such error is when you refer to a class you haven't imported yet. You can take advantage of NetBeans' helpfulness to stop typing in all those `import` statements at the top of each program.

Listing 19.2 contains the full text you should enter as the source code for the file `ZombieChicken.java`.

Go ahead and start doing that, but don't type all the lines. Instead, type in Line 1, skip Lines 3–13, and then type in Line 15. After you finish Line 15, an alert icon appears to the left of that line in the source code editor.

If you click this alert, a menu appears with two ways NetBeans can fix the error. This menu is shown in Figure 19.1.

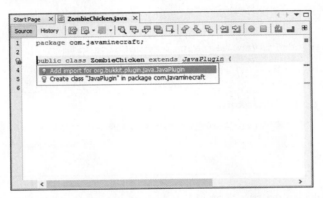

FIGURE 19.1

Letting NetBeans fix an error as you write a Java program.

One of the suggested fixes is Add Import for `org.bukkit.plugin.java.JavaPlugin`. Select this and the following import statement appears in the code:

```
import org.bukkit.plugin.java.JavaPlugin;
```

NOTE   This NetBeans feature is why all the programs for the rest of this book use `import` with individual classes instead of an entire package such as `org.bukkit.entity.*`.

Most Java programmers import single classes like this because it's a better practice. Making entire packages available in a program can lead to some confusion when two packages contain a class with the same short name. An example in the Java Class Library is that `java.util` and `java.sql` both have classes named `Date`.

If you imported both packages with *, you could not write a statement that referenced `Date` without using its full class name.

When you let NetBeans add an `import` statement for you, make sure the class is the correct one. For mods, the class should have a package that begins with `org.bukkit` in the name.

Begin the `ZombieChicken` program by following these steps:

1. Click File, New File. The New File dialog opens.

2. In the Categories pane, select Java.

3. In the File Types pane, select Empty Java File; then click Next.

4. In the Class Name field, enter `ZombieChicken`.

5. In the Package field, enter `com.javaminecraft`.

6. Click Finish.

Enter Listing 19.2 into the source code editor, skipping Lines 3–13 and letting NetBeans add the proper imports. Save the file when you're finished.

The new features in the code will be explained after the listing.

LISTING 19.2 The Full Text of `ZombieChicken.java`

```
 1: package com.javaminecraft;
 2:
 3: import java.util.logging.Logger;
 4: import org.bukkit.Location;
 5: import org.bukkit.World;
 6: import org.bukkit.command.Command;
 7: import org.bukkit.command.CommandSender;
 8: import org.bukkit.entity.Chicken;
 9: import org.bukkit.entity.Player;
10: import org.bukkit.entity.Zombie;
11: import org.bukkit.plugin.java.JavaPlugin;
12: import org.bukkit.potion.PotionEffect;
13: import org.bukkit.potion.PotionEffectType;
14:
15: public class ZombieChicken extends JavaPlugin {
16:     public static final Logger LOG = Logger.getLogger(
17:         "Minecraft");
18:
```

```
19:     @Override
20:     public boolean onCommand(CommandSender sender,
21:         Command command, String label, String[] arguments) {
22:
23:         if (label.equalsIgnoreCase("zombiechicken")) {
24:             if (sender instanceof Player) {
25:                 executeCommand(sender);
26:                 return true;
27:             }
28:         }
29:         return false;
30:     }
31:
32:     public void executeCommand(CommandSender sender) {
33:         Player me = (Player) sender;
34:         Location spot = me.getLocation();
35:         World world = me.getWorld();
36:
37:         // spawn 1-10 chicken-riding zombies
38:         int quantity = (int) (Math.random() * 10) + 1;
39:         for (int i = 0; i < quantity; i++) {
40:             // set chicken and zombie location
41:             Location cSpot = new Location(world,
42:                 spot.getX() + (Math.random() * 15),
43:                 spot.getY() + 5,
44:                 spot.getZ() + (Math.random() * 15));
45:             // create the mobs
46:             Chicken clucky = world.spawn(cSpot, Chicken.class);
47:             Zombie rob = world.spawn(cSpot, Zombie.class);
48:             rob.setBaby(true);
49:             clucky.setPassenger(rob);
50:             // increase the chicken's speed
51:             int speed = (int) (Math.random() * 10);
52:             PotionEffect potion = new PotionEffect(
53:                 PotionEffectType.SPEED,
54:                 Integer.MAX_VALUE,
```

```
55:                        speed);
56:                   clucky.addPotionEffect(potion);
57:              }
58:         LOG.info("[ZombieChicken] Created " + quantity +
59:              " chicken-riding zombies");
60:    }
61: }
```

The ZombieChicken mod spawns 1–10 chickens and an equal number of zombies and then turns the zombies into babies and makes them passengers of those chickens.

The Math.random() class is utilized in Line 38 to generate the random quantity of mobs.

The location of each mob also is random in the X and Z dimensions. In the Y dimension, which tracks how far a player is up or down, the mob's starting position is five blocks higher than the player. This statement in Lines 41–44 creates a Location object for that spot:

```
Location cSpot = new Location(world,
     spot.getX() + (Math.random() * 15),
     spot.getY() + 5,
     spot.getZ() + (Math.random() * 15));
```

A zombie is created and spawned the same way as a chicken during Chapter 18, "Spawn a Mob." A factory method is called in Line 47 with the location and class to spawn:

```
Zombie rob = world.spawn(cSpot, Zombie.class);
```

This creates a zombie in the variable rob.

Zombies are one of the only hostile mobs in Minecraft that can appear in child or adult forms (zombie villagers and zombie pigmen are two others). In a mod, you must create an adult zombie object and call its setBaby(Boolean) method with an argument of true to turn it into a youngster:

```
rob.setBaby(true);
```

A mob can take a passenger on its back by calling that mob object's setPassenger(Entity) method with the passenger as the argument. The argument is an Entity object from the org.bukkit.entity package. All mobs in the game are subclasses of `Entity`. This statement makes the zombie ride the chicken:

```
clucky.setPassenger(rob);
```

This mod adds one new wrinkle to mobs by altering the speed at which the chickens move. You can customize a mob by adding a potion effect to it, just like when your player in the game drinks a potion to become invisible, see clearly under the ocean surface, and heal.

Potion effects are created in a mod with the `PotionEffect` and `PotionEffectType` classes in the `org.bukkit.potion` package.

A `PotionEffect` can be created by calling its constructor with three arguments:

- A `PotionEffectType` class variable indicating the type of effect (`PotionEffectType.SPEED` in this mod)

- The duration of the effect

- An integer value called the *amplifier* that represents how strong the effect is

Line 51 sets the chicken's `speed` from 0 to 9:

```
int speed = (int) (Math.random() * 10);
```

Lines 52–55 create the potion effect:

```
PotionEffect potion = new PotionEffect(
    PotionEffectType.SPEED,
    Integer.MAX_VALUE,
    speed);
```

A mob has an `addPotionEffect(PotionEffect)` method to apply the effect:

```
clucky.addPotionEffect(potion);
```

Potions in the game typically run out after a certain amount of time, but you often will want a mob's potion effect to last forever. The closest thing you can do to achieve this is to set the duration to the largest possible integer in Java, which is 2,147,483,647. A class variable in the `Integer` class, `Integer.MAX_VALUE`, is an easy way to refer to this number.

NOTE   In Minecraft and the Spigot class library, the duration of everything is measured in ticks. A tick is approximately one-twentieth of a second when the game is running at full speed. Setting a potion effect to the maximum will make it last at least 1,200 days in real time.

That's probably sufficient for your speedy chicken.

The third argument to the `PotionEffect()` constructor is the amplifier, an integer value that determines the strength of the effect. An amplifier of 1 is the normal effect, so an amplifier of 4 is four times as strong and 8 is eight times.

Deploying the Mod

Now that the mod has been developed, you must deploy it to the Minecraft server. The Java Archive (JAR) file `ZombieChicken.jar` must be copied from the project folder to the server after the server has been stopped.

Follow these steps:

1. In NetBeans, choose the menu command Run, Clean and Build Project. The project is created as `ZombieChicken.jar`.

2. In your computer's file system, open the file folder where you installed the Spigot server.

3. Open the `ZombieChicken` subfolder.

4. Open that folder's `dist` subfolder.

5. Select the `ZombieChicken` JAR file, and then press Ctrl+C to copy that file.

6. Go back to the Minecraft server folder.

7. Open the `plugins` subfolder.

8. Press Ctrl+V to copy `ZombieChicken.jar` into that folder.

When you start the server again and run the mod with the command **/zombiechicken**, you see a stampede of chicken-riding zombies, some of whom are alarmingly fast (see Figure 19.2). This would be a good time to run away.

FIGURE 19.2

The baby zombie says, "Giddy up, chicken!"

THE ABSOLUTE MINIMUM

The last two mods that you created, `ChickenStorm` and `ZombieChicken`, exploited the ability of the Spigot class library to represent any mob in Minecraft as a Java object.

You create the mob with a factory method that needs only the class of the mob—represented by its class name followed by `.class`—and the `Location` object where that mob should appear in the game world.

Mobs have a lot of methods that customize the mob, such as when the `Zombie` object's `setBaby()` method was called in `ZombieChicken` to make it a young zombie instead of an adult.

Mobs also have methods to interact with other mobs. The `setPassenger()` method gives a mob a rider.

So far you have just begun to tap into the potential of the Spigot class library. The next chapter digs into it more deeply so you can create a mod and then customize it in unexpected ways.

TAKE A CENSUS OF MOBS AND VILLAGES

A useful application of mods is to discover more about Minecraft in real time as the game is being played. This chapter's mod takes a census of the mobs that are active in the world in the vicinity of the player.

Mobs are loaded and unloaded by the game as players explore the world. The world is divided into chunks that are 16 blocks long, 16 blocks wide, and 256 blocks deep. The chunks nearest the player are loaded and another 440 chunks are loaded in memory at any time in multiplayer mode. The number of chunks loaded is more variable in single-player mode and depends on player movement and the view distance (how far a player can see blocks).

Information about mobs can be retrieved in a Minecraft mod in lists, a data structure you learned about during Chapter 14, "Store Objects in Data Structures." Another data structure proves helpful in this chapter: hash maps.

Although the mods you have programmed thus far each took one user command, a mod can handle multiple commands.

This chapter's project supports a second command to take a census of nearby villages.

Starting the Project

The `MobCensus` mod adds two commands to a Minecraft game: `/census`, which reports the count and type of all mobs currently loaded in the game world, and `/villager`, which reports the count and type of villagers and the iron golems who protect them.

Take these steps to create the project:

1. Select File, New Project. The New Project dialog opens.

2. Select the project category `Java` and project type `Java Application`; then click Next.

3. Enter the project name **MobCensus**.

4. Deselect Create Main Class in the check box (if necessary), and click Finish. The project is created, as you can see in the Projects pane.

5. In that Projects pane, right-click the `Libraries` folder and select the command Add Library. That dialog opens.

6. In the Available Libraries pane, select Spigot.

7. Click Add Library.

After creating the project and adding the Spigot library, you must create the mod's plug-in configuration file `plugin.yml` in the proper project folder:

1. Select File, New File. The New File dialog opens.

2. In the Categories pane, select Other.

3. In the File Types pane, select YAML File and click Next.

4. In the File Name field, enter **plugin** (without the `.yml`).

5. In the Folder field, enter **src**.

6. Click Finish.

The new file `plugin.yml` opens in the source code.

Because this mod implements more than one user command, it is different from the mod configuration files you have worked with before. Enter the text of Listing 20.1 in the editor, and save it when you're done.

LISTING 20.1 The Full Text of `plugin.yml`

```
 1: name: MobCensus
 2:
 3: author: Your Name Here
 4:
 5: main: com.javaminecraft.MobCensus
 6:
 7: commands:
 8:     census:
 9:         description: Count the current mobs.
10:     villager:
11:         description: Count the nearby villagers.
12:
13: version: 1.0
```

The commands are configured in Lines 7–11 of Listing 20.1. The first command is defined in Lines 8–9, and the second in Lines 10–11. A `plugin.yml` file can define as many commands as necessary. The first line is the command followed by a colon (:). The second line is the field name `description` followed by a colon, a space, and a short description of what the command does. This line is indented four spaces to the right of the line that precedes it.

After all commands have been defined, there should be a blank line. The last field defined in `plugin.yml` is `version`, which sets the version number of the mod.

Creating the Project

The `MobCensus` mod defines two methods that implement user commands: `executeCensusCommand()` and `executeVillagerCommand()`. The class has three new instance variables (compared to past mods): the `Player` object `me`, the `Location` object `spot`, and the `World` object `world`. These variables are used in both execute methods.

The `onCommand()` method that's inherited from `JavaPlugin` in the `org.bukkit.plugin.java` package sets the value of these instance variables and checks whether the user has entered the command `census` or `villager`. If the user has, the proper method is called to execute that command.

A method of the `World` class, `getLivingEntities()`, returns all current mobs in an object that implements the `List` interface:

```
List<LivingEntity> current = world.getLivingEntities();
```

The `ArrayList` class you learned about during Chapter 14 implemented the `List` interface. The techniques you learned to access array lists also work with lists.

The `current` list holds `LivingEntity` objects from the `org.bukkit.entity` package. (Mobs also are called *entities* in Spigot.)

Because the `census` command counts mobs, you need a place to store the count of each type of mob. The mod stores this count in a hash map called `mobs`:

```
HashMap<EntityType, Integer> mobs = new HashMap<>();
```

A hash map has a key and a value for each entry in the map. The keys for this map are values in the `EntityType` class, which has a value for each mob as well as other entities. The following mobs are types:

- BAT
- BLAZE
- CAVE_SPIDER
- CHICKEN
- COW
- CREEPER
- ENDER_DRAGON
- ENDERMAN
- ENDERMITE
- GHAST
- GIANT
- GUARDIAN
- HORSE
- IRON_GOLEM
- MAGMA_CUBE
- MUSHROOM_COW
- OCELOT

- PIG
- PIG_ZOMBIE
- PLAYER
- RABBIT
- SHEEP
- SILVERFISH
- SKELETON
- SLIME
- SNOWMAN
- SPIDER
- SQUID
- VILLAGER
- WITCH
- WITHER
- WOLF
- ZOMBIE

In Java, a set of constants like this are called an *enumeration* and have the enum data type. They can be referenced in a statement just like a static class variable, as in the following example:

```
int zombieCount = mobs.get(EntityType.ZOMBIE);
me.sendMessage("There are " + zombieCount + " zombies");
```

Because me is a Player object, calling its sendMessage(*String*) method displays a message to the player in Minecraft. The message appears on the screen, as shown in Figure 20.1. The arrow points to the message.

FIGURE 20.1

Sending a message to a player with a mod.

An enhanced for loop can be used to iterate through each element in a data structure. Here's the loop for each entity in the current list:

```
for (Entity mob : current) {
    // ...
}
```

During each trip through the loop, the next entity is stored in the Entity object named mob.

An Entity has a getType() method that returns its type as an EntityType. This can be used as the key in the hash map that keeps a current count of each mob:

```
int count = 1;
if (mobs.containsKey(mob.getType())) {
    count = mobs.get(mob.getType());
    count++
}
mobs.put(mob.getType(), count);
```

This code does two things:

- If the mob type is not found in `mobs`, the count for that type is set to 1.
- If the mob type is found, the count is increased by 1.

After every mob in `current` has been examined for its type, the loop ends. The count of each mob in the `mobs` hash map can be displayed.

Another enhanced `for` loop iterates through every entry in the hash map:

```
for (Entry entry : mobs.entrySet()) {
    // ...
}
```

The hash map's `entrySet()` method returns a `Set` of every element in the map, which includes each key and value. An `Entry` object holds the key and value for a single element.

The entity type can be retrieved from that entry by calling its `getKey()` method and casting the value that is returned to an `EntityType` object:

```
EntityType type = (EntityType) entry.getKey();
```

The value is retrieved by calling the entry's `getValue()` and casting it to an integer:

```
int count = (int) entry.getValue();
```

The mod displays the type and count in a message to the player:

```
me.sendMessage(type + ": " + count);
```

With that, the `census` command has been fully implemented.

The mob's second command, `villager`, also uses the `world` object's `getLivingEntities()` method to get all mobs, storing them in a `mobs` list.

A `for` loop checks all these mobs, storing each one in a `LivingEntity` object named `mob`:

```
for (LivingEntity mob : mobs) {
    // ...
}
```

This command ignores all mobs further than 400 blocks away from the player, so the distance between the player and each mob must be determined.

First, the mob's location is retrieved by calling its `getLocation()` object:

```
Location mobSpot = mob.getLocation();
```

Next, the distance between the player and mob is calculated in the X, Y, and Z dimensions:

```
double xd = mobSpot.getX() - spot.getX();
double yd = mobSpot.getY() - spot.getY();
double zd = mobSpot.getZ() - spot.getZ();
```

The Pythagorean theorem in math states that for any right triangle, the square of the hypotenuse (the side opposite the right angle) is equal to the sum of the square of the other two sides. The formula is $a^2 + b^2 = c^2$.

This theorem comes in handy when you need to calculate the distance between the player and mob, which is the square root of the X, Y, and Z distances squared:

```
double distance = Math.sqrt(xd * xd + yd * yd + zd * zd);
```

If `distance` is greater than 400, this mob is skipped:

```
if (distance > 400) {
    continue;
}
```

After the too-distant mobs have been excluded, the mod checks whether the mob's type is a villager:

```
if (mob.getType() == EntityType.VILLAGER) {
    Villager dude = (Villager) mob;
    // ...
}
```

The `Villager` class represents villagers in the game. A `Villager` object has an `isAdult()` method that returns `true` for adults and `false` for children.

Another check determines whether the mob is an iron golem:

```
if (mob.getType() == EntityType.IRON_GOLEM) {
    // ...
}
```

The counts for adult villagers, child villagers, and iron golems are displayed in a player message.

Put all of this together in the MobCensus program, which you begin with the following steps:

1. Click File, New File. The New File dialog appears.

2. In the Categories pane, select Java.

3. In the File Types pane, select Empty Java File and click Next.

4. For the Class Name field, enter **MobCensus**.

5. For the Package field, enter **com.javaminecraft**.

6. Click Finish.

The MobCensus.java file opens in the NetBeans source code editor. Enter the text of Listing 20.2, and save it afterwards.

LISTING 20.2   The Full Text of MobCensus.java

```
 1: package com.javaminecraft;
 2:
 3: import java.util.HashMap;
 4: import java.util.List;
 5: import java.util.Map.Entry;
 6: import java.util.logging.Logger;
 7: import org.bukkit.Location;
 8: import org.bukkit.World;
 9: import org.bukkit.command.Command;
10: import org.bukkit.command.CommandSender;
11: import org.bukkit.entity.Entity;
12: import org.bukkit.entity.EntityType;
13: import org.bukkit.entity.LivingEntity;
14: import org.bukkit.entity.Player;
15: import org.bukkit.entity.Villager;
```

```
16: import org.bukkit.plugin.java.JavaPlugin;
17:
18: public class MobCensus extends JavaPlugin {
19:     public static final Logger LOG = Logger.getLogger(
20:         "Minecraft");
21:     Player me; // player
22:     Location spot; // player's location
23:     World world; // game world
24:
25:     @Override
26:     public boolean onCommand(CommandSender sender,
27:         Command command, String label, String[] arguments) {
28:
29:         if (sender instanceof Player) {
30:             me = (Player) sender;
31:             spot = me.getLocation();
32:             world = me.getWorld();
33:
34:             if (label.equalsIgnoreCase("census")) {
35:                 executeCensusCommand();
36:                 return true;
37:             }
38:
39:             if (label.equalsIgnoreCase("villager")) {
40:                 executeVillagerCommand();
41:                 return true;
42:             }
43:         }
44:         return false;
45:     }
46:
47:     // count all mobs around the player
48:     public void executeCensusCommand() {
49:         // store the mobs in a list
50:         List<LivingEntity> current = world.getLivingEntities();
```

```
51:          // store the mob count in a hash map
52:          HashMap<EntityType, Integer> mobs = new HashMap<>();
53:
54:          // loop through all the mobs found
55:          for (Entity mob : current) {
56:              int count = 1;
57:              if (mobs.containsKey(mob.getType())) {
58:                  // mob type found in hash map, so get count
59:                  count = mobs.get(mob.getType());
60:                  count++;
61:              }
62:              // store new count in hash map
63:              mobs.put(mob.getType(), count);
64:          }
65:          // display the count for each mob
66:          for (Entry entry : mobs.entrySet()) {
67:              EntityType type = (EntityType) entry.getKey();
68:              int count = (int) entry.getValue();
69:              me.sendMessage(type + ": " + count);
70:          }
71:      }
72:
73:      // count villagers within a 400-block radius
74:      public void executeVillagerCommand() {
75:          List<LivingEntity> mobs = world.getLivingEntities();
76:          int adultCount = 0;
77:          int kidCount = 0;
78:          int golemCount = 0;
79:          // loop through all mobs
80:          for (LivingEntity mob : mobs) {
81:              Location mobSpot = mob.getLocation();
82:              // calculate mob's distance away from player
83:              double xd = mobSpot.getX() - spot.getX();
84:              double yd = mobSpot.getY() - spot.getY();
85:              double zd = mobSpot.getZ() - spot.getZ();
```

```
 86:            double distance = Math.sqrt(xd * xd + yd * yd
 87:                + zd * zd);
 88:            if (distance > 400) {
 89:                // skip mobs too far away
 90:                continue;
 91:            }
 92:            // see if the mob is a villager
 93:            if (mob.getType() == EntityType.VILLAGER) {
 94:                Villager dude = (Villager) mob;
 95:                if (dude.isAdult()) {
 96:                    adultCount++;
 97:                } else {
 98:                    kidCount++;
 99:                }
100:            }
101:            // see if the mob is an iron golem
102:            if (mob.getType() == EntityType.IRON_GOLEM) {
103:                golemCount++;
104:            }
105:        }
106:        me.sendMessage("There are " + adultCount
107:            + " adult villagers and " + kidCount
108:            + " children nearby, protected by "
109:            + golemCount + " iron golem");
110:    }
111: }
```

After you have created the mod, build it by selecting the menu command Run, Clean and Build Project. The message `Finished building MobCensus (clean, jar)` appears in the lower-left corner of the NetBeans interface, and a file called `MobCensus.jar` is created in the `dist` subfolder of this project.

You are ready to deploy the mod.

Deploying a Mod

The Java Archive (JAR) file `MobCensus.jar` must be copied from the project folder to the Spigot server while the server is not running.

Follow these steps:

1. If the Minecraft server is running, stop it by going to the server window and typing the command **stop**. You will see messages related to the shutdown until it is finished.

2. Press any key to close the server window.

3. In your computer's file system, open the folder where you installed the Minecraft server.

4. Open the MobCensus subfolder.

5. Open that folder's dist subfolder.

6. Select the MobCensus JAR file and press Ctrl+C to copy it.

7. Return to the Minecraft server folder.

8. Open the plugins subfolder.

9. Press Ctrl+V to copy MobCensus.jar into it.

When you run the mod, enter the /census command to see a count of the nearby mobs (see Figure 20.2). (To see all of this mod's output, enter / as if you were beginning another command.)

FIGURE 20.2

Conducting a census of Minecraft mobs.

Enter the `/villager` command to find out how nearby villages are doing (see Figure 20.3).

There are 13 adult villagers and 0 children nearby, protected by 0 iron golem

FIGURE 20.3

Counting the village people.

THE ABSOLUTE MINIMUM

Learning how to develop mods is largely a process of building on what you've done before. With each new mod, you learn something new about the Spigot class library. Each technique you acquire will be part of your tool set when you tackle the next mod.

So far, you have created and customized a mob, made mobs interact with each other, and learned how to find and examine all the mobs that share the Minecraft game world with the player at any given time.

During this chapter, you used the skills you have developed with data structures. All living mobs in the game world—also called *living entities*—were stored in a `List` and accessed using the same methods you've used on array lists. A count of those mobs was kept in a hash map.

The `List` data structure turns up throughout the Spigot class library, so you'll be seeing it again.

IN THIS CHAPTER

- Work with materials in Minecraft
- Define command-line arguments in plugin.yml
- Read arguments in a mod
- Get the items in a player's inventory
- Loop through the items
- Transform one material into another
- Use the Spigot Javadoc documentation

TRANSMUTE MATERIALS IN AN INVENTORY

This chapter moves away from mobs into materials, the inanimate stuff that takes up space in the Minecraft world. Writing a mod that manipulates the physical world in the game requires a thorough grounding in the `Material` class in the `org.bukkit` package of the Spigot class library.

The `Transmuter` mod you create transforms material from one type to another at the control of the player. The original material must be present in the player's inventory for it to work.

All materials in the game are represented in Spigot by `Material`, an enumeration of constants. Some of the materials are blocks that can be built, such as `Material.DIRT`, `Material.AIR`, and `Material.DIAMOND_ORE`. Others are objects that can be held in an inventory or found on the ground, such as `Material.ROTTEN_FLESH` and `MATERIAL.RAW_CHICKEN`.

Working with a player's inventory requires the use of the `PlayerInventory` and `ItemStack` classes in the `org.bukkit.inventory` package.

Starting the Project

Minecraft mods can take command-line arguments just like Java programs.

The `Transmuter` mod puts an immense amount of power in the player's hands. Any material currently in the player's inventory can be transmuted to another with a command that specifies both materials as arguments (as shown in Figure 21.1):

```
/transmute ROTTEN_FLESH DIAMOND
```

FIGURE 21.1

Transmuting one material to another.

The first argument is the input material to transmute and the second argument is the output, so the preceding command turns rotten zombie flesh into diamonds. (Ka-ching!)

If you decide you'd rather have zombie flesh, this command changes it back:

```
/transmute DIAMOND ROTTEN_FLESH
```

With this version of the mod, players have to guess at the names of materials, but many of them are pretty intuitive. Here's another command:

```
/transmute GRAVEL CLAY
```

If no command-line arguments are specified or the materials are not named correctly, the mod's default behavior is to transmute dirt into cobblestone.

Create the new mod project by performing these steps:

1. Select File, New Project.

2. Select the project category Java and project type Java Application; then click Next.

3. Enter the project name **Transmuter**.

4. Make sure Create Main Class is deselected and click Finish. The project is created.

5. In the Projects pane, right-click the Libraries folder and select the command Add Library.

6. In the Available Libraries pane, select Spigot.

7. Click Add Library.

This creates the new project. Next, you must create the mod's configuration file plugin.yml in the src project folder:

1. Select File, New File.

2. In the Categories pane, select Other.

3. In the File Types pane, select YAML File; then click Next.

4. In the File Name field, enter **plugin** (without .yml).

5. In the Folder field, enter **src**.

6. Click Finish.

The new file plugin.yml opens for editing. Because this mod takes arguments, you need to add a new field to this configuration that tells players what the arguments specify. Enter the text of Listing 21.1 into the NetBeans source code editor, and save it with File, Save All or some other means.

LISTING 21.1   The Full Text of plugin.yml

```
1: name: Transmuter
2:
3: author: Your Name Here
4:
5: main: com.javaminecraft.Transmuter
6:
7: commands:
```

```
 8:      transmute:
 9:          description: Transmute an inventory material.
10:          usage: /<command> [inputMaterial] [outputMaterial]
11:
12: version: 1.0
```

The new field in `plugin.yml` is usage in Line 10. It describes how the command is correctly used and what the arguments do. This line states that the command is followed by a first argument that identifies the input material and a second argument that identifies the output material.

The square brackets (`[]`) around the argument descriptors are meaningful. A convention among programmers in documenting command-line arguments is to put these brackets around arguments that are optional and omit them from arguments that must be specified.

Here's an alternate version of Line 10:

```
usage: /<command> inputMaterial outputMaterial
```

This indicates that the input material and output material arguments are required, so if a user did not include those arguments, the program would fail with an error.

The `Transmuter` mod does not require arguments. If none are specified, the `/transmute` command turns dirt into cobblestone. Because of this, the brackets are used in Line 10.

Creating the Project

Now that the `plugin.yml` file is set up properly, it's time to develop the Java program that implements the mod.

The mod has a single `executeCommand(String[])` method that carries out the `/transmute` command. This method has one argument, a `String` array that holds the command-line arguments (if any).

The first thing the method does is define the default input and output materials:

```
Material input = Material.DIRT;
Material output = Material.COBBLESTONE;
```

Each material is a constant in the `Material` class. There are over 340 materials defined in `Material` as of the current version of the Spigot library, and you'll be introduced to many of them later in this chapter. The name of each material consists of letters, numbers, and underscore (_) characters. There are no spaces in the names, so `Material.DIAMOND_SWORD` is correct and `Material.DIAMOND SWORD` is not.

A class method of `Material` can find a material using its name as a string: `getMaterial(String)`.

The following code uses this method to take a command-line argument and find the material that matches that name:

```
if (arguments.length > 1) {
    input = Material.getMaterial(arguments[0]);
    output = Material.getMaterial(arguments[1]);
}
```

An `if` conditional ensures that the arguments exist by checking the `length` variable of the `String` array. If this was not done, the program would fail with an error indicating that an array index was out of bounds.

The `getMaterial()` method returns a `Material` if a valid material was named and `null` otherwise.

That `null` causes the command to end prematurely with a message indicating an invalid material was specified. Here's the code to reject a bad input material:

```
if (input == null) {
    me.sendMessage(arguments[0] + " is not a known material");
    return;
}
```

The `return` statement ends the `executeCommand()` method.

When both the `input` and `output` objects contain a valid material, the mod proceeds to load the player's inventory by calling a `Player` object's `getInventory()` method. This method sends back a `PlayerInventory` object that contains a bunch of `ItemStack` objects, each representing 1 of the 40 slots in the inventory (4 armor slots, 9 hotkey slots, and 27 other slots).

There's a `getSize()` method to find out how many slots the `PlayerInventory` object holds. The following code loops through the inventory, calling `getItem(int)` on each slot to get its `ItemStack`:

```
for (int i = 0; i < stuff.getSize(); i++) {
    ItemStack items = stuff.getItem(i);
    // ...
}
```

When an `ItemStack` object has no items in it—in other words, the slot is empty— calling `getItem()` returns the value `null`.

The mod ignores these empty slots by exiting the loop with `continue`:

```
if (items == null) {

    continue;

}
```

The loop continues for slots that have a stack of items in them. Each stack has a `getType()` method that returns the `Material` of the stack. This can be compared to the `input` material:

```
if (items.getType() == input) {

    // ...

}
```

When a match occurs, the stack's `setType(Material)` method changes that stack to the new material:

```
items.setType(output);
```

Each stack also has a `getAmount()` method that returns a count of how many of the item are in the stack. In addition, a `setAmount(int)` method changes the quantity.

Many items can have a quantity of 64 in an inventory slot, others 16, and some only one. Calling a material's `getMaxStackSize()` method returns the maximum number of the material that can be contained in an item stack.

After the mod transmutes a material, it fills that inventory slot with the maximum quantity of that material:

```
items.setAmount(output.getMaxStackSize());
```

Begin coding the `Transmuter` program by performing these steps in NetBeans:

1. Click File, New File.

2. In the Categories pane, select Java.

3. In the File Types pane, select Empty Java File; then click Next.

4. In Class Name, enter **Transmuter**.

5. In Package field, enter **com.javaminecraft**.

6. Click Finish.

Enter the text of Listing 21.2 in the source code editor.

LISTING 21.2 The Full Text of `Transmuter.java`

```
 1: package com.javaminecraft;
 2:
 3: import java.util.logging.Logger;
 4: import org.bukkit.Material;
 5: import org.bukkit.command.Command;
 6: import org.bukkit.command.CommandSender;
 7: import org.bukkit.entity.Player;
 8: import org.bukkit.inventory.ItemStack;
 9: import org.bukkit.inventory.PlayerInventory;
10: import org.bukkit.plugin.java.JavaPlugin;
11:
12: public class Transmuter extends JavaPlugin {
13:     public static final Logger LOG = Logger.getLogger(
14:         "Minecraft");
15:     Player me; // player
16:
17:     @Override
18:     public boolean onCommand(CommandSender sender,
19:         Command command, String label, String[] arguments) {
20:
21:         me = (Player) sender;
22:
23:         if (label.equalsIgnoreCase("transmute")) {
24:             if (sender instanceof Player) {
25:                 executeCommand(arguments);
26:             }
27:             return true;
28:         }
29:         return false;
30:     }
31:
32:     public void executeCommand(String[] arguments) {
33:         // set default to transmute dirt into cobblestone
34:         Material input = Material.DIRT;
35:         Material output = Material.COBBLESTONE;
36:         if (arguments.length > 1) {
```

```
37:              // turn player arguments into materials
38:              input = Material.getMaterial(arguments[0]);
39:              output = Material.getMaterial(arguments[1]);
40:          }
41:      if (input == null) {
42:              me.sendMessage(arguments[0]
43:                  + " is not a known material");
44:              return;
45:          }
46:      if (output == null) {
47:              me.sendMessage(arguments[1]
48:                  + " is not a known material");
49:              return;
50:          }
51:
52:      // get the player's current inventory
53:      PlayerInventory stuff = me.getInventory();
54:      for (int i = 0; i < stuff.getSize(); i++) {
55:          // examine each stack of items
56:          ItemStack items = stuff.getItem(i);
57:          if (items == null) {
58:              // this inventory slot is empty
59:              continue;
60:          }
61:          if (items.getType() == input) {
62:              // slot matches input material, so transmute
63:              items.setType(output);
64:              // fill slot with maximum amount possible
65:              items.setAmount(output.getMaxStackSize());
66:          }
67:      }
68:      // write a message to the player
69:      me.sendMessage(input.name() + " transmuted into "
70:              + output.name());
71:      }
72: }
```

If the mod's source code has been saved and there are no errors, you can deploy the mod. Build it: Choose Run, Clean and Build Project and look for the message `Finished building Transmuter (clean, jar)` in the lower-left corner of the NetBeans interface.

Deploying the Mod

Using your file system, copy the JAR file `Transmuter.jar` from this project's folder to the Spigot server through these steps:

1. Stop the Minecraft server (if necessary).

2. Open the folder where you installed the Minecraft server, and then open the `Transmuter` subfolder.

3. Open that folder's `dist` subfolder.

4. Select the `Transmuter` JAR file, and press Ctrl+C to copy it.

5. Open the Minecraft server folder again, and then open its `plugins` subfolder.

6. Press Ctrl+V to copy `Transmuter.jar` into it.

When you run the mod and play Minecraft, look at the items in your inventory and try to find the correct command-line arguments to use with `/transmute` to change them.

In Figure 21.2, emerald ore has been transformed into poisonous potatoes. That's a terrible trade!

Try the `/transmute` command with different materials to see which ones you can guess. When you'd like to see the real names for all the materials, you can read the Spigot class library's official documentation for the `Material` class.

Visit Spigot's website at http://hub.spigotmc.org/javadocs/spigot. The home page of the Spigot class library documentation loads for the current version. This page has a link in a frame at the lower left for every class in the library, including `Material`.

Scroll down in that frame until you find that link, and click `Material`. The documentation for that class appears. The first things on that page are the `enum` values for each `Material`, as shown in Figure 21.3.

FIGURE 21.2

Using a mod to transmute items in an inventory.

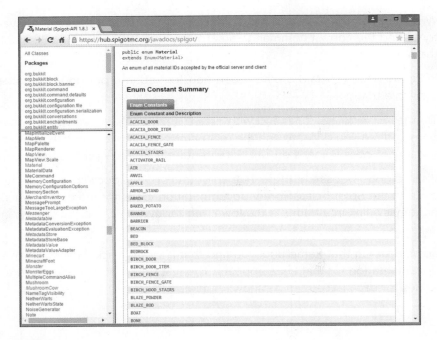

FIGURE 21.3

Reading the Java documentation for `Material`.

These values match the material names to use in the `Transmuter` mod. They also will be used any time you need to identify a material in a mod or change the material at a specific block in the game.

You will learn more about the Spigot documentation and how to make the most of it in Chapter 25, "Display a Mob's Health During Combat."

 CAUTION The `Material.getMaterial(String)` class method requires that the material be capitalized exactly like the constants for each material. Because constants in Java have names with all capital letters, `SANDSTONE` is correct and `Sandstone` and `sandstone` are not.

THE ABSOLUTE MINIMUM

Although it's fun to kill mobs and finish achievements in Minecraft, the most addictive aspect of the game is building and destroying stuff. Like a small child with a stack of wooden blocks or Godzilla clambering ashore in Tokyo, a Minecraft player has great power to wreak havoc on the world—and not necessarily great responsibility.

What a player can do, a mod can do with the Spigot Java class library.

The first step in the process of learning how to build and destroy the world in a mod was completed during this chapter. You were introduced to the `Material` class and discovered how to examine materials and transform them.

You also took your first look at the Spigot documentation.

It won't be the last.

Minecraft mod programming is a moving target. The Minecraft game is still getting cool new upgrades from Mojang, and the developers of the Spigot class library and server do their best to keep up with them, feature by feature.

Becoming a mod programmer is an exploratory process. Instead of attempting to memorize all the classes and methods before you put them to use, it is generally more effective to stumble around learning things as you code mods and examine mods created by other programmers who share their source code.

When you hit something that's perplexing or completely new to you, the Spigot documentation helps you puzzle it out and achieve the effect you seek.

22

DIG A GIANT HOLE

One of the things that makes Minecraft distinct is that it can be played and enjoyed without any specific goals being pursued. Though the game has a path to pursue to reach an end level and kill a supreme boss called the ender dragon, many players enjoy the game without ever trying to accomplish that.

You can play Minecraft with no long-term purpose at all. It is the ultimate sandbox game, where venturing around the world to build and destroy things and interact with the environment is its own reward.

Minecraft mods can enhance that experience by manipulating the materials of the world. As you know, the core of this functionality is the `Material` class in the `org.bukkit` package.

In this chapter, you develop a mod that enhances the digging capabilities of a player. The `BigDig` mod digs a circular hole around the player with a size determined by the player. The hole can be as small as 5 blocks in radius or as large as 30.

Starting the Project

Begin this chapter's mod project with these steps:

1. Select File, New Project.

2. Select project category `Java` and the project type `Java Application`; then click Next.

3. Enter the project name **BigDig**.

4. Deselect Create Main Class and click Finish.

5. In the Projects pane, right-click the `Libraries` folder and select the command Add Library.

6. In the Available Libraries pane, select Spigot.

7. Click Add Library.

The `BigDig` project is created with no files in it. This mod requires only a simple one-command mod configuration. To create the `plugin.yml` configuration file for the mod in the `src` project folder, follow these steps:

1. Select File, New File.

2. In the Categories pane, select Other.

3. In the File Types pane, select YAML File and click Next.

4. In the File Name field, enter **plugin** (leave off the `.yml`).

5. In the Folder field, enter **src**.

6. Click Finish.

The NetBeans source code editor opens with `plugin.yml` ready to be created. Enter the text of Listing 22.1 into the NetBeans source code editor, and save it when you're done.

LISTING 22.1   The Full Text of `plugin.yml`

```
1: name: BigDig
2:
3: author: Your Name Here
4:
5: main: com.javaminecraft.BigDig
6:
```

```
 7: commands:
 8:     bigdig:
 9:         description: Scoop away land around the player.
10:         usage: /<command> radius
11:
12: version: 1.0
```

Creating the Project

The BigDig mod digs out a circular globe around the player with a radius from 5 to 30 blocks in size. The player determines the size by following the /bigdig command with a space and a number, as in this command:

```
/bigdig 10
```

Mods can take arguments just like Java applications can. The arguments are stored in the fourth argument to the onCommand() method, a String array.

After a double called rad is created and given the value 15, the following statement sets the radius to the value of the first argument:

```
rad = Double.parseDouble(arguments[0]);
```

The parseDouble() method of Java's standard Double class converts a string to a double value, if such a conversion is possible.

To guard against bad input from a user, parseDouble() is put inside a try-catch block. A NumberFormatException occurs when the user's value isn't numeric.

If the user's value is a number, that becomes the dig radius. But there's one more check to ensure the input is acceptable. An if conditional ensures that the radius falls into an acceptable range of values:

```
if ((rad < 5) || (rad > 30)) {
    rad = 15;
}
```

Now that the proper radius has been established, the BigDig class has code that digs out the circle.

Like other mods, this one requires Player, Location, and World.

Different techniques can be used to dig out a circle around a player in a three-dimensional grid like the Minecraft world.

This mod accomplishes it by looking at every block in a square around the player that has sides a little bigger than twice the radius. The center of the square is the spot where the player is standing.

Three nested `for` loops loop through all the squares. There's a loop for the x-axis, one for the y-axis, and one for the z-axis:

```
for (double x = spot.getX() - rad; x < spot.getX() + rad;
    x++) {

    for (double y = spot.getY() - rad; y < spot.getY() + rad;
        y++) {

        for (double z = spot.getZ() - rad; z < spot.getZ() + rad;
            z++) {

            // ...
        }
    }
}
```

A `Location` object is created to represent the spot that's being examined in one trip through the loop:

```
Location loc = new Location(world, x, y, z);
```

The player's location was previously stored in the `spot` object:

```
Location spot = me.getLocation();
```

CAUTION   Minecraft worlds have a bottom level that can be dug, which has a Y value of 1. You can't dig through this in the game's survival mode because one or more bedrock blocks exist at that level and above it—and bedrock can't be mined by any pick axe in the game.

You can dig right through it in creative mode, which drops the player into a dark void and is fatal if you fall too far.

Mods are not prevented from destroying bedrock, so you must be sure in your mod not to dig through this layer.

The mod checks to see whether the current (x,y,z) position in the loop is at Y level 1, the lowest level a block can be dug in the game. If it is at this level, the loop ends this pass through the loop with the `continue` keyword:

```
if (y < 2) {
    continue;
}
```

This prevents any block at Y level 1 from being dug by this mod.

Now that that problem has been avoided in the loop, three statements measure the distance between the current spot and the player, on all three axes:

```
double xd = x - spot.getX();
double yd = y - spot.getY();
double zd = z - spot.getZ();
```

Using the same distance formula as the Transmuter mod in Chapter 21, "Transmute Materials in an Inventory," the distance can be calculated by squaring xd, yd, and zd; adding them together; and using the Math method sqrt() to get the square root of that sum:

```
double distance = Math.sqrt(xd * xd + yd * yd + zd * zd);
```

If the distance from the current block to the player is within the player's designated radius, that block is turned into air with these two statements:

```
Block current = world.getBlockAt(loc);
current.setType(Material.AIR);
```

First, a Block object is created that represents the block.

Next, the block's setType(*Material*) method is called with Material.AIR, one of several dozen values that represent the things a block can be made of in Minecraft.

The same technique that's used to destroy a block by turning it into air can be used to build things. The only thing that changes is the type of material. If you had wanted to dig out a circle of the game and turn it into diamond ore instead of air, this statement would be used:

```
current.setType(Material.DIAMOND_ORE);
```

When a circle has been dug from the world, the mod does two things to note the accomplishment: A sound is played and a message is sent to the server log window.

Sounds are played by calling a World object's playSound() method with four arguments: the sound's location, type, volume, and pitch. Here's the statement:

```
world.playSound(spot, Sound.BURP, 30, 5);
```

As you might have guessed, the sound is a burp. There are dozens of possible sounds that could be used.

A message is logged on the server by calling the `Logger` object's `info()` command with the text of the message:

```
LOG.info("[BigDig] Dug at ("
    + (int) spot.getX() + ", "
    + (int) spot.getY() + ", "
    + (int) spot.getZ() + ")");
}
```

Follow these steps in NetBeans to start developing the `BigDig` program:

1. Click File, New File.

2. In the Categories pane, select Java.

3. In the File Types pane, select Empty Java File and click Next.

4. For Class Name, enter **BigDig**.

5. For Package, enter **com.javaminecraft**.

6. Click Finish.

The new file opens for editing. Enter the text of Listing 22.2 into that file.

LISTING 22.2 The Full Text of `BigDig.java`

```
 1: package com.javaminecraft;
 2:
 3: import java.util.logging.Logger;
 4: import org.bukkit.Location;
 5: import org.bukkit.Material;
 6: import org.bukkit.Sound;
 7: import org.bukkit.World;
 8: import org.bukkit.block.Block;
 9: import org.bukkit.command.Command;
10: import org.bukkit.command.CommandSender;
11: import org.bukkit.entity.Player;
12: import org.bukkit.plugin.java.JavaPlugin;
13:
14: public class BigDig extends JavaPlugin {
```

```
15:        public static final Logger LOG = Logger.getLogger(
16:            "Minecraft");
17:
18:        @Override
19:        public boolean onCommand(CommandSender sender,
20:            Command command, String label, String[] arguments) {
21:
22:            if (sender instanceof Player) {
23:                if (label.equalsIgnoreCase("bigdig")) {
24:                    executeCommand(sender, arguments);
25:                }
26:                return true;
27:            }
28:            return false;
29:        }
30:
31:        public void executeCommand(CommandSender sender,
32:            String[] arguments) {
33:
34:            // set the default dig radius
35:            double rad = 15;
36:            if (arguments.length > 0) {
37:                try {
38:                    // get the user's choice of radius (if any)
39:                    rad = Double.parseDouble(arguments[0]);
40:                    // make sure it's from 5 to 30
41:                    if ((rad < 5) || (rad > 30)) {
42:                        rad = 15;
43:                    }
44:                } catch (NumberFormatException exception) {
45:                    // do nothing
46:                }
47:            }
48:
49:            Player me = (Player) sender;
50:            Location spot = me.getLocation();
```

```
51:        World world = me.getWorld();
52:
53:        // loop through square twice as big as radius
54:        for (double x = spot.getX() - rad; x < spot.getX()
        ➥+ rad;
55:            x++) {
56:
57:            for (double y = spot.getY() - rad; y < spot.getY()
58:                + rad; y++) {
59:
60:                for (double z = spot.getZ() - rad; z <
61:                    spot.getZ() + rad; z++) {
62:
63:                    // get a location in that square
64:                    Location loc = new Location(world, x, y, z);
65:                    // is it close to the bottom of the world?
66:                    if (y < 2) {
67:                        // yes, so don't dig here
68:                        continue;
69:                    }
70:                    // see how far it is from the player
71:                    double xd = x - spot.getX();
72:                    double yd = y - spot.getY();
73:                    double zd = z - spot.getZ();
74:                    double distance = Math.sqrt(xd * xd + yd
                    ➥* yd
75:                        + zd * zd);
76:                    // is it within the radius?
77:                    if (distance < rad) {
78:                        // yes, so turn that block into air
79:                        Block current = world.getBlockAt(loc);
80:                        current.setType(Material.AIR);
81:                    }
```

```
82:                           }
83:                      }
84:                 }
85:
86:                 // play a sound after the dig is dug
87:                 world.playSound(spot, Sound.BURP, 30, 5);
88:                 LOG.info("[BigDig] Dug at ("
89:                      + (int) spot.getX() + ", "
90:                      + (int) spot.getY() + ", "
91:                      + (int) spot.getZ() + ")");
92:            }
93: }
```

If the mod's source code has been saved and there are no errors, you can build the `BigDig` mod's JAR file (choose Run, Clean and Build Project) and deploy it on the Spigot server.

Deploying the Mod

The mod implements a `/bigdig` command on the server after it's deployed.

Within your file system, copy the JAR file `BigDig.jar` from its project folder to the Minecraft server through these steps:

1. Stop the Minecraft server if it is running.

2. Open the folder where you installed the Spigot server, and then open the `BigDig` subfolder.

3. Open the `dist` subfolder.

4. Select the `BigDig` JAR file, and then press Ctrl+C to copy it.

5. Open the Minecraft server folder again, and open its `plugins` subfolder.

6. Press Ctrl+V to copy `BigDig.jar` into it.

Figure 22.1 shows the results of the BigDig mod being used to dig a hole with a 12-block radius. Six startled pigs survived the fall.

FIGURE 22.1

Digging gigantic holes in the Minecraft world.

Backing Up a Minecraft World

This mod has more potential for creating havoc in the Minecraft game world than any other you've developed thus far. You can create very strange landscapes with holes that alter the path of oceans, ponds, and lava pools and send mobs toppling down many blocks to their doom, taking other mobs suddenly into the surface world.

Before you cause too much chaos, you might want to learn how to save a copy of the Minecraft world your server is running.

The Spigot server saves its world in three subfolders under the main folder. The base name of these three folders is the name of the world, which is called world by default when you first run the server.

So for the game world named world, it is stored in the subfolders world, world_nether, and world_nether_the_end. These folders hold the main world, the Nether dimension, and the dimension called The End.

If the game world was named godfather, the subfolders would be godfather, godfather_nether, and godfather_nether_the_end.

To save a backup copy of a Minecraft world, copy all three of the world's subfolders to new folder locations. It is better to do this while the Spigot server is not running, but it is not impossible to restore a world from a copy made off a running server.

The name of a world can be determined by opening the `server.properties` file in the main server folder with any text editor. This is a Java properties file that has a series of field names—one per line—followed by an equal sign and the value for that field. The following line sets the world name:

```
level-name=world
```

If you change this name, the server will look for world subfolders matching the new name. Finding them causes that world to become the current game world. The old game world will still exist in its three folders, but it won't be loaded by the server.

If the Spigot server can't find any subfolders matching the new world name, a new one will be created and stored in newly created subfolders.

While you're puttering around in the `server.properties` file, there's another field you should learn about because it's a cool way to share and explore Minecraft worlds with other players who have their own servers.

The `level-seed` field defines a special number called the *random number seed* for the world. A random number seed is a value that controls how random numbers are generated in a computer program. If the same seed is used, the same random numbers are generated in the same sequence.

Here's the default value for `level-seed` in `server.properties`:

```
level-seed=
```

The seed has not been specified, so the server chooses one at random when the game world is created the first time it is played.

To find the seed when one has not been specified as a server property, run the server, play the game, and enter the command `/seed`. You will see a sequence of numbers that could be ridiculously long, as shown in Figure 22.2.

The seed for the world I've been playing in while writing this book is the following number: 8562810125796183076. If you want to explore the same world on your server, use this line in the `server.properties` file:

```
level-seed=8562810125796183076
```

If you do that and teleport to the location (6659, 126, 328), you should see the same island landscape depicted in Figure 22.2 with only a few small differences. (I built a house at the far left and covered it with a grass roof and knocked down a few trees.)

FIGURE 22.2

Finding a Minecraft world's random number seed.

NOTE   Are you wondering why a Minecraft world would be called `godfather`? That's a reference to 834266025, which has been dubbed "the Godfather of Survival Island Seeds" among players of the XBox 360 version of Minecraft.

Players who find a seed that produces a world that's exceptionally challenging or interesting often share its value on Minecraft message boards so other players can check it out.

If you stumble upon an interesting seed, visit the book's website at www.javaminecraft.com and post a message on the help board to let me know the seed and what makes it distinct.

THE ABSOLUTE MINIMUM

The mod you created in this chapter begins to dig into the potential for writing a Java program that makes alterations to the Minecraft world.

All such changes involve the `Material` class, which has dozens of materials that represent blocks and other objects in the game.

Changing the material of a block to `Material.AIR` is how you dig that block. An idea for how to enhance the `BigDig` mod would involve accessing the player's inventory using `PlayerInventory` and `ItemStack` objects from the `org.bukkit.inventory` package. You could take the blocks that were dug up by the mod and store them in slots in the player's inventory.

In the next chapter, you will use the `Material` class to clear out a forest of trees.

23

IN THIS CHAPTER

- Examine the blocks in a large area of the game world
- Find the block at an (x,y,z) location
- Discover trees by checking for blocks that hold logs
- Store locations that have been searched in an array list
- Avoid server lag by using less memory in a mod
- Create an inner class to represent an (x,y,z) location
- Use the programming technique of recursion

CHOP DOWN A FOREST OF TREES

Minecraft mods that add a new command to the game all start with the same basic framework. You extend the `JavaPlugin` class from the `org.bukkit.plugin.java` package; store the player, world, and server in instance variables; and override the superclass method `onCommand()`.

When the player enters a command, `onCommand()` is called. If the command was entered by a player and it is a command this particular mod knows how to handle, an `executeCommand()` method (or something similar) is called to respond to the command and the value `true` is returned when it's finished.

Within that simple framework, you branch out to do new things with the Spigot class library, working with the classes and interfaces in the library to interact with the Minecraft player, the game world, and the mobs that occupy that world.

This chapter branches out into trees. You create a mod that chops down trees and explores the capabilities of three classes: `Location`, `Block`, and `Material`.

Along the way, you learn how to employ a powerful programming technique called *recursion* and make use of inner classes in Java.

You also run into an issue that will be increasingly important in your mod programming: how to do cool things without taking up too much memory and causing the Minecraft server to lag.

Starting the Project

This chapter describes how to write a mod that deforests a large chunk of the Minecraft landscape with a single command. When the `TreeChopper` mod is deployed on the Minecraft server and a `/choptrees` command is entered, a 3D cube around the player that's 40×40×40 blocks in size is completely denuded of logs.

When the logs of all those trees are chopped down, the leaves of those trees gradually disappear as if the player cleared the forest with an ax.

Begin this chapter's mod project with these steps:

1. Select File, New Project.

2. Select project category `Java` and project type `Java Application`, and click Next.

3. Enter the project name **TreeChopper**.

4. Deselect Create Main Class (if necessary) and click Finish.

5. In the Projects pane, right-click the `Libraries` folder and select the command Add Library.

6. In the Available Libraries pane, select Spigot.

7. Click Add Library.

The `TreeChopper` project is created with no files in it. This mod requires only a simple one-command mod configuration. To create the `plugin.yml` configuration file for the mod in the `src` project folder, follow these steps:

1. Select File, New File.

2. In the Categories pane, select Other.

3. In the File Types pane, select YAML File and click Next.

4. In the File Name field, enter **plugin** (leave off the `.yml`).

5. In the Folder field, enter **src**.

6. Click Finish.

The NetBeans source code editor opens with `plugin.yml` ready to be created. Enter the text of Listing 23.1 into the NetBeans source code editor, and save it when you're done.

LISTING 23.1 The Full Text of `plugin.yml`

```
 1: name: TreeChopper
 2:
 3: author: Your Name Here
 4:
 5: main: com.javaminecraft.TreeChopper
 6:
 7: commands:
 8:     choptrees:
 9:         description: Chop down all trees in a 40x40x40 cube.
10:
11: version: 1.0
```

Creating the Project

The `TreeChopper` mod chops down the wood of all trees in a three-dimensional 40×40×40 cube around the player when the `/choptrees` command is issued. The `executeCommand()` method does the work.

The 3D cube is centered on the player, so the player's (x,y,z) location is stored in the integer variables `spotX`, `spotY`, and `spotZ`.

Nested `for` loops cycle through all the possible x, y, and z locations in the cube:

```
for (int x = spotX - 20; x < spotX + 21; x++) {
    for (int z = spotZ - 20; z < spotZ + 21; z++) {
```

```
for (int y = spotY - 20; y < spotY + 21; y++) {
   // interior of loop here
}
   }
}
```

Inside the loop, a `Location` and `Block` object are created for the current location:

```
Location searchLoc = new Location(world, x, y, z);
Block here = searchLoc.getBlock();
```

The material type of a block can be determined by calling its `getType()` method. There are two values in the `Material` class for logs in Minecraft: `Material.LOG` and `Material.LOG2`. If the current block is made of either material, it is cut down by setting that block's material to air:

```
if (here.getType() == Material.LOG
   | here.getType() == Material.LOG_2) {

   here.setType(Material.AIR);
}
```

This is all the code required to remove every log from a 3D cube that's 40 blocks tall, wide, and deep. But cutting down trees in Minecraft is more complicated than that because some trees might extend beyond the borders of the cube.

CAUTION   You might be tempted to solve this problem by enlarging the size of the 3D cube covered by the `TreeChopper` mod. For instance, you could make the cube 80×80× 80 by changing the values in the three nested `for` loops for x, y, and z.

This biggest drawback to this approach is that it is much more resource intensive. The mod takes up a lot of memory as it examines blocks and turns some of them from logs into air. The more memory required in a mod, the slower it runs and the more likely it will cause lag for all players in the world until it completes its work.

When writing mods, it's important to keep these concerns in mind. The greatest enemy of any dedicated Minecraft player is server lag.

Minecraft has some extra-tall species of trees such as the mega spruce trees, also called *redwoods*. They could extend above the top surface of the cube, as could other trees on an incline above the player when the /choptrees command is used.

This mod looks for trees that extend outside of the cube and will keep looking until every log in the tree has been chopped down no matter how far it extends.

The TreeChopper mod tackles the problem of the outside-the-cube trees by tracking two things with array lists:

- An array list called trees holds the (x,y,z) location of every log block found inside the 3D cube.

- An array list called searched holds every (x,y,z) location in the game world that has been searched looking for logs.

Array lists hold objects, so you might assume that the trees and searched data structures would hold Location objects.

That approach was attempted the first time the mod was developed for this chapter, but it requires a huge number of Location objects to be stored in the program's memory by the Java Virtual Machine (JVM). A 40×40×40 cube contains 64,000 locations, and this mod looks for even more than that because it searches beyond the edges of the cube.

NOTE To learn more about the kinds of trees you might find in the Minecraft world, visit the Minecraft wiki at http://minecraft.gamepedia.com/Tree. The wiki has grown into an enormous user-edited reference for the game, which is extremely useful for mod programmers.

One word of caution, though: If you like to discover things about the game world on your own while exploring as a player, the wiki will spoil some of that experience. Players who edited the wiki have tackled hundreds of the game's mysterious inner workings and figured them out.

When I encountered a desert temple for the first time, I spoiled the surprise because I already read what the wiki says about them.

The mod defines an inner class called Loc that is the simplest possible representation of an (x,y,z) location. An inner class is defined inside a class as if it was an instance variable:

```
class Loc {
    int x, y, z;
```

```
    Loc(int x, int y, int z) {
    this.x = x;
    this.y = y;
    this.z = z;
    }
}
```

The `Loc` class has `x`, `y`, and `z` instance variables that hold the integer (x,y,z) values. It also has a `Loc(int, int, int)` constructor for creating a `Loc` object for the specified location.

This class is much smaller and simpler than the `Location` class. Holding 64,000 or more `Loc` objects in memory causes no noticeable lag.

When the `executeCommand()` method loops through every location in the 3D cube, it creates a `Loc` object each time and adds it to the `searched` array list:

```
Loc loc = new Loc(x, y, z);
searched.add(loc);
```

If a location contains a log, after the log is removed, the `Loc` object is added to the `trees` array list:

```
trees.add(loc);
```

So at this point, every log inside the 3D cube has been chopped down. A `searched` array list contains every (x,y,z) location in the game world that was searched. A `trees` array list contains every (x,y,z) location that used to hold a log.

The last work the `executeCommand()` method does is to loop through the `trees` array list looking for adjacent logs to chop down:

```
for (Loc loc : trees) {
    chopAdjacentTrees(loc);
}
```

The `chopAdjacentTrees(Loc)` method will look at every block adjacent to the specified location to see whether it contains a log. If it does, it will chop down that log by turning it into air.

The method creates a `Location` object and `spotX`, `spotY`, and `spotZ` integers for the x, y, and z coordinates of that location:

```
int spotX = spot.getBlockX();
int spotY = spot.getBlockY();
int spotZ = spot.getBlockZ();
```

Nested `for` loops search a 3×3×3 3D cube around the location:

```
for (int x = spotX - 1; x < spotX + 2; x++) {
    for (int y = spotY - 1; y < spotY + 2; y++) {
        for (int z = spotZ - 1; z < spotZ + 2; z++) {
            // interior of loop here
        }
    }
}
```

A new `Loc` object is created for the location being searched:

```
Loc loc = new Loc(x, y, z);
```

If this location has been searched already, it will be found in the `searched` array list. When this is the case, the loop skips to the next location by using `continue`:

```
if (searched.contains(loc)) {
    continue;
}
```

At this point, if the loop didn't skip, it indicates the location has never been searched. It is added to the array list so it won't be searched again later:

```
searched.add(loc);
```

This location is checked for logs using the same technique as the `executeCommand()` method: A `Location` and `Block` object are created for that location, the block's `getType()` method looks for `Material.LOG` or `Material.LOG_2`, and if one of them is found, the block is turned to `Material.AIR`.

The only task left to do for this location is to call `chopAdjacentTrees(Loc)` for that location because it contains a log:

```
chopAdjacentTrees(loc);
```

Calling a method inside itself is called *recursion*. It's an extremely powerful technique that can do a lot of work in a short amount of code.

Here, recursion makes it possible to keep searching the Minecraft world for logs that grew outside of a 3D cube until there are no more logs adjacent to a log already discovered. So if a tree has 10 logs growing above the cube's top side and some branches that extend to the left and right, calling `chopAdjacentTrees(Loc)` finds them all.

A simpler example of recursion in Java code will illustrate the concept.

The following method is designed to keep doubling an integer until it is greater than 100:

```java
public int doubleNumber(int number) {
    if (number < 100) {
        return doubleNumber(number * 2);
    }
    return number;
}
```

If the method was called with 13 as the initial value (`doubleNumber(13)`), it produces the value 104. The reason is because it doubles 13 to 26, 26 to 52, and 52 to 104 and then is done because 104 is greater than 100.

Here are the method calls it performs, in order:

1. `doubleNumber(13);`

2. `doubleNumber(26);`

3. `doubleNumber(52);`

4. `doubleNumber(104);`

The fourth call to the method makes the `if` conditional false because 104 is greater than 100. So the method returns the value 104, and its work is complete.

The last thing the `TreeChopper` mod does is display a server message noting that the command was performed:

```java
LOG.info("Chopping down trees around (" + spotX + ", " + spotY + ", "
    + spotZ + ")");
```

You're ready to code the mod and see it in action.

Undertake these steps in NetBeans to start developing the `TreeChopper` program:

1. Click File, New File.

2. In the Categories pane, select Java.

3. In the File Types pane, select Empty Java File and click Next.

4. For Class Name, enter **TreeChopper**.

5. For Package, enter **com.javaminecraft**.

6. Click Finish.

The new file opens for editing. Enter the text of Listing 23.2 into that file.

LISTING 23.2 The Full Text of `TreeChopper.java`

```
 1: package com.javaminecraft;
 2:
 3: import java.util.ArrayList;
 4: import java.util.logging.Logger;
 5: import org.bukkit.Location;
 6: import org.bukkit.Material;
 7: import org.bukkit.World;
 8: import org.bukkit.block.Block;
 9: import org.bukkit.command.Command;
10: import org.bukkit.command.CommandSender;
11: import org.bukkit.entity.Player;
12: import org.bukkit.plugin.java.JavaPlugin;
13:
14: public class TreeChopper extends JavaPlugin {
15:     public static final Logger LOG = Logger.getLogger(
16:         "Minecraft");
17:     Player me;
18:     World world;
19:     Location spot;
20:     // trees found inside the 40 by 40 by 40 cube
21:     ArrayList<Loc> trees = new ArrayList<>();
22:     // locations that have been searched for trees
23:     ArrayList<Loc> searched = new ArrayList<>();
24:     // inner class to hold (x,y,z) coordinates
25:     class Loc {
26:         int x, y, z;
27:
28:         Loc(int x, int y, int z) {
29:             this.x = x;
30:             this.y = y;
31:             this.z = z;
32:         }
```

```
33:        }
34:
35:        public boolean onCommand(CommandSender sender,
36:            Command command, String label, String[] arguments) {
37:
38:            me = (Player) sender;
39:            world = me.getWorld();
40:            spot = me.getLocation();
41:
42:            if (label.equalsIgnoreCase("choptrees")) {
43:                if (sender instanceof Player) {
44:                    executeCommand();
45:                }
46:                return true;
47:            }
48:            return false;
49:        }
50:
51:        // chop down trees in 40 by 40 by 40 cube around player
52:        private void executeCommand() {
53:            int spotX = spot.getBlockX();
54:            int spotY = spot.getBlockY();
55:            int spotZ = spot.getBlockZ();
56:            // loop through all possible (x,y,z) locations in cube
57:            for (int x = spotX - 20; x < spotX + 21; x++) {
58:                for (int z = spotZ - 20; z < spotZ + 21; z++) {
59:                    for (int y = spotY - 20; y < spotY + 21; y++) {
60:                        Location searchLoc = new Location(world,
61:                            x, y, z);
62:                        Block here = searchLoc.getBlock();
63:                        Loc loc = new Loc(x, y, z);
64:                        // remember this location was searched
65:                        searched.add(loc);
66:                        if (here.getType() == Material.LOG
67:                            | here.getType() == Material.LOG_2) {
```

```
68:
69:                                    // this is a tree, so chop it down
70:                                    here.setType(Material.AIR);
71:                                    // remember where the tree was found
72:                                    trees.add(loc);
73:                                }
74:                            }
75:                        }
76:                    }
77:                for (Loc loc : trees) {
78:                    chopAdjacentTrees(loc);
79:                }
80:                LOG.info("Chopping down trees around (" + spotX + ", "
81:                    + spotY + ", " + spotZ + ")");
82:            }
83:
84:            // finish chopping down trees that grew outside the cube
85:            private void chopAdjacentTrees(Loc chopLoc) {
86:                Location spot = new Location(world, chopLoc.x,
87:                    chopLoc.y, chopLoc.z);
88:                int spotX = spot.getBlockX();
89:                int spotY = spot.getBlockY();
90:                int spotZ = spot.getBlockZ();
91:                // examine all locations adjacent to this one
92:                for (int x = spotX - 1; x < spotX + 2; x++) {
93:                    for (int y = spotY - 1; y < spotY + 2; y++) {
94:                        for (int z = spotZ - 1; z < spotZ + 2; z++) {
95:                            Loc loc = new Loc(x, y, z);
96:                            if (searched.contains(loc)) {
97:                                // skip locations searched previously
98:                                continue;
99:                            }
100:                           // remember this location was searched
101:                           searched.add(loc);
102:                           Location searchLoc = new Location(world,
103:                               x, y, z);
```

```
104:                              Block here = searchLoc.getBlock();
105:                              if (here.getType() == Material.LOG
106:                                  | here.getType() == Material.LOG_2) {
107:
108:                                  // this is a tree, so chop it down
109:                                  here.setType(Material.AIR);
110:                                  // recursion looks for adjacent trees
111:                                  chopAdjacentTrees(loc);
112:                              }
113:                          }
114:                      }
115:                  }
116:              }
117: }
```

If the mod's source code has been saved and there are no errors, you can build the `TreeChopper` mod's Java Archive (JAR) file and deploy it on the Spigot server

Deploying the Mod

The mod implements a `/choptrees` command on the server after it's deployed.

Within your file system, copy the JAR file `TreeChopper.jar` from its project folder to the Minecraft server through these steps:

1. Stop the Minecraft server if it is running.

2. Open the folder where you installed the Spigot server, and then open the `TreeChopper` subfolder.

3. Open the `dist` subfolder.

4. Select the `TreeChopper` JAR file, and then press Ctrl+C to copy it.

5. Open the Minecraft server folder again, and open its `plugins` subfolder.

6. Press Ctrl+V to copy `TreeChopper.jar` into it.

Figure 23.1 and Figure 23.2 show a top-down look at a snowy forest before and after the `/choptrees` command has been used.

FIGURE 23.1

Looking down from the sky at a forest of trees.

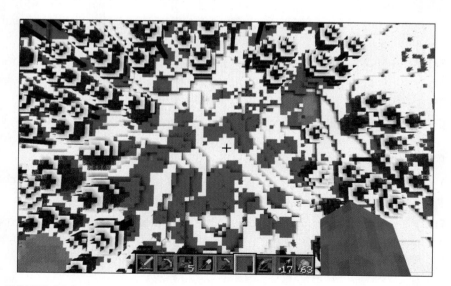

FIGURE 23.2

Looking down again with a new clearing in the middle of the forest.

The command was entered at the ground level directly below the vantage point.

THE ABSOLUTE MINIMUM

The mods described in this book are by necessity simple. It is easier to learn and master the concepts required of a Minecraft mod coder in a 100-line program than in the mods you'll find shared on websites, which can be 1,000 or even 10,000 lines long.

A lot of mod programming is iterative. You do something simple, such as looping through every block in a 3D cube and turning every block of log into air. In a flash, the cube contains no trees and leaves for those trees begin to disappear, dropping their apples and saplings on the ground.

When the mod's simple task has been accomplished, you notice that there are limitations which make it less useful.

Some trees only have been partially chopped down, leaving log blocks floating in the air. That's not good.

So you return to the mod and figure out how to solve that problem.

But sometimes your solution introduces problems of its own. The mod begins to run noticeably slower. Messages in the server window indicate that it is suffering from lag.

The most likely culprit for this problem is that the mod is taking up way too much memory. The array list you created that holds thousands of Location objects in the 3D cube is probably the problem, you surmise.

Finally, you try another approach and create an inner class that holds the simplest possible object to represent an (x,y,z) location. You rewrite the mod to use it in the array list.

Eureka! The mod clears a forest in an instant. You find a way to make it chase a tree outside the 3D cube and chop all of its logs.

Programming a mod is a lot like making a building in Minecraft. At first your home is just a small, square building made of dirt or cobblestone with a door that keeps the mobs out at night. Over time you find ways to improve it and make it cooler.

Mods go through the same stages of growth, and at some point you have finished something you are proud of and want to share with your friends, and perhaps the whole community of Minecraft players.

24

RESPOND TO EVENTS IN THE GAME

Mods can do something once when a command is entered by a player. Enter a `/choptrees` command and chop down a forest of trees.

Mods can do something that affects game play for a sustained time. Enter `/petwolf` multiple times and attract a pack of wolves who come to your defense whenever mobs attack.

Mods also can do nothing.

The mod you create during this chapter does nothing until an event happens in the game.

An *event* is an object that represent things that can happen as a program runs. When a user clicks a Save button, that's an event. When a user closes a window, that's another event. Waiting for an event to happen and doing something in response is a kind of programming called *event handling*. A Java class that handles an event is called an *event listener*.

In Minecraft, hundreds of different events take place during game play. The mod you develop in this chapter does nothing—until a player moves.

Starting the Project

This chapter's `StoneWalker` mod turns the ground under the player into stone if that block is dirt, grass, gravel, or cobblestone.

Unlike other mods that changed blocks on a one-time basis in response to a user command, the `StoneWalker` mod will continue to transform blocks in real time as the player moves around. This requires event handling, a technique that enables a Java program to respond to events as they happen.

A `/stonewalk` command turns the mod on, and a `/stopstonewalk` command turns it off.

Begin this chapter's mod project with these steps:

1. Select File, New Project.
2. Select project category `Java` and project type `Java Application`, and click Next.
3. Enter the project name **StoneWalker**.
4. Deselect Create Main Class and click Finish.
5. In the Projects pane, right-click the `Libraries` folder and select the command Add Library.
6. In the Available Libraries pane, select Spigot.
7. Click Add Library.

The `StoneWalker` project is created with no files in it. This mod requires only a simple one-command mod configuration. To create the `plugin.yml` configuration file for the mod in the `src` project folder, follow these steps:

1. Select File, New File.
2. In the Categories pane, select Other.
3. In the File Types pane, select YAML File and click Next.
4. In the File Name field, enter **plugin** (leave off the `.yml`).
5. In the Folder field, enter **src**.
6. Click Finish.

The NetBeans source code editor opens with `plugin.yml` ready to be created. Enter the text of Listing 24.1 into the NetBeans source code editor, and save it when you're done. This configuration file defines the two commands supported by the `StoneWalker` mod. Because neither command takes any command-line arguments, no `usage` field appears in the file.

LISTING 24.1 The Full Text of `plugin.yml`

```
 1: name: StoneWalker
 2:
 3: author: Your Name Here
 4:
 5: main: com.javaminecraft.StoneWalker
 6:
 7: commands:
 8:     stonewalk:
 9:         description: Turn ground to stone as player walks over.
10:     stopstonewalk:
11:         description: Turn off this effect.
12:
13: version: 1.0
```

Creating the Project

The `StoneWalker` mod declares a Boolean instance variable called `isStoneWalking` that tracks whether the mod is on or off:

```
private boolean isStoneWalking = false;
```

The variable is `true` when the mod is on, which causes the ground under the player to be transformed into stone. It is `false` when the mod is off.

The other instance variables for the class are the `Player`, `World`, and `Location` objects.

Like all mods that respond to commands, `StoneWalker` overrides the `onCommand()` method.

After checking to make sure the command was issued by a `Player` object, the method looks for the `/stonewalk` and `/stopstonewalk` commands. When it finds one, it sets the value of `isStoneWalking` and displays a message to the Minecraft server window:

```
if (label.equalsIgnoreCase("stonewalk")) {
    isStoneWalking = true;
    LOG.info("[StoneWalker] Command on");
    return true;
}
if (label.equalsIgnoreCase("stopstonewalk")) {
    isStoneWalking = false;
    LOG.info("[StoneWalker] Command off");
    return true;
}
```

That's all the `onCommand()` method requires. It does not call any other methods, unlike the other mods you have created in previous chapters.

The reason for such a simple method is that the work the `StoneWalker` mod performs is in response to an event in the game. When a player moves to a new block, it is an event in the Minecraft game.

The `JavaPlugin` class that is the superclass of all Minecraft mods in the Spigot class library can monitor events and call methods to indicate they have happened. This is called event handling, and it is a common practice in programming.

 NOTE Java programs that have a graphical user interface require event handling through the `java.awt.event` package. A class implements a listener interface for the events it wants to monitor and is registered as a listener. Any time a user clicks a button, moves a slider, enters text with the keyboard, or interacts with the interface in some other way, the listener that monitors that type of interaction is called.

A mod indicates that it is listening for events through the `Listener` interface in the `org.bukkit.event` package. When the class is declared with a `class` statement, an `implements` keyword is followed by the name of the interface. Here's the statement that this mod requires:

```
class StoneWalker extends JavaPlugin implements Listener {
```

The mod must be registered as an event listener when the mod loads. This can be accomplished by overriding the `onEnable()` method from the `JavaPlugin` superclass:

```
@Override
    public void onEnable() {
        // ...
    }
}
```

The `@Override` annotation notes that this method overrides the same method in its superclass.

Inside the method, a `Server` object is created from the `org.bukkit` package. As you might have guessed, this represents the Minecraft server and enables a mod to learn more about it. The `Server` object has a `getPluginManager()` method that returns an object that controls how mods function inside the server:

```
PluginManager manager = server.getPluginManager();
```

The `PluginManager` object is from the `org.bukkit.plugin` package. It has a method called `registerEvents(Listener, Plugin)` that tells the manager two things necessary for event handling:

- The class that will handle the events, which must implement `Listener`

- The mod's class, which is a subclass of `JavaPlugin`

For this mod, both of these things are the `StoneWalker` class, so the `this` keyword is used as both arguments:

```
manager.registerEvents(this, this);
```

 NOTE   The concept of `this` can be difficult for new Java programmers to figure out the first time it is encountered. It's a keyword that refers to the object in which a statement exists. So when `this` is used in a statement in the `StoneWalker` class, it refers to the `StoneWalker` object that executes the statement when the program is run.

Here's the finished `onEnable()` method, which is called when the mod is loaded and enabled by the Minecraft server:

```
@Override
public void onEnable() {
    Server server = getServer();
    PluginManager manager = server.getPluginManager();
    manager.registerEvents(this, this);
}
```

The final step is to add the event handler method associated with the in-game event the mod needs to monitor. A mod can have more than one such method, but `StoneWalker` only needs one that listens when a player moves onto a new block.

There are hundreds of events in the Spigot class library, grouped into packages that begin with `org.bukkit.event` in their names. The list of current packages provides a clue to the type of events they cover:

- `org.bukkit.event.block`
- `org.bukkit.event.enchantment`
- `org.bukkit.event.entity`
- `org.bukkit.event.hanging`
- `org.bukkit.event.inventory`
- `org.bukkit.event.painting`
- `org.bukkit.event.player`
- `org.bukkit.event.server`
- `org.bukkit.event.vehicle`
- `org.bukkit.event.weather`
- `org.bukkit.event.world`

Events caused by a player are grouped into the `org.bukkit.event.player` package. There are 50 different classes for events in this package as of the current Spigot version. One is `PlayerMoveEvent`.

The event handler method that receives an event has a standard name in Spigot: The lowercase text on followed by the event's class name. So for `PlayerMoveEvent`, the method is `onPlayerMove()`.

This method must be `public` and does not return a value. The method has only one argument, a `PlayerMoveEvent` object.

Putting this together, the mod needs this method:

```
@EventHandler
public void onPlayerMove(PlayerMoveEvent event) {
    // ...
}
```

The method is preceded by a new annotation called `@EventHandler`. This annotation belongs to the `org.bukkit.event` package, so NetBeans will offer to import it (if you don't add it yourself). This annotation indicates that the method handles an event generated as a Minecraft game is played.

The argument to an event handler method represents the event. The first thing you often will do in the method is to find out more about an event.

A `PlayerMoveEvent` object has a `getPlayer()` method that identifies the player who moved:

```
Player player = event.getPlayer();
```

This is compared to the mod's `Player` instance variable to make sure it's the player running the mod:

```
if (player != me) {
    return;
}
```

The `return` statement exits the method, causing nothing to happen in response to the event.

The method also must ensure that the mod is currently on by checking the Boolean instance variable `isStoneWalking`:

```
if (!isStoneWalking) {
    return;
}
```

The event has `getFrom()` and `getTo()` methods that return the `Location` objects for the locations the player came from and went to, respectively.

This mod transforms a block to stone after the player leaves it, so the `getFrom()` method is called:

```
Location from = event.getFrom();
```

The block at this location is retrieved by calling the `Location` method `getBlock()`:

```
Block block = from.getBlock();
```

The purpose of this mod is to transform blocks under the player, not the ones the player occupies.

A `Block` object has a `getRelative(BlockFace)` method that retrieves an adjacent block through one of the faces (sides) of that block. These faces are indicated by the `BlockFace` enumeration from the `org.bukkit.block` package. There are values DOWN, UP, NORTH, SOUTH, EAST, and WEST, as well as NORTH_EAST, NORTH_WEST, SOUTH_EAST, and SOUTH_WEST. Finally, there are EAST_NORTH_EAST, EAST_SOUTH_EAST, NORTH_NORTH_EAST, NORTH_NORTH_WEST, SOUTH_SOUTH_EAST, SOUTH_SOUTH_WEST, WEST_NORTH_WEST, and WEST_SOUTH_WEST.

This mod needs the block right below the player:

```
Block down = block.getRelative(BlockFace.DOWN);
Material below = down.getType();
```

Only four types of material are turned to stone: `Material.DIRT`, `Material.COBBLESTONE`, `Material.GRAVEL`, and `Material.GRASS`. The mod checks for this with a new `okToTransform(Material)` method that returns `true` if the specified material should be transformed and `false` otherwise. Here's part of that method:

```
private boolean okToTransform(Material mat) {
    if (mat == Material.DIRT) {
        return true;
    }
    // ...
}
```

The `onPlayerMoveEvent()` method calls `okToTransform()` and transforms the stone if the method returns `true`:

```
if (okToTransform(below)) {
    down.setType(Material.STONE);
}
```

Undertake these steps in NetBeans to start developing the `StoneWalker` program:

1. Click File, New File.

2. In the Categories pane, select Java.

3. In the File Types pane, select Empty Java File and click Next.

4. For Class Name, enter **StoneWalker**.

5. For Package, enter **com.javaminecraft**.

6. Click Finish.

The new file opens for editing. Enter the text of Listing 24.2 into that file.

LISTING 24.2   The Full Text of StoneWalker.java

```
 1: package com.javaminecraft;
 2:
 3: import java.util.logging.Logger;
 4: import org.bukkit.Location;
 5: import org.bukkit.Material;
 6: import org.bukkit.Server;
 7: import org.bukkit.World;
 8: import org.bukkit.block.Block;
 9: import org.bukkit.block.BlockFace;
10: import org.bukkit.command.Command;
11: import org.bukkit.command.CommandSender;
12: import org.bukkit.entity.Player;
13: import org.bukkit.event.EventHandler;
14: import org.bukkit.event.Listener;
15: import org.bukkit.event.player.PlayerMoveEvent;
16: import org.bukkit.plugin.PluginManager;
17: import org.bukkit.plugin.java.JavaPlugin;
18:
19: public class StoneWalker extends JavaPlugin
20:     implements Listener {
21:
22:     public static final Logger LOG = Logger.getLogger(
23:         "Minecraft");
24:     private boolean isStoneWalking = false;
25:     Player me;
26:     World world;
27:     Location spot;
28:
29:     @Override
30:     public boolean onCommand(CommandSender sender,
31:         Command command, String label, String[] arguments) {
32:
33:         me = (Player) sender;
34:         world = me.getWorld();
```

```
35:            spot = me.getLocation();
36:
37:        if (sender instanceof Player) {
38:            if (label.equalsIgnoreCase("stonewalk")) {
39:                isStoneWalking = true;
40:                LOG.info("[StoneWalker] Command on");
41:                return true;
42:            }
43:            if (label.equalsIgnoreCase("stopstonewalk")) {
44:                isStoneWalking = false;
45:                LOG.info("[StoneWalker] Command off");
46:                return true;
47:            }
48:        }
49:        return false;
50:    }
51:
52:    @Override
53:    public void onEnable() {
54:        // make this class an event listener
55:        Server server = getServer();
56:        PluginManager manager = server.getPluginManager();
57:        manager.registerEvents(this, this);
58:    }
59:
60:    @EventHandler
61:    public void onPlayerMove(PlayerMoveEvent event) {
62:        Player player = event.getPlayer();
63:        Location from = event.getFrom();
64:        if (player != me) {
65:            // some other player is moving, ignore
66:            return;
67:        }
68:        if (!isStoneWalking) {
69:            // stonewalk is off
70:            return;
```

```
71:             }
72:             LOG.info("[StoneWalker] Player moved to ("
73:                 + from.getBlockX() + ", " + from.getBlockY() + ", "
74:                 + from.getBlockZ() + ")");
75:             // get block player is in
76:             Block block = from.getBlock();
77:             // get block and material underfoot
78:             Block down = block.getRelative(BlockFace.DOWN);
79:             Material below = down.getType();
80:             if (okToTransform(below)) {
81:                 // turn underfoot block to stone
82:                 LOG.info("[StoneWalker] Transforming to stone");
83:                 down.setType(Material.STONE);
84:             }
85:         }
86:
87:     private boolean okToTransform(Material mat) {
88:         if (mat == Material.DIRT) {
89:             return true;
90:         }
91:         if (mat == Material.COBBLESTONE) {
92:             return true;
93:         }
94:         if (mat == Material.GRAVEL) {
95:             return true;
96:         }
97:         if (mat == Material.GRASS) {
98:             return true;
99:         }
100:        return false;
101:     }
102: }
```

If the mod's source code has been saved and there are no errors, you can build the StoneWalker mod's Java Archive (JAR) file and deploy it on the Spigot server.

Deploying the Mod

Within your file system, copy the JAR file `StoneWalker.jar` from its project folder to the Minecraft server through these steps:

1. Stop the Minecraft server if it is running.

2. Open the folder where you installed the Spigot server, and then open the `StoneWalker` subfolder.

3. Open the `dist` subfolder.

4. Select the `StoneWalker` JAR file, and then press Ctrl+C to copy it.

5. Open the Minecraft server folder again, and open its `plugins` subfolder.

6. Press Ctrl+V to copy `StoneWalker.jar` into it.

After the mod is loaded, type **/stonewalk** to turn on the mod's stone-transforming abilities and **/stopstonewalk** to turn them off.

Figure 24.1 shows a floor of stone created by a player who ran across a grassy field in an extremely orderly path.

FIGURE 24.1

Turning the ground underfoot to stone with player movement.

THE ABSOLUTE MINIMUM

During this chapter, you were introduced to an entirely different kind of mod.

Instead of doing something in response to a command, you made the mod wait to take action until a player generated an event by moving from one block to another.

The mod is an event listener waiting for the class of event it handles: the `PlayerMoveEvent` class from the `org.bukkit.player` package. A class becomes an event listener by using `implements` in the class declaration and registering to monitor events in the Minecraft server's mod manager.

When a player moves, the event occurs and is detected when the `onPlayerMoveEvent()` method is called in the event listener class.

A mod that listens to events can have a large impact on the play experience of Minecraft. They're one of the most entertaining ways to extend the game by programming mods.

IN THIS CHAPTER

- Track damage to mobs during combat
- Listen to events when a mob targets a player
- Listen to events when a player attacks a mob
- Display information about a mob in the game
- Retrieve a mob's current health and maximum health
- Select different colors for text output in game text
- Use NetBeans to learn about the Spigot class library

25

DISPLAY A MOB'S HEALTH DURING COMBAT

Although Minecraft is commonly described as a building game, there's also a lot of enjoyment to be had from facing off in combat against mobs, other players, and the occasional unfortunate animal when you need food, a leather hide, chicken feathers, or some other item.

The mod for this chapter enhances combat by adding a feature to Minecraft that appears in many MMORPGs and other games: a health bar above a foe that indicates how much damage it has taken in battle.

The mod displays the bar with the help of two more event-handling methods for objects in the org.bukkit.entity package: onEntityDamage() and onEntityTarget(). The method names tell you the names of the event classes, which are EntityDamageEvent and EntityTargetEvent. Just drop the on at the start of the method name and add Event to the end. This convention is followed throughout the event-handling classes in the Spigot class library.

It's time to enter the fray.

Starting the Project

The `HealthChecker` mod enhances combat in Minecraft by showing the player the current health state of mobs during a battle. A health bar appears above the mob, with green bars for health and red bars for damage.

Figure 25.1 shows a zombie that is not long for this world.

FIGURE 25.1

Showing a mob's health bar during Minecraft combat.

With 9 green exclamation points and 11 red exclamation points displayed in Figure 25.1, the zombie has 45 percent of its health remaining—a healthy zombie would have all 20 in green.

Begin this chapter's mod project with these steps:

1. Select File, New Project.

2. Select project category `Java` and project type `Java Application`, and click Next.

3. Enter the project name **HealthChecker**.

4. Deselect Create Main Class and click Finish.

5. In the Projects pane, right-click the `Libraries` folder and select the command Add Library.

6. In the Available Libraries pane, select Spigot.

7. Click Add Library.

The `HealthChecker` project is created with no files in it. This mod requires only a simple one-command mod configuration. To create the `plugin.yml` configuration file for the mod in the `src` project folder, follow these steps:

1. Select File, New File.

2. In the Categories pane, select Other.

3. In the File Types pane, select YAML File and click Next.

4. In the File Name field, enter `plugin` (leave off the `.yml`).

5. In the Folder field, enter `src`.

6. Click Finish.

The mod has one command, `/healthcheck`, that turns the health bar display on and off (the default is off). The command `/healthcheck on` turns it on, and `/healthcheck off` turns it off, as you will see in the `plugin.yml` file.

The NetBeans source code editor opens with `plugin.yml` ready to be created. Enter the text of Listing 25.1 into the NetBeans source code editor, and save it when you're done.

LISTING 25.1 The Full Text of `plugin.yml`

```
 1: name: HealthChecker
 2:
 3: author: Your Name Here
 4:
 5: main: com.javaminecraft.HealthChecker
 6:
 7: commands:
 8:    healthcheck:
 9:       description: Toggle display of mob health
10:       usage: /<command> [on|off]
11:
12: version: 1.0
```

Creating the Project

The `HealthChecker` mod handles events, which requires three things in the program to support this functionality:

- The class must `implement` the `Listener` interface from the package `org.bukkit.event`.

- In the `onEnable()` method, the mod must be designated as the class listening to events.

- An event handler method must be defined for each event that will be monitored, each preceded by an `@EventHandler` annotation.

The mod has a `display` Boolean instance variable that controls whether the health points of a mob are displayed (`true`) or not (`false`):

```
private boolean display = false;
```

This variable is declared `private` because it is used only within this Java class.

The `onCommand()` method's only job is setting `display` to `true` when the command /healthcheck on is entered and `false` when /healthcheck off is entered:

```
if (arguments.length > 0) {
    if (arguments[0].equals("on")) {
    display = true;
}
    if (arguments[0].equals("off")) {
        display = false;
    }
}
```

The `HealthChecker` mod doesn't display the health of all mobs all the time. Instead, it shows up only when that information would be useful to a player.

Two events in Spigot are appropriate times for a mob's health to be displayed—`EntityDamageEvent`, which occurs when a mob takes damage, and `EntityTargetEvent`, which occurs when a mob targets a player for attack.

An `EntityDamageEvent` object is the argument to an `onEntityDamage()` method. The event has a `getEntity()` method that returns the mob which has been damaged.

A check to make sure this mob really is a `LivingEntity` begins the code in the event-handling method. If it is, a `LivingEntity` object is created by casting the object returned by `getEntity()` so that it can be the only argument to the mod's `showHealth(LivingEntity)` method:

```
@EventHandler
public void onEntityDamage(EntityDamageEvent event) {
    if (event.getEntity() instanceof LivingEntity) {
        LivingEntity entity = (LivingEntity) event.getEntity();
        showHealth(entity);
    }
}
```

The same thing happens with an `EntityTargetEvent` object in an `onEntityTarget()` method. The `showHealth()` method is called with the mob that caused the event.

This mod has two methods that display a health points bar above a mob:

- The `showHealth(LivingEntity)` method is called to display the mob's health points.

- The `makeBarGraph(int, int, String)` method builds the health bar.

In the `showHealth()` method, the first thing that happens is a check whether the mod's functionality is on. If not, the method ends without doing anything:

```
if (!display) {
    return;
}
```

A mob's current and maximum health can be determined by calling its `getHealth()` and `getMaxHealth()` methods, respectively. These methods return `double` values, which this mod casts to integers:

```
int maxHealth = (int) entity.getMaxHealth();
int currentHealth = (int) entity.getHealth();
```

The type of mob is returned as an `EntityType` object by calling the mob's `getType()` method. This can be converted to a string with the `toString()` method:

```
String entityName = entity.getType().toString();
```

These three pieces of information—the current health, maximum health, and mob type as a string—are the three arguments required to make the health bar. The `makeBarGraph()` method is called:

```
String text = makeBarGraph(currentHealth, maxHealth,
    entityName);
```

The bar graph returned by the method is displayed above the mob by calling the mob's `setCustomName(String)` method:

```
entity.setCustomName(text);
```

The last method to implement in this project is `makeBarGraph()`. Here's the declaration for the method:

```
public String makeBarGraph(int x, int y, String prefix) {
    // ...
}
```

This method uses an instance variable of the class to define the scale of the graph, which is the number of exclamation points that are displayed in the bar:

```
private static int SCALE = 20;
```

The variable's name is in all caps to show that it's a constant that does not change in value anywhere in the program.

The first statement in the `makeBarGraph()` method calculates the number of exclamation points that represent the mob's current health:

```
int percent = (int) ((x / (float) y) * SCALE);
```

The zombie shown earlier in Figure 25.1 had 9 out of 20 health points. So, when `makeBarGraph()` was called, the first 2 arguments to the method were an x current health of 9 and a y maximum health of 20.

With those values, `percent` will equal 9 because (9 / 20) × 20 equals 9. So 9 exclamation points ("!!!!!!!!!") will be in the zombie's health bar.

A new `StringBuilder()` object is created to hold the health bar's output text:

```
StringBuilder output = new StringBuilder(12 + SCALE +
➥prefix.length());
```

The output is set to different colors using `ChatColor`, an enumeration in the `org.bukkit` package that holds the 22 colors permitted in Minecraft chat messages.

This statement sets the current output color to white:

```
output.append(ChatColor.WHITE);
```

The mob type and the additional text ": [" is output:

```
output.append(prefix);
output.append(": [");
```

This text will be displayed in the current color, white.

Next, the health bar will display the exclamation points for the mob's current health, which will be green:

```
output.append(ChatColor.GREEN);
```

This code ensure that `percent` is greater than 0, which means at least one exclamation point should be displayed; then it uses a `for` loop to display the green exclamation points:

```
if (percent > 0) {
    for (int i = 0; i < (percent); i++) {
        output.append("!");
    }
}
```

The rest of the mob's health bar represents how much damage it has taken and is shown in red:

```
output.append(ChatColor.RED);
```

This code ensures that `percent` is less than `SCALE`, which indicates the mob is not 100% healthy. Another `for` loop displays the red exclamation points:

```
if (percent < SCALE) {
    for (int i = 0; i < (SCALE - percent); i++) {
        output.append("!");
    }
}
```

Finally, the text "]" is displayed in white:

```
output.append(ChatColor.WHITE);
output.append("]");
```

The method completes its work by returning the finished `StringBuilder` output as a string:

```
return output.toString();
```

Undertake these steps in NetBeans to start developing the `HealthChecker` program:

1. Click File, New File.

2. In the Categories pane, select Java.

3. In the File Types pane, select Empty Java File and click Next.

4. For Class Name, enter **HealthChecker**.

5. For Package, enter **com.javaminecraft**.

6. Click Finish.

The new file opens for editing. Enter the text of Listing 25.2 into that file.

LISTING 25.2 The Full Text of `HealthChecker.java`

```
 1: package com.javaminecraft;
 2:
 3: import java.util.logging.Logger;
 4: import org.bukkit.ChatColor;
 5: import org.bukkit.Server;
 6: import org.bukkit.command.Command;
 7: import org.bukkit.command.CommandSender;
 8: import org.bukkit.entity.LivingEntity;
 9: import org.bukkit.entity.Player;
10: import org.bukkit.event.EventHandler;
11: import org.bukkit.event.Listener;
12: import org.bukkit.event.entity.EntityDamageEvent;
13: import org.bukkit.event.entity.EntityTargetEvent;
14: import org.bukkit.plugin.PluginManager;
15: import org.bukkit.plugin.java.JavaPlugin;
16:
17: public class HealthChecker extends JavaPlugin
18:     implements Listener {
19:
20:     public static final Logger LOG = Logger.getLogger(
21:         "Minecraft");
22:     private boolean display = false;
23:     private static int SCALE = 20;
```

```
24:
25:      @Override
26:      public boolean onCommand(CommandSender sender,
27:          Command command, String label, String[] arguments) {
28:
29:          if (sender instanceof Player) {
30:              if (label.equalsIgnoreCase("healthcheck")) {
31:                  if (arguments.length > 0) {
32:                      if (arguments[0].equals("on")) {
33:                          display = true;
34:                      }
35:                      if (arguments[0].equals("off")) {
36:                          display = false;
37:                      }
38:                  }
39:                  return true;
40:              }
41:          }
42:          return false;
43:      }
44:
45:      @Override
46:      public void onEnable() {
47:          Server server = getServer();
48:          PluginManager manager = server.getPluginManager();
49:          manager.registerEvents(this, this);
50:      }
51:
52:      // display a mob's current health
53:      public void showHealth(LivingEntity entity) {
54:          if (!display) {
55:              return;
56:          }
57:          int maxHealth = (int) entity.getMaxHealth();
58:          int currentHealth = (int) entity.getHealth();
59:          String entityName = entity.getType().toString();
```

```
60:            String text = makeBarGraph(currentHealth, maxHealth,
61:                entityName);
62:            entity.setCustomName(text);
63:        }
64:
65:    // make the health bar graph (x=current, y=maximum
66:    public String makeBarGraph(int x, int y,
67:        String prefix) {
68:
69:        int percent = (int) ((x / (float) y) * SCALE);
70:        StringBuilder output = new StringBuilder(12 + SCALE
71:            + prefix.length());
72:        output.append(ChatColor.WHITE);
73:        output.append(prefix);
74:        output.append(": [");
75:        output.append(ChatColor.GREEN);
76:        if (percent > 0) {
77:            // show bars in graph
78:            for (int i = 0; i < (percent); i++) {
79:                output.append("!");
80:            }
81:        }
82:        output.append(ChatColor.RED);
83:        if (percent < SCALE) {
84:            // show bars in graph
85:            for (int i = 0; i < (SCALE - percent); i++) {
86:                output.append("!");
87:            }
88:        }
89:        output.append(ChatColor.WHITE);
90:        output.append("]");
91:        return output.toString();
92:    }
93:
94:    // monitor when an entity takes damage
95:    @EventHandler
```

```
96:        public void onEntityDamage(EntityDamageEvent event) {
97:            if (event.getEntity() instanceof LivingEntity) {
98:                // a living mob has been damaged
99:                LivingEntity entity = (LivingEntity)
100:                    event.getEntity();
101:                showHealth(entity);
102:            }
103:        }
104:
105:        // monitor when an entity is targeted by a mob
106:        @EventHandler
107:        public void onEntityTarget(EntityTargetEvent event) {
108:            if (event.getEntity() instanceof LivingEntity) {
109:                LivingEntity entity = (LivingEntity)
110:                    event.getEntity();
111:                showHealth(entity);
112:            }
113:        }
114: }
```

If the mod's source code has been saved and there are no errors, you can build the `HealthChecker` mod's Java Archive (JAR) file and deploy it on the Spigot server.

Deploying the Mod

Within your file system, copy the JAR file `HealthChecker.jar` from its project folder to the Minecraft server through these steps:

1. Stop the Minecraft server if it is running.

2. Open the folder where you installed the Spigot server, and then open the `HealthChecker` subfolder.

3. Open the `dist` subfolder..

4. Select the `HealthChecker` JAR file, and then press Ctrl+C to copy it.

5. Open the Minecraft server folder again, and open its `plugins` subfolder.

6. Press Ctrl+V to copy `HealthChecker.jar` into it.

CAUTION One thing I learned during the development of the `HealthChecker` mod was that the health bar doesn't always appear as promptly as you might expect. Sometimes a mob will target you and the bar isn't seen until you hit the mob in combat. This might be happening when the server isn't processing events as quickly because it is occupied with other tasks.

This is something you'll have to learn through testing as you create mods. The Minecraft world is juggling an enormous amount of tasks as the game is played—not only from mods, but also from its own code.

When the mod has been deployed, type this command to active its functionality:

```
/healthcheck on
```

When a mob targets you for attack or you damage a mob by attacking it, the health bar appears preceded by the type of mob. May all your health bars be red.

Learning Spigot Methods from NetBeans

You will spend a lot of time on the Web reading the Spigot Javadoc documentation as you learn how to become an expert at Minecraft mod programming.

You can find out more on the events that mobs generate during the game by loading your web browser and following these steps:

1. Visit the documentation home page at https://hub.spigotmc.org/javadocs/spigot.

2. In the Packages frame at the upper left, click `org.bukkit.event.entity`. The classes and interfaces in the package are loaded in the frame at the lower left.

3. Scroll through that list until you find one that sounds interesting, such as `EntityExplodeEvent`, and click it.

The official documentation for the class appears in the main frame. You can learn an enormous amount about the class, including the superclasses above it in the Spigot class hierarchy, the constructor to use when creating an object of this class, and the methods you can call.

Different events have different methods that pertain to what the event does.

For an explosion, there's a `setYield(float)` method that determines the percentage of blocks that will be dropped to the ground after the explosion instead of being completely destroyed. There also is a `getYield()` method that reveals the current yield percentage.

The documentation's description for the `getLocation()` method, which returns the spot where the explosion occurred, has this amusingly grim sentence: "It is not possible to get this value from the Entity as the Entity no longer exists in the world."

Reading the Javadoc documentation is enormously helpful, but there's another, quicker way you can find out some things about the Spigot classes you use in a Minecraft mod.

NetBeans will pop up helpful information about the classes as you enter the source code of a mod.

To see this in action, go back to the `HealthChecker.java` class you entered from Listing 25.2 and add a blank line after Line 56.

On this line, type the variable name **entity** and follow it with a period (.) character, which tells NetBeans you might be starting to call a method of that object.

NetBeans pops up a window below the line you're typing. This window contains a list of all of that object's methods. You can scroll up and down the window to learn these things about each method:

- The method name

- The arguments it takes, if any

- The primitive type or class of those arguments

- The primitive type or class returned by the method, or `void` if none is returned

You can select one of these methods by scrolling to it and pressing Enter or clicking the method name. It will be entered for you in the source code editor.

In Figure 25.2, the window has scrolled to the `damage()` method. This method takes a `double` value as an argument and does not return a value, as indicated by `void` at the right margin of the window.

The Spigot class library is well-designed, and many methods have names that make their purpose pretty clear. The `damage()` method takes the specified number of health points away from the mob as if it was struck by a player's sword.

By paying attention to this feature of NetBeans, you can learn a lot about Spigot without leaving the source code editor.

Before you leave the NetBeans editor, either take out that line you just typed or finish the statement by calling one of the mob's methods.

Current Line

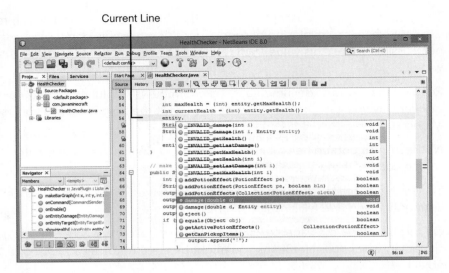

FIGURE 25.2
Learning about an object's methods in the NetBeans source code editor.

THE ABSOLUTE MINIMUM

The battle is over and you have emerged victorious with another mod to put in your warchest.

The `HealthChecker` mod showed how to write an event-handling class that listens to two new types of events related to mobs. Because mobs are called *entities* in the Spigot class library, these events are `EntityDamageEvent` and `EntityTargetEvent`, both from the `org.bukkit.entity` package.

The event-handling methods for the classes can be inferred from those class names. Add the text `on` to the front and drop the `Event` from the end, giving you `onEntityDamage()` and `onEntityTarget()`.

Like all the other event-handling methods, these take the associated event object as their only argument.

There are 11 different event packages in Spigot. The biggest is the one for mobs, `org.bukkit.event.entity`, which has 42 classes.

Because you'll be spending a lot of time poring over the Javadoc documentation for Spigot, this chapter showed how to get a head start on that as you write Java programs in the NetBeans source code editor.

26

MAKE A WORLD CHANGE OVER TIME

The world in a Minecraft game is incredibly huge. A player can walk in the same direction for 30 million blocks before reaching an edge.

But as big as it is, the world remains almost entirely the same without a player's actions. If you left an area and didn't come back to it for weeks while exploring elsewhere, when you returned, the hills, trees, and other objects would be the same—aside from the occasional block moved at random by the inexplicable whims of an enderman. The mobs would be in different places, of course, but they would be the same types of mobs who occupied that area originally.

One way to introduce some variability into the game is with mods.

You can make changes to the world over time that aren't caused, directly or indirectly, by a player.

This chapter's mod can fill a clearing with trees through an unlikely source: an army of mutated chickens.

Starting the Project

This chapter's mod, `JohnnyApplechicken`, turns ordinary chickens into mutants that lay trees instead of eggs.

Begin this chapter's mod project with these steps:

1. Select File, New Project.

2. Select project category `Java`, project type `Java Application`, and click Next.

3. Enter the project name **JohnnyApplechicken**.

4. Deselect Create Main Class and click Finish.

5. In the Projects pane, right-click the `Libraries` folder and select the command Add Library.

6. In the Available Libraries pane, select Spigot.

7. Click Add Library.

The `JohnnyApplechicken` project is created with no files in it. This mod requires only a simple one-command mod configuration with a `usage` field to explain the arguments that are supported. To create the `plugin.yml` configuration file for the mod in the `src` project folder, follow these steps:

1. Select File, New File.

2. In the Categories pane, select Other.

3. In the File Types pane, select YAML File and click Next.

4. In the File Name field, enter **plugin** (leave off the .yml).

5. In the Folder field, enter **src**.

6. Click Finish.

The NetBeans source code editor opens with `plugin.yml` ready to be created. Enter the text of Listing 26.1 into the NetBeans source code editor, and save it when you're done.

LISTING 26.1 The Full Text of `plugin.yml`

```
1: name: JohnnyAppleChicken
2:
3: author: Your Name Here
4:
```

```
 5: main: com.javaminecraft.JohnnyApplechicken
 6:
 7: commands:
 8:     applechicken:
 9:         description: Spawn 100 chickens.
10:         usage: /<command> [on | off]
11:
12: version: 1.0
```

Creating the Project

Unlike the other mods you have created, JohnnyApplechicken responds to both a user command and an event.

The /applechicken command with no arguments spawns 100 chickens around the player, filling the area with a giant, clucking mass of birds.

The /applechicken on and /applechicken off commands toggle the functionality of the mod's other feature—an event-handling method that causes all chickens in the game to lay trees instead of eggs.

A for loop is used to spawn 100 chickens:

```
for (int i = 0; i < 100; i++) {
    world.spawn(spot, Chicken.class);
}
```

The spot variable is a Location object declared as an instance variable. As in other mods, it holds the player's location.

A commandOn Boolean instance variable equals true when chickens lay trees and false when they lay eggs. Here's the code to turn on the command:

```
if (arguments[0].equals("on")) {
    commandOn = true;
    LOG.info("[JohnnyApplechicken] On!");
    return true;
}
```

The use of return true tells the Minecraft server the mod has handled a command successfully. Every mod you write that implements a user command should return true in the onCommand() method.

The last line of the method is `return false`, which is reached only when no command was executed by the mod.

This mod registers itself as an event handler in the `onEnable()` method just like the mods created in Chapter 24, "Respond to Events in the Game," and Chapter 25, "Display a Mob's Health During Combat."

One event-handling method is defined in this program's class file, `onItemSpawn()`, which has an `ItemSpawnEvent` object as its argument:

```
public void onItemSpawn(ItemSpawnEvent event) {
    // ...
}
```

The ItemSpawnEvent class is in the `org.bukkit.event.entity` package.

A check to the `commandOn` instance variable ensures that the mod's tree-laying capabilities are turned on:

```
if (!commandOn) {
    return;
}
```

After that check, the item that was spawned to trigger the event is examined. The `ItemSpawnEvent` object's `getEntity()` method returns the item that was spawned, which is cast to the `Item` class.

An item can be in a quantity of more than one when encountered in Minecraft, so you must retrieve the item stack by calling the `Item` object's `getItemStack()` method. It returns an `ItemStack` object.

This mod cares about only one type of item that can be spawned: eggs. The type is represented by the `Material` enumeration, and it is retrieved with the item stack's `getType()` method.

This code examines the item:

```
Item item = (Item) event.getEntity();
ItemStack stack = item.getItemStack();
Material type = stack.getType();
```

A freshly laid chicken egg is `Material.EGG`.

After checking to ensure this event laid an egg, it cancels the normal event by calling the event object's `setCancelled(Boolean)` method with `true` as the argument:

```
event.setCancelled(true);
```

Sometimes in an event-handling method, you don't want the normal behavior to happen. In this mod, you don't want an egg to be laid, so the event is cancelled.

If the event was not cancelled, the chicken would lay a tree and an egg.

This mod places the new tree as a sapling on the spot where the egg would have dropped. A tree can be planted on only two types of blocks that are supported by the current Spigot version—DIRT and GRASS.

CAUTION   A third type of block in Minecraft supports tree saplings: podzol. This block appears in the mega taiga biome and looks like a darker dirt block with green and orange flecks of color.

The block can't be used in a mod (yet) because the current version of Spigot does not support it. Podzol was introduced in Minecraft version 1.7.2, but Spigot 1.8.3 does not include a Material.PODZOL enum value.

When you are developing a mod, don't assume that everything in the game is supported in the Spigot class library. Though the volunteer programmers who designed Spigot have done an excellent job of keeping up with new features as they appear in Minecraft, some things are not yet implemented.

Learning about the block where the egg would have been laid begins by retrieving the Location and Block object for that spot:

```
Location cloc = item.getLocation();
Block block = cloc.getBlock();
```

These objects are used to get the block underneath that one and retrieve its material:

```
Block under = block.getRelative(BlockFace.DOWN);
Material below = under.getType();
```

An if conditional checks whether the below object is Material.DIRT or Material.GRASS. If it is, that block gets a tree sapling through its setType(Material) method:

```
if (below == Material.DIRT || below == Material.GRASS) {
    block.setType(Material.SAPLING);
}
```

The mod completes its work with a server window message:

```
LOG.info("[JohnnyAppleChicken] Tree planted");
```

Undertake these steps in NetBeans to start developing the `JohnnyApplechicken` program:

1. Click File, New File.

2. In the Categories pane, select Java.

3. In the File Types pane, select Empty Java File and click Next.

4. For Class Name, enter **JohnnyApplechicken**.

5. For Package, enter **com.javaminecraft**.

6. Click Finish.

The new file opens for editing. Enter the text of Listing 26.2 into that file.

LISTING 26.2 The Full Text of `JohnnyApplechicken.java`

```
 1: package com.javaminecraft;
 2:
 3: import java.util.logging.Logger;
 4: import org.bukkit.Location;
 5: import org.bukkit.Material;
 6: import org.bukkit.Server;
 7: import org.bukkit.World;
 8: import org.bukkit.block.Block;
 9: import org.bukkit.block.BlockFace;
10: import org.bukkit.command.Command;
11: import org.bukkit.command.CommandSender;
12: import org.bukkit.entity.Chicken;
13: import org.bukkit.entity.Item;
14: import org.bukkit.entity.Player;
15: import org.bukkit.event.EventHandler;
16: import org.bukkit.event.Listener;
17: import org.bukkit.event.entity.ItemSpawnEvent;
18: import org.bukkit.inventory.ItemStack;
19: import org.bukkit.plugin.PluginManager;
20: import org.bukkit.plugin.java.JavaPlugin;
21:
22: public class JohnnyApplechicken extends JavaPlugin
23:     implements Listener {
```

```
24:
25:     public static final Logger LOG = Logger.getLogger(
26:         "Minecraft");
27:     private boolean commandOn = true;
28:     Player me;
29:     World world;
30:     Location spot;
31:
32:     @Override
33:     public boolean onCommand(CommandSender sender,
34:         Command command, String label, String[] arguments) {
35:
36:         me = (Player) sender;
37:         world = me.getWorld();
38:         spot = me.getLocation();
39:
40:         if (sender instanceof Player) {
41:             if (label.equalsIgnoreCase("applechicken")) {
42:                 if (arguments.length == 0) {
43:                     for (int i = 0; i < 100; i++) {
43:                         world.spawn(spot, Chicken.class);
44:                     }
45:                     return true;
46:                 }
47:                 if (arguments[0].equals("on")) {
48:                     commandOn = true;
49:                     LOG.info("[JohnnyApplechicken] On!");
50:                     return true;
51:                 }
52:                 if (arguments[0].equals("off")) {
53:                     commandOn = false;
54:                     LOG.info("[JohnnyApplechicken] Off!");
55:                     return true;
56:                 }
57:             }
58:         }
```

```
59:            return false;
60:        }
61:
62:        @Override
63:        public void onEnable() {
64:            // make this class an event listener
65:            Server server = getServer();
66:            PluginManager manager = server.getPluginManager();
67:            manager.registerEvents(this, this);
68:            LOG.info("[JohnnyApplechicken] On!");
69:        }
70:
71:        @EventHandler
72:        public void onItemSpawn(ItemSpawnEvent event) {
73:            if (!commandOn) {
74:                // the command is not active, so ignore
75:                return;
76:            }
77:            // get the item that was spawned
78:            Item item = (Item) event.getEntity();
79:            ItemStack stack = item.getItemStack();
80:            Material type = stack.getType();
81:            if (type == Material.EGG) {
82:                // it is a newly laid egg
83:                event.setCancelled(true);
84:                Location cloc = item.getLocation();
85:                Block block = cloc.getBlock();
86:                Block under = block.getRelative(BlockFace.DOWN);
87:                Material below = under.getType();
88:                if (below == Material.DIRT
89:                    || below == Material.GRASS) {
90:
91:                    // plant a tree sapling
92:                    block.setType(Material.SAPLING);
93:                }
94:                LOG.info("[JohnnyAppleChicken] Tree planted");
```

```
95:            }
96:        }
97: }
```

If the mod's source code has been saved and there are no errors, you can build the `JohnnyApplechicken` mod's Java Archive (JAR) file and deploy it on the Spigot server.

Deploying the Mod

Within your file system, copy the JAR file `JohnnyApplechicken.jar` from its project folder to the Minecraft server through these steps:

1. Stop the Minecraft server if it is running.
2. Open the folder where you installed the Spigot server, and then open the `JohnnyApplechicken` subfolder.
3. Open the `dist` subfolder.
4. Select the `JohnnyApplechicken` JAR file, and then press Ctrl+C to copy it.
5. Open the Minecraft server folder again, and open its `plugins` subfolder.
6. Press Ctrl+V to copy `JohnnyApplechicken.jar` into it.

Figure 26.1 shows two chickens and a tree that the one on the left just hatched.

FIGURE 26.1

What came first, the chicken or the tree?

THE ABSOLUTE MINIMUM

The `Johnny Applechicken` mod is a simple demonstration of how these programs can be an instigator of change in a Minecraft world. This enhances the gameplay experience by giving the player something new to observe in the game.

The tree-laying chickens can turn a grassy clearing or valley into a forest over the course of weeks in game time.

If the mod is used to spawn 100 chickens, they can quickly turn areas into dense—and sometimes impassable—forests.

There are, of course, some drawbacks to consider when writing a mod that alters the world. Players build cool things in Minecraft, and a mod could wreck them like a griefer.

During testing, I discovered that tree-laying chickens can obliterate fences and enable animals to escape a farm. An egg can be laid on a fence block, so if a tree is placed there instead, the fence vanishes.

27

IN THIS CHAPTER

- Make a powerful new friend
- Try to write a mod on your own
- Hit any spot in the Minecraft world with lightning
- Monitor when a mob targets a player for attack
- Learn the reason a mob chose its target
- Join the Spigot mod programmer's community
- Examine the source code of a sophisticated mod
- Take your skills further on www.javaminecraft.com

BEFRIEND THE GOD OF LIGHTNING

Minecraft is a dangerous place.

From the moment you start the game, there's a mob of mobs eager to kill you and pick up your stuff—even if it's of no use to them at all. I'm still looking for the zombie who has my Fortune III diamond pick axe.

When I find him, vengeance will be mine. As will my pick axe.

Because of the game's many dangers, it's good to have friends in high places. For this final chapter of the book, you will have one of those.

Your friend will be able to throw lightning bolts from on high at any mob that even thinks about attacking you. The second you are targeted for attack by a mob, boom.

Evil eye from an enderman? Boom.

Cross countenance of a creeper? Boom.

Malevolent mug of a magma cube? Boom.

We'll call your new friend Zeus.

Starting the Project

There are two ways you can write the mod that has been named `BestFriendOfZeus`.

One is to read along in the chapter as the code and programming techniques are explained, as you've done throughout this book.

The other is to try to do it yourself first, with only your brain stuffed with newly acquired programming knowledge and one hint.

If you'd like to see whether you can code it before reading, here's the hint:

The `World` class in the `org.bukkit` package has a `lightningStrike()` method.

Your mod should strike every mob with lightning the moment it targets the player.

The mod should have a command that turns this help on and turns it off. It should be off when the mod starts.

If you are going to try coding it yourself, now is the time to start. The next chapter heading will be waiting for you to get back.

Stepping Through Mod Development

Here's how the book's version of `BestFriendOfZeus` is created.

Create the project:

1. Select File, New Project.

2. Select project category `Java` and project type `Java Application`, and click Next.

3. Enter the project name **BestFriendOfZeus**.

4. Deselect Create Main Class; then click Finish.

5. In the Projects pane, right-click the `Libraries` folder and select the command Add Library.

6. In the Available Libraries pane, select Spigot.

7. Click Add Library.

The BestFriendOfZeus project is created with no files in it and needs the mod's configuration file for the command /zeus. The command has an "on" argument that calls on the help of Zeus and an "off" argument that asks for Zeus to chill out.

Create the plugin.yml configuration file for the mod in the src project folder by doing this:

1. Select File, New File.

2. In the Categories pane, select Other.

3. In the File Types pane, select YAML File; then click Next.

4. In the File Name field, enter **plugin** (leave off .yml).

5. In the Folder field, enter **src**.

6. Click Finish.

The NetBeans source code editor opens with plugin.yml ready to be written. Enter the text of Listing 27.1 into the editor, and save it when you're done.

CAUTION   You probably don't need to be reminded to save your work 27 chapters into the book, but like a parent I worry. What if you forget to save it and there's a lightning strike?

LISTING 27.1   The Full Text of plugin.yml

```
 1: name: BestFriendOfZeus
 2:
 3: author: Your Name Here
 4:
 5: main: com.javaminecraft.BestFriendOfZeus
 6:
 7: commands:
 8:     zeus:
 9:         description: Ask Zeus to be your best friend.
10:         usage: /<command> [on | off ]
11:
12: version: 1.0
```

The usage field in Line 10 defines that the two accepted arguments are "on" and "off".

Creating the Project

The `BestFriendOfZeus` mod must listen to events to know when a mob targets a player in order to rain down lightning on the unfortunate entity.

Three things must happen to make a mod an event handler:

1. The mod's class declaration includes `implement Listener`.

2. The mod's `onEnable()` method registers itself as an event listener and has the `@Override` annotation.

3. The `onEntityTargetEvent()` method receives the event and has the `@EventHandler` annotation.

The `onEnable()` method uses the same three statements as the other event-handling mods you have developed. Create a `Server` object, use it to get the `PluginManager` object, and then use it to register as an event listener:

```
manager.registerEvents(this, this);
```

The `onEntityTarget()` method takes an `EntityTargetEvent` object as its only argument. This class is from the `org.bukkit.event.entity` package.

Here's the start of the method with two event method calls:

```
public void onEntityTarget(EntityTargetEvent event) {
    Entity entity = event.getEntity();
    Entity target = event.getTarget();
    // ...
}
```

The `getEntity()` method retrieves the mob that found somebody it wants to attack.

The `getTarget()` method retrieves that somebody.

The method must check whether the target is a player using the `instanceof` keyword:

```
if (target instanceof Player) {
    // ...
}
```

If it is, the method casts the target to a `Player` object:

```
Player playa = (Player) target;
```

Because the mod has a `Player` instance variable called `me` (like most in the book), this can be compared to `playa` to ensure the player was targeted and not some other player:

```
if (playa == me) {
    // ...
}
```

A mob can select a target of attack for 12 reasons that are spelled out in the `EntityTargetEvent.TargetReason` enumeration. The names explain the reasons pretty well:

- `CLOSEST_PLAYER`

- `COLLISION`

- `DEFEND_VILLAGE`

- `FORGOT_TARGET`

- `OWNER_ATTACKED_TARGET`

- `PIG_ZOMBIE_TARGET`

- `RANDOM_TARGET`

- `REINFORCEMENT_TARGET`

- `TARGET_ATTACKED_ENTITY`

- `TARGET_ATTACKED_NEARBY_ENTITY`

- `TARGET_ATTACKED_OWNER`

- `TARGET_DIED`

The event has a `getReason()` method that returns one of these values. This mod looks for `TargetReason.CLOSEST_PLAYER`. When it finds that a mob has targeted a player for that reason, it calls the mob's `getLocation()` method to find out where it is and then uses the coolest method in the `World` class:

```
if (event.getReason() == TargetReason.CLOSEST_PLAYER) {
    Location loc = entity.getLocation();
    // here comes the boom!
    world.strikeLightning(loc);
}
```

The (x,y,z) location of a lightning strike is a bad place to hang out.

That's how a Minecraft player gets a new friend named Zeus.

With the `plugin.yml` configuration file formatted properly and in the right subfolder, it's time to create `BestFriendOfZeus.java` so you can put this all together:

1. Click File, New File.

2. In the Categories pane, select Java.

3. In the File Types pane, select Empty Java File; then click Next.

4. For Class Name, enter **BestFriendOfZeus**.

5. For Package, enter **com.javaminecraft**.

6. Click Finish.

The new file opens for editing. Enter the text of Listing 27.2 into that file.

LISTING 27.2   The Full Text of `BestFriendOfZeus.java`

```
 1: package com.javaminecraft;
 2:
 3: import java.util.logging.Logger;
 4: import org.bukkit.Location;
 5: import org.bukkit.Server;
 6: import org.bukkit.World;
 7: import org.bukkit.command.Command;
 8: import org.bukkit.command.CommandSender;
 9: import org.bukkit.entity.Entity;
10: import org.bukkit.entity.Player;
11: import org.bukkit.event.EventHandler;
12: import org.bukkit.event.Listener;
13: import org.bukkit.event.entity.EntityTargetEvent;
14: import org.bukkit.event.entity.EntityTargetEvent.TargetReason;
15: import org.bukkit.plugin.PluginManager;
16: import org.bukkit.plugin.java.JavaPlugin;
17:
18: public class BestFriendOfZeus extends JavaPlugin
19:     implements Listener  {
20:
21:     public static final Logger LOG = Logger.getLogger(
22:         "Minecraft");
```

```
23:      Player me;
24:      World world;
25:      Location spot;
26:      boolean on = false;
27:
28:      @Override
29:      public boolean onCommand(CommandSender sender,
30:          Command command, String label, String[] arguments) {
31:
32:          me = (Player) sender;
33:          world = me.getWorld();
34:          spot = me.getLocation();
35:
36:          if (sender instanceof Player) {
37:              if (label.equalsIgnoreCase("zeus")) {
38:                  if (arguments.length > 0) {
39:                      if (arguments[0].equals("on")) {
40:                          // Zeus powers activate!
41:                          on = true;
42:                          me.sendMessage("Zeus is yer friend!");
43:                      } else {
44:                          // Zeus powers deactivate!
45:                          on = false;
46:                          me.sendMessage(
47:                              "Zeus is not yer friend!");
48:                      }
49:                      return true;
50:                  }
51:              }
52:          }
53:          return false;
54:      }
55:
56:      // make this class listen to events
57:      @Override
58:      public void onEnable() {
```

```
59:            Server server = getServer();
60:            PluginManager manager = server.getPluginManager();
61:            manager.registerEvents(this, this);
62:        }
63:
64:        @EventHandler
65:        public void onEntityTarget(EntityTargetEvent event) {
66:            Entity entity = event.getEntity();
67:            Entity target = event.getTarget();
68:
69:            if (!on) {
70:                // don't do it, Zeus!
71:                return;
72:            }
73:
74:            LOG.info("Target " + target + " chosen by " + entity);
75:            if (target instanceof Player) {
76:                // the mob's target is a player
77:                Player playa = (Player) target;
78:                if (playa == me) {
79:                    // the mob's target is this player
80:                    if (event.getReason() ==
81:                        TargetReason.CLOSEST_PLAYER) {
82:
83:                        Location loc = entity.getLocation();
84:                        // here comes the boom!
85:                        world.strikeLightning(loc);
86:                    }
87:                }
88:            }
89:        }
90: }
```

If the mod's source code has been saved and there are no errors, you can build the BestFriendOfZeus mod's Java Archive (JAR) file and deploy it on the Spigot server.

Deploying the Mod

Within your file system, copy the JAR file `BestFriendOfZeus.jar` from its project folder to the Minecraft server through these steps:

1. Stop the Minecraft server if it is running.

2. Open the folder where you installed the Spigot server, and then open the `BestFriendOfZeus` subfolder.

3. Open the `dist` subfolder.

4. Select the `BestFriendOfZeus` JAR file, and then press Ctrl+C to copy it.

5. Open the Minecraft server folder again, and open its `plugins` subfolder.

6. Press Ctrl+V to copy `BestFriendOfZeus.jar` into it.

Figure 27.1 shows a witch being struck by lightning long before it gets close enough to throw one of those aggravating potions.

FIGURE 27.1

That has gotta hurt!

After the mod has been loaded and you're back in the Minecraft world, use `/zeus on` to begin the friendship.

Play with the mod for a while to experience the good and the bad of friendship with Zeus.

At first, you might think it's all good. You can go about your business building, farming, and mining without worrying about mobs sneaking up on you.

But there are some bad things you will discover, too. You might not want to get too attached to your player, at least until you've revised the mod's code to make Zeus a better friend.

Joining the Community of Mod Developers

You now can create and deploy mods with the skills you attained in this book. There's a lot more to try in the Spigot class library, which you can explore by perusing the Javadoc documentation at the website https://hub.spigotmc.org/javadocs/spigot.

There are thousands of mods that other programmers have shared on the Web. You can find many of them in the Spigot Resources directory at https://www.spigotmc.org/resources.

Many of these mods have their Java source code available, so you can view how they were written and find out about new techniques for interacting with Minecraft in your own programs.

The TreeAssist mod is an interesting one I discovered when I was first finding out how trees can be chopped down in Minecraft mods. It has two handy features for pixelated lumberjacks:

- When the player chops the lowest log block in a tree, the rest of its logs are chopped down automatically.

- When a tree is chopped down, a sapling of the same type is planted at that location.

Each mod in the directory has its own page. The main page for TreeAssist is http://www.spigotmc.org/resources/treeassist.4657.

Click the Download Now link on that page to download the JAR file that you can use to deploy the mod on your own server. Put the `TreeAssist.jar` file in the same folder where your own mods have been saved—the `plugins` subfolder of the server. When you next restart the server, the mod's commands will be available.

Go to https://github.com/itsatacoshop247/TreeAssist to see to the GitHub repository, a site that contains the code that comprises the program.

You will see a page with a folder and file listing, as shown in Figure 27.2.

src Folder

FIGURE 27.2

Examining a mod's source code on GitHub.

The listing will likely be different by the time you visit, but you will see a `src` folder like the one pointed out in Figure 27.2. This is the place where the mod's source code is found.

This mod has multiple files and folders. The `TreeAssist.java` file is the starting place because it is the class that extends `JavaPlugin`.

THE ABSOLUTE MINIMUM

The final chapter of *Absolute Beginner's Guide to Minecraft Mods Programming* is only the first chapter of your mod programming career.

With the skills you have developed over these 27 chapters, you have a strong foundation for writing mod programs. You can take these skills further on the website that I launched for readers of this book at www.javaminecraft.com.

Visit to see the source code files for this book, read answers to questions I've been posed by readers, and share tips and techniques for all new mod programmers who are venturing out into the world.

There's a lot more to try in Spigot, which in its current version has 718 Java classes. By the time you read this, there likely will be more because Mojang regularly releases new versions of Minecraft with a lot of additional mobs, objects, and features that mod programmers will be eager to code for. The volunteers who created the Spigot class library strive to keep up with everything added to the game.

It might sound grandiose to call Minecraft mod programming a career, but Markus "Notch" Persson didn't think Minecraft was a career either when he began it in 2009—and now he's rich enough to buy 57.4 million copies of this book for his closest friends. At full retail price!

In addition to having skills you can use in a colorful, block-based 3D world, you will find them pretty useful in the real world. Java is currently the world's most widely used programming language, and there's strong demand for software developers who know the language in many fields.

So if anyone questions the amount of time you spend writing mods, or the time you're playing Minecraft, tell them it's for your career.

Appendix A

VISIT THIS BOOK'S WEBSITE

As much as I'd like to think otherwise, there are undoubtedly some things you're not clear about after completing this book.

Programming is a specialized technical field that throws strange concepts and jargon at you, such as "instantiation," "ternary operators," and "big- and little-endian byte order."

If you're unclear about any of the topics covered in the book, or if I was unclear about a topic (sigh), visit the book's website at www.javaminecraft.com for assistance.

The website offers the following:

- **Help message board**—A forum where readers can report problems and ask questions about the book, Minecraft mod programming, and Java programming in general. I post messages there to answer readers, and the other forum members often assist each other. Visit the forum directly at `http://help.javaminecraft.com`.

- **Error corrections and clarifications**—When errors are brought to my attention, they are described on the site with the corrected text and any other material that could help.

- **Updated links to the sites mentioned in this book**—If a site mentioned in the book has changed addresses and I know about the new link, I'll offer it on the website.

Feel free to voice all opinions positive, negative, indifferent, undecided, enraged, enthused, peeved, amused, irked, intrigued, bored, captivated, enchanted, disenchanted, flummoxed, and flabbergasted.

—Rogers Cadenhead

Index